REPTILES

BIOLOGICAL SCIENCES EDITOR
A. J. Cain
M.A. D.Phil.
*Professor of Zoology
in the University of Liverpool*

Reptiles

ANGUS d'A. BELLAIRS

Professor of Vertebrate Morphology in the
University of London at St Mary's Hospital
Medical School and Honorary Herpetologist to
the Zoological Society of London

J. ATTRIDGE

Senior Lecturer in Zoology at Birkbeck College
University of London

HUTCHINSON
UNIVERSITY LIBRARY
LONDON

Hutchinson & Co (Publishers) Ltd
3 Fitzroy Square London W1

London Melbourne Sydney Auckland
Wellington Johannesburg Cape Town
and agencies throughout the world

First published 1957
Reprinted 1966
Second edition 1968
Third edition 1970
Fourth (revised) edition 1975
© Angus d'A. Bellairs 1957, 1968 and 1970
   Angus d'A. Bellairs and John Attridge 1975

The photograph on the cover of the paperback
edition and on the front panel of the cased edition
shows a marine iguana from Hood Island, Galapagos.
Photograph by Peter Nightingale.

Set in Monotype Times
Printed in Great Britain by the Anchor Press Ltd
and bound by Wm Brendon & Son Ltd
both of Tiptree, Essex

ISBN 0 09 123210 4 (cased)
     0 09 123211 2 (paper)

470058465

Contents

Preface to Fourth Edition

Since the first edition of this book appeared in 1957 the study of reptiles has been virtually transformed by the explosive evolution of modern biology. There has been a tremendous increase in the number of publications dealing with reptiles, and important contributions are being made not only in traditional fields such as systematics and anatomy, but in such areas as ethology, physiology and even molecular biology. Much of this work is being done in the USA and it is perhaps sad that there are so few students of living reptiles in England.

The first three editions of *Reptiles* were by A. d'A. Bellairs. However, the accelerating growth of knowledge and the fact that books of this type tend to deteriorate unless they periodically receive infusions of fresh blood suggested that it would be wise to recruit a second author for this new, fourth edition. One of us (J.A.) has been mainly concerned with revising the sections on palaeontology, a rapidly advancing field, while the other (A. d'A. B.) has done his best to bring the information on living reptiles up to date. The book as a whole, however, is a joint responsibility.

The length of *Reptiles* has been somewhat increased and many sections have been extensively revised; the information given in the last two editions in a final chapter on recent advances has been incorporated into the main text. All the figures have been re-drawn and new ones have been added. Nearly all the drawings are the work of Joyce Joffe; the authors owe much to her care and patience over the vital task of illustration. The bibliography has been re-cast and unavoidably a number of the older references have had to be omitted. Preference has been given to recent books of importance and to articles dealing with topics which seem of special current interest.

It remains the aim of this book to provide, however incompletely, a kind of synthesis of the different sorts of knowledge available on reptiles. Such, we hope, may be of interest to students of general zoology and to naturalists, as well as to herpetologists, as the specialists on reptiles and amphibians are called.

As far as possible we have tried to strike a proper balance in the treatment of the living and the far more numerous extinct forms, and we have also tried to regard the latter as animals with life-histories as well as bones. In our account of fossil reptiles and of certain aspects of reptile anatomy we should like to make a very full acknowledgement to the fine textbooks by A. S. Romer and E. H. Colbert, and to the impressive series of articles in the volumes of the *Biology of the Reptilia* produced under the editorship of Carl Gans and his collaborators.

We are conscious of having given very little space to the methods of distinguishing between different living species and genera by means of scale counts and other external features which play such a large part in museum work. This aspect of herpetology is, however, dealt with very fully in many books and catalogues which are well known to those who make reptilian systematics their special study.

Each chapter dealing with a particular group is preceded by a synoptic classification of its members. Almost all the genera and all the larger groups mentioned in the text are listed so that the reader can see fairly quickly where they belong. The classification of the living groups is given in greater detail than that of the extinct ones; we have listed all the surviving families, but it has only been possible to include a few representative genera, notably those referred to in the text. The geological period is given in the lists for all extinct genera; where no period is stated, the genus is alive today.

Our thanks remain to the many friends who gave useful advice in the preparation of the earlier editions; we should particularly like to mention the help of the late Professor H. Munro Fox, the former editor of the books on biological sciences in this series, and of Miss Ann Douglas, previously editor of the Hutchinson University Library.

Finally we must acknowledge the generosity of the many authors and publishing houses, and in particular of the American Museum of Natural History and Artia, Czechoslovakia, for allowing us to re-draw or adapt figures published by them. The Artia publication *Life Before Man* by Z. V. Špinar and Z. Burian (issued in England by Thames and Hudson) contains some of the best reconstructions of fossil reptiles available.

A. d'A. Bellairs
Department of Anatomy
St Mary's Hospital Medical School
London W2

J. Attridge
Department of Zoology
Birkbeck College
Malet Street
London WC1

Abbreviations

GEOLOGICAL
Often used with prefixes L. (Lower), M. (Middle) and U. (Upper). Carb., Carboniferous (U.Carb. = Pennsylvanian). Cret., Cretaceous. Jur., Jurassic., Perm., Permian. Tert., Tertiary. Trias., Triassic.

GEOGRAPHICAL
N., S., E., W. refer to points of the compass and indicate general regions only. Note that Sn.Am. indicates *southern* America—i.e. the American continent south of Mexico and including Central as well as South America. Af., Africa. Am., America., As., Asia., Aus., Australasia. Eur., Europe. Gal., Galapagos. Ind., Indies. Mad., Madagascar. O.W., Old World. N.W., New World. W.w., worldwide but mainly warmer countries; many fossil groups designated W.w. are not known from Aus.

1 | Introduction

The reptiles form a class of backboned or vertebrate animals which is represented today by the crocodiles, turtles, snakes, lizards and the rather lizard-like tuatara (*Sphenodon*) of New Zealand. It is not very difficult to distinguish any of these types of reptiles from existing members of other classes of vertebrates, but when one turns one's attention to extinct creatures, the problem of distinction becomes more complicated. The fossilized remains of these animals generally represent only the hard parts of their bodies such as bones and teeth, which have become mineralized and preserved through the course of geological time. Many of the characters which distinguish a reptile from an amphibian or a mammal refer to the soft tissues of the body, or to the life-history and mode of embryonic development. Of these even the best preserved fossils tell us comparatively little and such information as can be obtained from them is easily misinterpreted.

There is also a more fundamental difficulty in separating different classes of animals, one that is implicit in all man-made systems of classification. We know, both from the direct evidence of the fossil record and from the indirect evidence provided by the study of comparative anatomy, that during the course of evolution reptiles have originated from amphibians and have in turn given rise, by two collateral branches, to the birds and mammals. Animals must therefore once have existed which were intermediate in character between amphibians and reptiles, and between the latter and members of each of the two 'higher' groups of vertebrates, although no such transitional creatures have survived to the present time.

It is impossible, therefore, to draw an absolute dividing line between groups of animals which have been directly descended from, or are ancestral to, each other. Names such as Amphibia and Reptilia are only labels, made by men for their own convenience, and applied selectively to groups of members of a continuous series, the members of each group resembling one another on the whole more closely than they do the members of any other group. In practice, however, this difficulty is less important than it may seem. The great majority of animals, at least of vertebrates, living or extinct, fall fairly readily into one or other of these artificial groups, and each group can be seen to possess certain characteristic (though not necessarily exclusive) features, which are all or nearly all found among its members.

Reptiles are vertebrates and possess all the features which are characteristic of their phylum: bilateral symmetry, a skull, a backbone enclosing a tubular nerve cord which is expanded in the head region to form the brain; eyes, nose and ears, a heart, a blood system which is closed off from the body cavities, and a standard complement of viscera; alimentary tract, excretory and reproductive organs; and, usually, paired limbs or their vestiges.

The more particular features of the class Reptilia may be summarized as follows:

(1) 'Cold-bloodedness' or poikilothermy. These terms do not refer to the absolute temperature of the body, but signify the lack of an effective internal mechanism for regulating the body temperature in response to changes in the temperature of the environment. However, other methods of temperature control involving the utilization of external sources of heat are employed (p. 54). Generally speaking, fishes and amphibians are similar in these respects.

(2) As a rule reptiles breathe atmospheric air by means of lungs. They never possess gills like fishes and amphibian larvae (tadpoles).

(3) Almost all reptiles are covered by scales or scutes, a character which distinguishes them from most living amphibians.

(4) The eggs of reptiles have much yolk; thus they resemble those of birds but differ from those of many fish and amphibians and nearly all mammals. They possess extra-embryonic membranes which are important in terrestrial development. Most reptiles lay eggs and these are always deposited on land; many species, however, bear their young alive (p. 52).

(5) At hatching or birth young reptiles are essentially similar in shape and habits to their parents. They do not undergo a

larval stage and metamorphosis, like the change from tadpole to frog.

(6) The ventricle of the heart is usually only partly divided by a septum, and two separate aortic trunks arise from it. Some mixing of arterial and venous bloodstreams is likely to occur, at least under some circumstances—an important point of distinction from adult birds and mammals.

(7) Like amphibians (typically) and birds, reptiles have only one bone in the ear to conduct sound vibrations from the eardrum to the inner ear, and there are several bones in each side of the lower jaw (p. 65). In mammals there are three conducting bones in the ear (Fig. 3D) and only one bone in the lower jaw.

There are, of course, other features which characterize the Reptilia as a group, but the above are the most striking and among the most important. Some of them are present in other classes of vertebrates and hardly any of them is an exclusive possession of the reptiles; it is the combination of them all together in one animal that builds up the picture of reptilian organization.

The first reptiles appeared towards the end of the Palaeozoic era (Fig. 1), about 300 million years ago, and expanded tremendously during the Triassic, the first period of the Mesozoic era. Throughout the Mesozoic, which lasted from about 230 to 62 millions of years ago, the reptiles prospered and multiplied; in numbers of different kinds and in variety of size, shape and habits, they surpassed their amphibian ancestors and perhaps also their mammalian descendants, and became the dominant forms of terrestrial vertebrate life.

The end of the Mesozoic was a time of crisis in reptilian history. During the late Cretaceous, five out of the ten orders then existing became extinct; among the casualties were the dinosaurs and most of the other spectacular types. While some of these had disappeared before the end of the period, others lived on until its very close, vanishing with dramatic suddenness and for reasons which are not entirely understood. Of the four surviving orders of reptiles, only one, the Squamata (lizards, amphisbaenians and snakes), seems to have increased in the number of its representatives during the Tertiary era.

Despite the fact that they no longer occupy their once predominant position, the reptiles do not form a negligible pro-

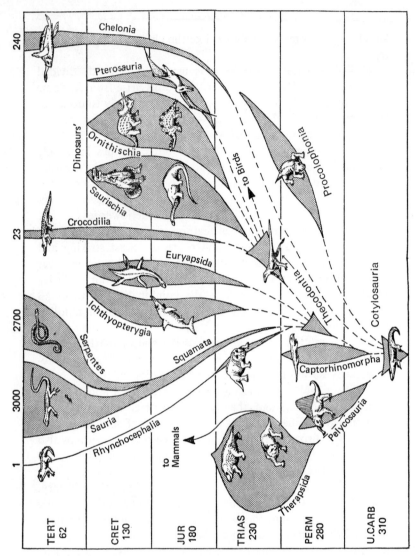

Fig. 1

History and relationships of the main groups of reptiles. The abundance of these groups is shown in a general way by the widths of the stippled areas representing them. The approximate time since the beignning of each geological period is given in millions of years, after Romer (1966). The Palaeozoic era ends with the Permian period, the Mesozoic with the Cretaceous. The different epochs of the Tertiary period are not shown. See p. 11 for abbreviations. Numbers of surviving species shown at top. Amphisbaenians included with Sauria.

portion of the total numbers of living vertebrates. Modern reptiles comprise nearly 6000 species (Carr, 1964); lower figures (mainly for Squamata) are given by some workers, but in number of living species the reptiles probably exceed the mammals and greatly exceed the amphibians. They are outnumbered by the birds, however, and greatly surpassed in number by the fishes.

In size reptiles show great variation, though most living forms are of modest size. Tiny lizards, the smallest of modern reptiles, may be under 5cm (2in) long, while the largest living crocodiles and snakes may reach lengths of at least 6 and 9m (20 and 30ft) respectively. The biggest dinosaurs were 18–27m (60–90ft) long and had weights estimated at up to 51 000kg (50 tons) or more.

One species of lizard (*Lacerta vivipara*) and at least one snake (*Vipera berus*) extend northwards just inside the Arctic Circle, while some lizards are found as far south as the tip of South America. The number of species and genera of reptiles is highest in the tropics, falling off abruptly as the temperate zones are reached. The pattern of geographical distribution suggests that the more widespread groups like the lizards and snakes and the tortoises and turtles originated within the tropics and have since colonized some of the colder parts of the earth. Even fully terrestrial reptiles (or their eggs) are sometimes able to cross wide tracts of ocean, being accidentally transported on driftwood; some of the smaller species have been introduced into foreign territory by the agency of man.

Reptiles inhabit many different sorts of terrain and have evolved diverse patterns of structure and behaviour. The wide range of adaptive radiation which they show is particularly impressive when extinct as well as living forms are considered.

Now, and probably for hundreds of millions of years in the past, reptiles have swarmed in tropical forests and along the edges of tropical beaches. They have flourished in warm seas

---

Some of the illustrations depict particular forms, as follows. Therapsida: dicynodont (top) and *Cynognathus*. Pelycosauria: *Dimetrodon*. Rhynchocephalia: *Sphenodon* (top) and a rhynchosaur. Thecodontia: *Euparkeria*. Saurischia: *Tyrannosaurus* (top) and *Diplodocus*. Ornithischia: *Triceratops* (top) and *Stegosaurus*. Procolophonia: *Pareiasaurus*.

and fresh waters and have made their homes in prairies and deserts. Only the tundra and the icy polar regions, the tops of high mountains and the depths of oceans and lakes, have remained inaccessible to them.

Many reptiles are terrestrial and walk, run or crawl on the surface of the earth. Some pursue a secretive existence under stones and among the roots of vegetation, or burrow underground, while others spend most of their lives among the foliage of trees. All degrees of aquatic adaptation are found among them, and some, as the extinct ichthyosaurs, were so highly modified for marine life that they could hardly have moved on land. No reptile living today has the power of true flight, but this was developed by the pterosaurs and probably by the ancestors of birds.

In so far as the reptiles have been able to exploit a much wider range of environmental conditions than the amphibians, and to follow a much wider variety of ways of life, they may be said to represent an advance on the latter group. In their range of adaptation they probably parallel the mammals within the limits of their climate tolerance. In one respect, however, even more important than their deficient powers of temperature regulation, they cannot compete with mammals. No reptiles, outside the realms of science fiction, have been able to evolve large brains and formidable intelligence. A few of their descendants did, in fact, manage to remedy this deficiency, but by the time they had done so they had ceased to be reptiles and had crossed the threshold of mammalian organization.

2 | The reptile body

This book is not intended as a treatise on reptilian anatomy and physiology and for detailed information on the subject the reader is referred to one of the general works cited in the bibliography, in particular to A. S. Romer's textbook, *The vertebrate body*. In this chapter we have selected for treatment certain aspects of structure and function which are of general importance in all members of the class, which are not too difficult to describe briefly, and without some consideration of which many aspects of reptilian biology cannot be discussed. The reader may think that undue emphasis has been laid here upon the skeleton, but this is largely unavoidable since our knowledge of extinct animals—and the vast majority of reptiles are extinct—is almost restricted to it. Features of interest which are found only in certain groups of reptiles, or which are related to special modes of life, are mainly dealt with elsewhere, under the appropriate chapter headings.

The skin

By comparison with the skin of an amphibian like a frog, the reptilian integument is comparatively waterproof; it is known however, that loss of water in appreciable amounts can take place through the skin of some reptiles, particularly of amphibious species (Bentley, 1971). As in other vertebrates, it is made up of two main layers, a superficial epidermis, derived in the embryo from the outermost germ-layer, the ectoderm, and an inner dermis, derived from the mesodermal tissues (Fig. 3F). The scales are formed mainly from thickenings of the epidermis the thinner, often folded regions of the skin between them are known as hinges. Large plate-like scales, such as those which form the outer layers of a turtle's shell, are often called scutes. Scales or scutes may be modified to form crests, horns or other

excrescences. Though reptilian scales do not become fossilized
the impressions which they leave in the surrounding matrix
of rock may sometimes be preserved, indicating that extinct
as well as living reptiles possessed this characteristic form of
covering.

The outer parts of the scales are composed of dead horny
tissues of which the protein keratin forms a large part. They
are continually being shed from the surface of the body, flaking
off piecemeal, or sometimes being sloughed off periodically in
one piece, as in snakes (p. 216). This loss is made good by the proliferation of living cells in the deepest layer of the epidermis. The
skin has few glands, and when present these are usually local in
distribution; it lacks the sweat glands which in many mammals
play an important part in the control of body temperature.

The dermal part of the skin consists mainly of connective
tissue and contains nerves, blood vessels and involuntary or
smooth muscle fibres. Traced inwards it becomes continuous
with the connective tissue around the skeleton and muscles. The
dermis contains most of the pigment cells, which are responsible
for the colour of the skin and may be involved in the process of
colour change (p. 219).

In many reptiles the horny parts of the scales are reinforced
by bony plates or osteoderms (Fig. 3F) which develop in the
dermis, and may become fused with the the bones of the skull. They
are found beneath the head and body scales of some lizards, and
beneath the scutes in crocodiles and tortoises. Osteoderms often
show a curious pitting or 'sculpturing' of their surfaces, which
may also be seen, as in crocodiles, on many of the skull bones.

The scales of a reptile constitute a series of units which may
vary in number and position only very slightly between individuals
of the same species and more markedly between different species.
Scale-counts are therefore much used as aids to identification.
Moreover, a study of scale variations in a reptile population
may provide information on the emergence of new subspecies,
a phenomenon of interest to the geneticist.

Teeth

Most reptiles possess teeth and in certain groups, such as the
snakes, these show remarkable modifications of their structure

and function. The tooth tip is usually capped with a thin layer of extremely hard, highly calcified enamel-like substance. This 'enamel' is nearly always homogeneous in structure unlike the enamel of mammals, which is characteristically made up of densely packed prism-like formations.

The bulk of the tooth is composed of dentine, a hard tissue permeated by fine tubules and in some respects akin to bone. Within the dentine is a pulp cavity, filled with connective tissue and supplied with nerves and nutrient blood vessels.

In most reptiles the teeth are shed and replaced throughout life, instead of there being only one or two sets, as in mammals. In some reptiles the replacement of teeth follows an alternating pattern. Between any two functional teeth there is often an empty tooth space. As the new tooth erupts into the space and begins to function the original teeth on either side of it are shed. This arrangement prevents large tracts of jaw being denuded of all their functional teeth at the same time. Recent work shows that the process is actually more complicated than this and that teeth are replaced in waves which sweep along the jaw (in lizards from back to front) through alternate tooth positions (A. G. Edmund, in Gans *et al.* 1969: Osborn, 1973).

The teeth usually have a fairly simple conical or peg-like form. Though they may vary in size and shape over different parts of the jaw, they are not, save in some mammal-like reptiles, clearly differentiated into incisors, canines and cheek teeth, neither do they develop complicated crown patterns like the cheek teeth of mammals.

In some reptiles the teeth are restricted to the bones along the edges of the jaws, the premaxillae and maxillae above, and the dentaries below, as in mammals. In others, including most of the more primitive forms, teeth are also present on some of the palate bones, such as the vomers, palatines and pterygoids. The teeth may be set in sockets or merely fused with the surface of the bone; sometimes there is a special tissue around the tooth root known as bone of attachment which is comparable in structure with the cementum of mammalian teeth. The teeth may be entirely absent, as in turtles, when they are usually replaced functionally by a horny beak.

Skeleton

The internal skeleton is composed of two kinds of tissue, cartilage and bone. Bones may arise in the embryo either by ossifying directly in connective tissue, or by ossification of a pre-existing cartilaginous framework. Those which develop in the first manner are known as membrane or dermal bones and mostly occur in the skull and shoulder girdle. Bones which develop in or replace cartilage are also found in the skull and shoulder girdle, while the vertebrae, true ribs, sternum, pelvic girdle and the skeleton of the free parts of both limbs are also of this type.

In the embryo the greater part of the skeleton is formed of cartilage and though much of this will later become ossified, cartilage persists throughout life in parts of the skull, limb girdles, and on the ends of the joint surfaces of bones.

Bones grow in length by the proliferation of their cartilaginous extremities, the tissue so formed being converted into bone. In mammals secondary centres of ossification usually develop in the cartilaginous growing ends of the bones, or epiphyses as they are called. When these centres have replaced most of the surrounding cartilage they fuse with the bone shaft so that no further increase in length can take place. Most reptiles do not possess these secondary centres so that their bones are free to grow throughout life, a fact which may partly explain the occurrence from time to time of individual snakes or crocodiles which greatly exceed the usual size-range of their species. Calcified or bony epiphyses have been demonstrated, however in *Sphenodon* and many lizards (Haines, in Gans *et al.*, 1969).

The skull

The vertebrate skull can be regarded as consisting of two shells, one inside the other. The outer one is made up of dermal bones which mostly lie just beneath the skin or the lining of the mouth The inner one surrounds the brain, the inner ear and the nose, and is perforated by canals for the cranial nerves as they enter and leave the brain.

This concept of the skull is, of course, an over-simplification, since in some places the outer shell is deficient and the inner one exposed on the surface, while in others the inner shell is lacking and the deficiency is made up by the outer one.

In reptiles the outer shell is represented by the bones of the skull roof and sides, those around the eyes, those in the upper jaw and palate, and most of those in the lower jaw; the more important ones are listed and shown in Fig. 5 which represents the skull of a primitive reptile (p. 65).

In the embryo the inner shell is cartilaginous and is known as the chondrocranium; in reptiles much of it remains unossified throughout the whole life-span. In the nasal region it forms a close investment for the membranous nasal sacs (p. 37) and lies inside the membrane bones of the snout and palate. Between the two nasal organs it forms a thin deep nasal septum in the midline which is generally continued back between the eyes as the interorbital septum. The upper edge of the latter is split into a kind of trough in which lie the long olfactory stalks and the front parts of the cerebral hemispheres. This trough is open above where the brain is roofed over by dermal bones and its sides may also be deficient in places and contain vacuities which are filled in by dura mater, the tough membrane which surrounds the cranial cavity. Towards the back of the orbits, however, small bones known as orbitosphenoids and laterosphenoids (or pleurosphenoids) may ossify in the side walls of the trough but often exist only as cartilages (Fig. 2F).

The back part of the inner shell, unlike the front part, always becomes ossified by replacement bones. The most important of these are the basisphenoid, which lies in the midline of the skull base and is attached to the back of the interorbital septum, the periotics, which surround the membranous organs of each inner ear, and the occipital complex of bones which makes up the back of the skull. There is a kidney-shaped knob on the back of the occiput, sometimes partly divided into a middle and two lateral lobes, known as the occipital condyle. This articulates with the first vertebra, the atlas. Above the condyle is the foramen magnum, through which the brain becomes continuous with the spinal cord.

A further series of cartilage bones and cartilages is associated with the skull and can be regarded as derivatives of the chondrocranium. These are the skeletal elements of the embryonic branchial arches which in air-breathing vertebrates have lost their original roles as supports for the gills and taken on other functions.

The skeleton of the first arch is related to the jaws and consists in the embryo of a palatoquadrate cartilage in the upper jaw and a cartilage of Meckel in the lower. In the adult reptile the front part of the palatoquadrate ossifies to form the epipterygoid, a bone which projects upwards on either side of the basisphenoid behind the orbits (Figs. 2F, 21A, B: p. 184) while the posterior part becomes the quadrate bone. The back end of Meckel's cartilage becomes the articular bone of the lower jaw and its longer, more anterior portion persists throughout life as a cartilaginous rod which is partly surrounded by the dermal bones of the lower jaw. The upper end of the quadrate is attached to the side of the skull while its lower end makes contact with the articular at the joint of the jaw.

In some reptiles, notably the lizards and snakes (Squamata), not only the lower jaw but the upper one also is movable on the cranium. This phenomenon, known as kinesis, is discussed on p. 186.

The cartilages of the second arch form the stapes or columella auris, which is the conducting bone of the middle ear (Fig. 3E), and part of the hyoid skeleton, which supports the tongue and gives attachment to some of its muscles.

The number of separate bones, particularly of dermal bones, in the reptilian skull is considerably greater than that in the mammal, and a much larger proportion of the total skull substance in reptiles remains cartilaginous. The preparation of the loosely knit skull of a reptile for the museum is more difficult than that of a mammal and large parts of it, notably the unossified nasal capsule and interorbital septum usually disappear in the macerating process. They are seldom or never preserved in fossil material.

Temporal openings and classification

The construction of the cheek region of the skull in reptiles is important in classification. In the earliest reptiles, the cotylosaurs, the outer shell of dermal bones behind the orbits had a continuous, unbroken surface. Inside this the jaw-closing muscles had their attachments (Fig. 2) and passed down through vacuities in the palate to be inserted on to the lower jaw. In the descendants of these reptiles there was a general tendency for the outer shell to become perforated by one or more temporal openings or fenestrae through which parts of the muscles migrated. Such an arrangement may have increased the efficiency of muscle action, for it allowed the contracting muscles to bulge outwards and also to transfer some of their attachments from the inner to the outer shell of bones, increasing their length and hence their mechanical advantage. More complex factors may be involved in the evolution of fenestrae (see Frazzetta, 1968). It is well known, however, that the different groups of reptiles show differences in the number and position of these temporal openings, which are indicative, up to a point, of the divergent evolutionary paths which they have taken.

Using such criteria it is possible to list the main groups of reptiles in the following way.

Number and position of temporal openings	*Term*	*Main groups showing the condition*
None	anapsid	cotylosaurs,[1] turtles,[2] etc.
One vacuity at side of cheek with postorbital and squamosal usually meeting above	synapsid	pelycosaurs, therapsids[2]
One vacuity, high on cheek, usually with postorbital and squamosal meeting below	euryapsid	protorosaurs, plesiosaurs and their allies, ichthyosaurs
Both vacuities present, usually with postorbital and squamosal meeting between them	diapsid	archosaurs (crocodiles, dinosaurs, pterosaurs, etc.), lepidosaurs (*Sphenodon*, lizards,[2] snakes,[2] etc.)

[1] Apart from some millerettids (p. 154).
[2] Sometimes or always show condition in a modified form.

Recent workers have tended to put less emphasis upon this system, since it has become clear that it does not reflect the real evolutionary relationships of certain important groups. Thus, the archosaurs and lepidosaurs, though both diapsid, seem to be widely separated; the term Diapsida is no longer used in formal classification, though the names Anapsida and Synapsida

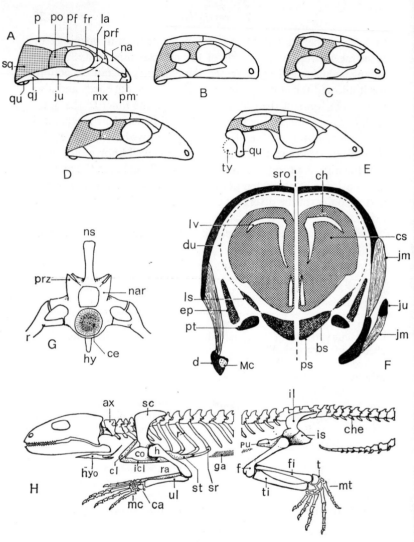

Fig. 2

A–E. Diagrams showing temporal region of skull in reptiles. Postorbital and squamosal stippled; bones of snout shown in Λ only.
A, anapsid. B, synapsid. C, diapsid. D, euryapsid. E, modified
diapsid (lizard).

F. Cross-section through temporal region of head showing anapsid
condition on left, synapsid on right. The dermal bones are in
black, cartilage bones in dark stipple.

G. Anterior thoracic vertebra of crocodile with part of two-headed
rib, seen from in front.

are still retained for two groups of subclass rank. The term 'parapsid' once used for the condition in ichthyosaurs and plesiosaurs has now been dropped, the two groups being placed in subclasses of their own (p. 105).

The vertebral column, ribs and sternum

The vertebral column supports the body along its length and gives attachment to the back muscles which play an important part in those types of locomotion, very general among reptiles, which involve undulations of the trunk and tail.

Each of the separate vertebrae which make up the column has a centrum and a neural arch; the latter surrounds the spinal canal and forms a dorsal spine (Fig. 2G). There is also a pair of processes at the front and back, the pre- and post-zygapophyses, which articulate with those of the adjacent vertebrae, and there is often a projecting 'transverse process' on either side which may articulate with a rib. In the caudal region there are usually V-shaped chevron bones beneath the vertebral centra which enclose the main blood vessels of the tail and give attachment to some of the tail muscles. They are well developed in water reptiles where the tail has become flattened from side to side as a swimming organ.

In the more primitive reptiles the vertebral centra are often hollowed out at both ends (amphicoelous), but in many groups

---

H. Skeleton of generalized reptile. Sections of the dorsal region and tail are removed. Based on Guibé in Grassé (1970).

ax, axis. *bs*, basisphenoid. *c*, canal for spinal cord. *ca*, carpals. *ce*, centrum of procoelous vertebra (hollowed in front). *ch*, cerebral hemisphere. *che*, chevron. *cl*, clavicle. *co*, coracoid. *cs*, corpus striatum. *d*, dentary. *du*, dura mater. *ep*, epipterygoid. *f*, femur. *fi*, fibula. *fr*, frontal. *ga*, gastralia (abdominal ribs). *h*, humerus. *hy*, hypapophysis. *hyo*, hyoid. *icl*, interclavicle. *il*, ilium. *is*, ischium. *jm*, jaw muscles. *ju*, jugal. *la*, lachrymal. *ls*, laterosphenoid. *lv*, lateral ventricle of brain. *mc*, metacarpal. *Mc*, Meckel's cartilage. *mt*, metatarsal. *mx*, maxilla. *na*, nasal. *nar*, neural arch. *ns*, neural spine. *p*, parietal. *pf*, pineal foramen. *pm*, premaxilla. *po*, postorbital. *prf*, prefrontal. *prz*, prezygapophysis. *ps*, parasphenoid. *pt*, pterygoid. *pu*, pubis. *qj*, quadratojugal. *qu*, quadrate. *r*, rib (dorsal segment). *ra*, radius. *sc*, scapula. *sq*, squamosal. *sr*, sternal rib. *sro*, skull roof. *st*, sternum. *t*, tarsals. *ti*, tibia. *ty*, tympanic membrane. *ul*, ulna.

procoelous vertebrae are found, where the cavity is only at the anterior surface (Figs. 2G, 22J). Into this fits a rounded projection from the vertebra in front, giving a ball and socket effect.

Since nearly all the vertebrae may carry ribs, precise definition of cervical, thoracic and lumbar regions of the spine is often difficult. The first two vertebrae, the atlas and the axis, are modified in shape to permit free movement of the head and are often devoid of ribs. In some forms, e.g. crocodiles and *Sphenodon*, there is a small element, the pro-atlas, between the atlas and the skull.

In some reptiles (e.g. crocodiles) each rib may have two heads articulating with its vertebra (Fig. 2G), but in many forms the dorsal head has merged with the ventral head, the combined structure articulating with the 'transverse process'. Most reptiles, apart from limbless forms, possess a sternum which may remain more or less cartilaginous. Some of the ribs in the thoracic region are usually connected with this by bars known as sternal ribs which correspond with the mammalian costal cartilages and are often unossified. Further back, opposite the hindlimbs, two or more modified ribs are usually attached to the limb girdle to form the sacrum. This arrangement helps to give the pelvis stability. Behind this level there may be a number of tail ribs which are usually firmly attached to the caudal vertebrae.

In many reptiles, for instance *Sphenodon* and crocodiles, a series of bony rods or gastralia (Figs. 2H, 23E) is found in the tissues of the belly wall. Unlike the true ribs these are dermal bones, perhaps remnants of the bony scales of the lobe-finned fishes. Many lizards have the belly reinforced by structures of a different type, formed in cartilage. These are called the parasternal ribs and seem to be detached parts of the true rib system.

The limbs

The majority of reptiles have four limbs though in some groups one or other, or both pairs, may be reduced or even entirely absent, as in most snakes.

The upper part of the shoulder girdle (Fig. 2H) is formed by the scapula. Ventral to this is a flattened plate, the coracoid, which makes contact with the sternum on each side. In some reptiles, such as the therapsids (p. 88), it can be divided into two or more parts (pre- and post-coracoid, etc.). The socket of the shoulder-joint or glenoid cavity lies at the junction of scapula with coracoid. The slender clavicle lies at the front edges of scapula and coracoid on each side, the inner ends of the two clavicles articulating with the dagger-shaped interclavicle which runs down the front of the sternum in the midline. An additional bone, the cleithrum, is found at the front of the upper part of the scapular blade in the earliest fossil reptiles. Clavicles, interclavicle and cleithrum are parts of the dermal skeleton.

In some primitive reptiles the humerus was short and massive with wide ends, the flat surface of the upper end being set nearly at a right angle with that of the lower; in many members of the class, however, the humerus has become fairly long and slender. Projections near the upper end of the bone give attachment to the powerful deltoid and pectoral muscles which originate from the shoulder girdle and sternum. The mechanism of the shoulder joint is described by Haines (1952).

The radius and the ulna articulate with the humerus at the elbow and with the inner row of carpal bones at the wrist. The wrist can rotate through about half a right angle, such movements being known as supination and pronation.

In the primitive reptilian carpus (Fig. 23E) there seems to have been a proximal row of three bones (apart from the pisiform): the radiale and ulnare opposite the radius and ulna respectively, with an intermedium between the two; a distal row of five bones opposite the metacarpals; and a third row consisting of two centralia sandwiched between the others. There is a good deal of variation in different reptile groups, some members of the primitive carpal series being suppressed or fused with their neighbours.

Beyond the carpals is a row of slender metacarpals embedded in the substance of the hand, and beyond these again are the bones of the fingers (digits), each consisting of a number of segments (phalanges). Primitive reptiles possessed pentadactyl limbs and a phalangeal formula (the number of phalanges in each digit from the inner or thumb side to the outer side of the hand) of 2:3:4:5:3. This arrangement still occurs very generally throughout the class, though in some groups, notably those in which the limbs have been converted into swimming paddles, it has become greatly modified (Fig. 12, p. 106).

Sesamoids or bones developed in muscle tendons may be found behind the elbow (i.e. the ulnar patella of many lizards) and at the outer side of the carpus (the pisiform).

The pelvic girdle (Fig. 2H) consists typically of three plates of bone: the ilium above, which is generally firmly connected with the sacral region of the vertebral column, and below the pubis in front and the ischium behind. The acetabulum or socket for the femur lies at the junction of these three bones. Pubis and ischium usually meet their fellows of the opposite side in a broad joint or symphysis in the midline of the belly. The pelvic bones give attachment not only to many of the muscles of the leg and thigh, but also to some of those of the ventral abdominal wall and tail, and sometimes also to those of the male organs of copulation.

The femur is usually stout with a cylindrical shaft and broad ends, and has prominent processes (trochanters) for muscle attachment near its head. Of the two leg bones, the inner or tibia is the larger and takes most of the weight of the body. The slender fibula usually articulates with the femur in reptiles but may be reduced or absent. A sesamoid bone, the patella is developed in the extensor muscle tendons at the front of the knee in some reptiles (e.g. some lizards).

The small tarsal bones in the ankle probably have a basically similar arrangement to the carpals, but there is no separate tibiale. The two elements in the inner row are known as the fibulare or calcaneum, and the astragalus which probably represents the fused tibilae, intermedium and a vanished centrale.

The foot of reptiles shows a greater tendency to part from its primitive pentadactyl pattern than the hand; not infrequently the inner and outer toes are reduced or absent. In the great majority of reptiles other than those on the mammalian line of evolution the fifth metatarsal tends to be shortened with its proximal extremity bent inwards, giving it a hook-like shape. This peculiarity is especially characteristic of the 'diapsid' groups and also of the Chelonia; it may in some cases help the foot to obtain a better grip of the ground (P. L. Robinson, personal communication).

The brain

The reptilian brain lies quite loosely within the cranial cavity, surrounded by a tough fibrous membrane, the dura mater.

It does not fill the cranium to nearly the same extent as the brain of a mammal, a fact to be considered in the interpretation of endocranial casts of fossil forms. The hinder part of the brain is well protected by the bones of the back and base of the skull as well as those of the roof. The front of the brain, however, is more lightly covered, for, as we have seen, the side walls of the cranial cavity in the region between and in front of the eyes are often mainly cartilaginous or membranous.

Both absolutely and relatively, the brain is small, and probably never accounts for more than about 1 %, at the most, of the body weight. In medium-sized lizards (*Lacerta viridis*) the brain accounts for about 0.5 % of the body weight and in large reptiles this proportion is very greatly reduced. In many dinosaurs with estimated weights of up to 30 480 kg (30 tons) or more, for example, the brain seems to have been only a few inches in length and a few ounces in weight.

The brains of reptiles, like those of other vertebrates, can be divided into fore-, mid- and hind-brain regions, the latter being continuous with the spinal cord (Fig. 3A). The fore-brain consists of the two cerebral hemispheres, which are hollow, surrounding cavities known as the lateral ventricles, and behind and between them a region known as the diencephalon which surrounds the cavity of the third ventricle. Each hemisphere is continuous in front with an olfactory stalk which ends in a blunt swelling, the olfactory bulb. Into this pass the nerves of smell from the nose. In many reptiles there is also a well developed vomeronasal nerve from the organ of Jacobson on each side (p. 37) which enters an accessory olfactory bulb just behind the main one. This primary association of the function of smell with the cerebral hemispheres is characteristic of reptiles, and indeed of most vertebrates.

In the dorsal part of each hemisphere is a small area which has been thought to correspond with the very extensive and dominant region of the mammalian cerebral cortex known as the neopallium, which receives sensory fibres from other parts of the brain, and which gives origin to motor fibres running back to the spinal cord. Experiments involving electrical stimulation or destruction of the cortex in reptiles have so far thrown no real light on its functions. It seems that the cortex plays a very small part in the neural activities of these animals (Goldby and Gamble, 1957).

By far the greater part of the reptilian cerebral hemisphere is formed by the corpus striatum, a solid mass of nervous tissue which bulges into the cavity of the lateral ventricle from the lower and outer part of its wall (Fig. 2F). This corpus striatum, which reaches even greater dimensions in birds, is generally regarded as being concerned in the elaboration of instinctive, as opposed to learned, behaviour, and in birds at least there is some experimental evidence for this view.

The corpus striatum is closely connected with the region of the brain which surrounds the third ventricle, the diencephalon. A part of this is made up by a small thalamus, which probably receives some sensory fibres from the brain-stem and spinal cord. Ventral to the thalamus is a large hypothalamic region closely connected with the pituitary. As in other vertebrates it is con-concerned with the integration of metabolic activities and perhaps plays some part in the animals' responses to changes in temperature (p. 55).

The roof of the mid-brain or tectum is extremely well developed, and forms a pair of prominent optic lobes which receive the great majority of the fibres from the optic nerves. This region is an important coordination centre and performs functions analagous with those of the cerebral cortex in mammals.

The hind-brain consists of the rather small cerebellum, devoid of lateral lobes, which is mainly concerned with balance and the maintenance of posture, and of the medulla oblongata. There is no region on the ventral surface of the medulla corresponding with the mammalian pons; the absence of this and of the lateral lobes of the cerebellum is correlated with the rudimentary nature of the cerebral cortex.

Cranial nerves corresponding with the twelve cranial nerves of mammals are present, mainly arising from the mid- and hind-brains. In reptiles, however, the vagus (X) and the cranial root of the XIth (accessory nerve) may be fused. A detailed account of the cranial anatomy including the nerves in a lizard has been given by Oelrich (1956).

The brain of a modern reptile has clearly become specialized along very different lines from that of mammals and the condition in the latter could not have been evolved from that in the former. The most striking differences between the two lie in the small size of the cerebral cortex and the absence of cerebellar lateral lobes, and the relatively enormous development of the corpus striatum and tectum in the reptilian brain. In these respects the brains of modern reptiles resemble those of birds, which show most of those features to a much higher degree. In birds, however, the cerebellum as a whole is large, but the lateral lobes are poorly developed.

As one would expect from their brain structure, reptiles lack the capacity for learning which mammals possess and at the same time they do not show the elaborate instinctive behaviour of birds. Under laboratory conditions they can learn to follow simple mazes and to remember the differences between various patterns and colours if these are associated with pleasant or unpleasant stimuli, such as food or electric shocks (Boycott and Guillery, 1962). Some reptiles, particularly certain lizards, show quite elaborate patterns of social behaviour (p. 209).

The pituitary gland

The pituitary or hypophysis is an important endocrine gland attached to the ventral surface of the diencephalon and often lodged in a fossa in the basisphenoid bone. The secretions of its various lobes, shed into the bloodstream, have far-reaching physiological effects, and probably in all vertebrates are concerned in the regulation of growth. In reptiles there is evidence that the pituitary plays some part in the control of skin pigmentation, in the regulation of water metabolism and in influencing the activity of other endocrine glands such as the ovaries. Partly by virtue of its association with the hypothalamus, it forms a functional link between the nervous and endocrine systems. Information about the environment (for example conditions of light or temperature) and also about the interior state of the animal (such as the state of the body fluids) can thus be transmitted to the appropriate endocrine gland (Bentley, 1971). Recent literature on the reptilian pituitary is vast, but the structure of the gland, the seasonal changes which it undergoes and some of its various physiological actions have been reviewed by Saint Girons (in Gans *et al.*, 1970, v. 3) and by Bentley (1971).

B

The pineal complex

Sphenodon and many lizards have a well-developed median eye-like structure situated beneath a foramen near the front of the parietal bone and covered only by skin and connective tissue. This eye has been variously called the parietal, pineal or third eye, and its homology with similar structures in other vertebrates is not yet fully understood. It is possible that it represents one of a pair of eye-like organs originally placed side by side on the primitive vertebrate head. Related to it is a gland-like structure known as the epiphysis (Fig. 3A), which together with the eye (and certain other structures) make up the pineal complex.

The parietal eye seems to have all the requisites for photo-reception: a lens, a retina and (usually) a nerve which enters the roof of the diencephalon. There are, however, no eye muscles or mechanism of accommodation. In recent years much interesting work on its functions has been done by R. C. Stebbins, R. M. Eakin and their collaborators, who have studied the effects of removing or inactivating it (see Stebbins and Cohen 1973). It seems that the eye acts as a kind of register of solar radiation, regulating the amount of time which the lizard spends in the sun, and thus influencing indirectly the extent of the creature's activity. Its functions are probably interrelated with those of the thyroid gland.

A pineal foramen, suggesting the presence of a parietal eye beneath it, was present in many fossil reptiles, though it had disappeared in the great majority of archosaurs. Among modern forms, this eye is absent or vestigial in all snakes and a few lizards, and also in chelonians and crocodilians. The epiphysis is present in all save the crocodilians. In mammals this structure, usually called the pineal body, is the only remaining part of the pineal complex. The functions of the epiphysis remain obscure.

The eyes

The eyes of reptiles are usually well developed and play an important part in the lives of their owners; a very interesting account of their structure and mode of action is given by Walls (1942), and Underwood (in Gans *et al.*, 1970, v.2) has contributed further information to this survey.

The eye colour, mainly due to pigmentation of the iris, is often bright, yellow or reddish hues being not uncommon. In some cases the colour of the eyes lends itself to a general camouflage pattern.

The sclerotic coat (sclera) of the eye (Fig. 23A, p. 200) is cartilaginous, except in snakes, whose eyes show many peculiarities (p. 206). At the junction of the sclera and cornea there is often a ring of small overlapping bony plates, often about fourteen in number, known as the scleral ossicles; these are surprisingly well preserved in many fossils (Fig. 12, p. 106).

Accommodation for near vision is brought about in a different way from that in mammals. In reptiles (other than snakes) the contraction of small muscles in the ciliary body presses this structure against the periphery of the lens, which is reinforced by a special pad, and deforms it into a more rounded shape suitable for close vision. The scleral ossicles help to resist the increase in pressure inside the eyeball which occurs during the accommodation process. Many reptiles (e.g. modern crocodiles) are able to do without these little bones, and their presence does not seem to be associated with an aquatic or any other particular mode of life.

The retina may contain both rods and cones of various types, the former predominating in nocturnal species. In most lizards, however, cones are the only visual cells present. A vertical pupil (which can contract more fully than a round one) is often seen in partly nocturnal animals which also bask by day and need to protect their nocturnally effective type of retina from bright light.

The fields of the two eyes in most reptiles overlap to some extent, giving a degree of binocular vision. Lizards (*Lacerta*) have been trained to distinguish coloured discs presented with normal mealworms and worms which have been rendered unpalatable by soaking in brine. They seem to prefer grey and white to colours, and among the latter, green, the commonest colour in their natural environment, was selected most often when four coloured discs bearing palatable food were offered simultaneously. Such experiments show that these lizards have the power of colour vision, and there is evidence that this is also the case with tortoises and possibly snakes, though probably not with crocodiles.

The optic nerve leaves the retina at the back of the eye, perforating the sclera. Projecting from the nerve into the eye is the conus papillaris, a structure richly supplied with blood vessels from which nutritive substances diffuse through the vitreous humour to the inner layers of the retina. It is comparable with the pecten of birds. The conus papillaris is reduced in turtles.

The optic nerve fibres cross over from one side of the head to the other at the optic chiasma, beneath the brain just in front of the pituitary, those from the right eye going to the left side of the brain and vice versa. It is generally believed that the fibres cross completely, but it has been shown that a few fibres remain on the same side in some Squamata, so that each eye is represented on both sides of the brain, though only on the same side to a very limited extent. Most of the optic fibres enter the mid-brain.

Of the two eyelids, the lower is the larger and more mobile, except, of course, in forms with a spectacle (p. 205). There is usually also a third eyelid, the nictitating membrane, at the front of the eye, which is more or less transparent and can sweep backwards very rapidly across the cornea, presumably cleaning it and lubricating its surface. There are generally two main conjunctival glands, a Harderian gland at the front of the eye associated with the nictitating membrane and a lachrymal gland at the upper and posterior aspect. The lachrymal or tear duct as a rule originates by two little canals at the front of the lower eyelid, superficial to the nictitating membrane, and drains into the nose, as in crocodiles, or ends in close relationship with the mouth and organ of Jacobson, as in Squamata (p. 207) and *Sphenodon*. It is absent in turtles.

In addition to the standard vertebrate complement of six eye muscles, there are others such as the retractor bulbi, and its derivatives which work the nictitating membrane, supplied by the abducent nerve. Beneath the orbit is a flat sheet of muscle, the levator bulbi, which is supplied by the trigeminal nerve and seems to be a modified jaw muscle; a separated portion of this forms the depressor of the lower eyelid. In certain lizards, notably the monitors, some of the eye muscles are partly attached inside the pituitary fossa on either side of the gland. The size of the fossa in the bony skull, therefore, is not necessarily a guide to the size of the gland itself. This condition is of some interest since attempts have been made to correlate the supposed size of this gland, which is concerned with the regulation of growth, with the body size of certain large extinct reptiles.

The nose and organ of Jacobson

The nose consists of a membranous sac on each side, opening in front at the external nostril and behind on to the palate at the internal nostril (Fig. 23F, p. 200). The front of each nasal sac generally has a simple tubular form; it leads back into a more extensive olfactory chamber which in some forms is twisted sideways on itself into a U-shape. On the outer wall of this chamber there is usually a shelf-like projection known as a concha, covered with epithelium and supported by cartilage.

Only a fairly small part of the lining of the nose has the function of smell, probably just the region over and adjoining the roof of the olfactory chamber. Elsewhere much of the epithelium is 'respiratory' in type with ciliated and mucous-secreting cells. It is well supplied with blood vessels, and probably plays some part in regulating the body temperature, imperfect though such regulation may be, since heat can presumably be lost or gained through it, and water evaporated from its surface.

Another sense organ associated with the nose is the paired organ of Jacobson. This is a modified part of the nasal sac which in the course of embryonic development comes to be more or less separated off from the latter and in lizards and snakes acquires a separate opening into the mouth (Fig. 23F). Its nerve supply is in effect a separate branch of the olfactory nerve and the sensation which it subserves it probably akin to that of smell. The organ is vestigial in crocodiles, fairly large in *Sphenodon* and reaches its highest development in the lizards and snakes. In turtles it is confluent with the nasal cavity and differs basically from that in other forms (see T. S. Parsons, in Gans *et al.*, 1970, v.2),

The ear

In many reptiles the eardrum or tympanic membrane is visible on the surface of the head; in some primitive fossil forms there was a conspicuous otic notch at the back of the skull across which it was probably stretched. In modern reptiles such as lizards it is attached to the concave surface of the back of the quadrate (Fig. 2E, p. 26).

Behind the eardrum lies the cavity of the middle ear which contains the stapes, or columella auris, and communicates with the pharynx by means of the eustachian tube. The outer part of the stapes which is in contact with the eardrum is cartilaginous and is termed the extra-stapes or extra-columella (Fig. 3E). The inner part is expanded to form the footplate and is applied to an opening in the ear capsule known as the oval window. Vibrations of the stapes due to sound waves impinging on the eardrum are transmitted to the inner ear fluids and stimulate the special sense organs which the latter bathe. In some reptiles the eardrum and middle ear are degenerate and methods of hearing involving bone conduction are employed.

The inner ear is a complicated system of tubes, all ultimately continuous with each other, containing fluid, the endolymph. It is surrounded by the skeletal otic capsule, from which it is separated in many places by more fluid, the perilymph. The tubes are arranged in two groups, the utricle and semicircular canals which are concerned in equilibration, and the saccule and its derivatives which are at least in part concerned with hearing. The special receptor organs are located in various places on the walls of the tubes. Arising from the saccule is an outgrowth known as the ductus endolymphaticus which ends in a blind endolymphatic sac. In some Squamata this is large and filled with calcareous matter; in the geckos and a few other lizards it escapes from the skull through an opening (variously situated in different species) and extends back among the neck muscles. It has been suggested that it serves as a calcium-secreting gland, pouring calcium salts into the bloodstream before the time of egg-laying when these are needed for the formation of the calcareous eggshell.

The lagena or cochlear duct is another outgrowth from the saccule: unlike the cochlea of mammals it is not coiled. The special organ of hearing, the papilla basilaris, is situated on the wall of the cochlear duct and corersponds with the organ of Corti in mammals. (See I. L. Baird in Gans *et al.*, 1970, v.2.) Many important studies on the hearing of reptiles have been made by E. G. Wever and his collaborators.

The blood and lymphatic systems

The reptilian heart (Fig. 3) possesses two separate auricles and a ventricle which is usually incompletely divided by a septum. The pulmonary veins, carrying oxygenated blood from the lungs, enter the left auricle. The two anterior venae cavae and the posterior vena cava, returning deoxygenated blood from the systemic circulation, convey blood to the small sinus venosus which opens into the right auricle.

It is a characteristic feature of all living reptiles that three separate arterial trunks are given off directly from the ventricle. These are the pulmonary trunk which arises from the right side of the ventricle and divides into the two pulmonary arteries, and the left and right aortae or systemic arches. The latter are designated according to their courses outside the heart and not according to their sites of origin from the ventricle, for the left aorta arises on the right side of the right aorta, between it and the pulmonary trunk (Fig. 3). The right aorta is often somewhat larger than the left and gives rise to the carotid vessels which supply the head and usually to both the fore-limb arteries (subclavians).

The two aortic arches sweep backwards round the oesophagus and meet above it in the midline to form the dorsal aorta from which the vessels to the viscera and hinder part of the body are derived.

Channels connecting the aortae with the carotid arteries (ductus carotici) and the aortae with the pulmonary arteries (ductus arteriosi) are present in the embryo. The former often and the latter sometimes persist into adult life in certain species of reptiles.

The way in which the ventricle is partly divided by septa is very complicated and determines the extent to which the arterial and venous bloodstreams mix inside the heart. The circulation in the reptilian heart has been studied by a number of investigators, notably by Foxon *et al.* (1956) who have used radiographic techniques involving the injection of the radiopaque substance thorotrast into the bloodstream.

In reptiles other than crocodiles the main interventricular septum lies in the horizontal rather than the vertical plane and partly divides the ventricle into dorsal and ventral cavities, the

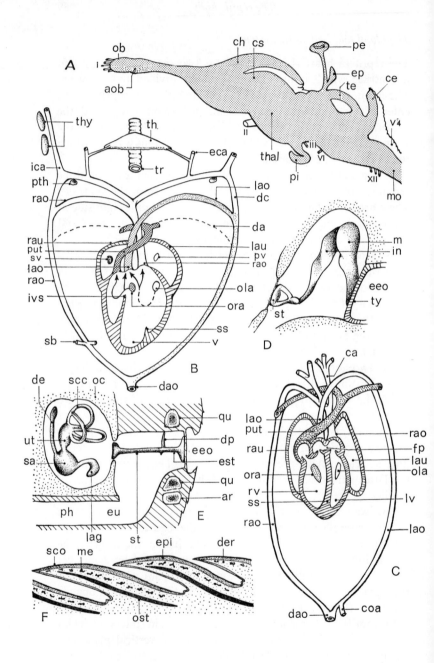

former being the larger of the two. Embryological studies show that the dorsal cavity represents the original left side of the ventricle, while the ventral one represents the right. For convenience the terms 'left' and 'right' will be used here, but it should be emphasized that these cavities are generally and more properly called the cavum dorsale and cavum ventrale by other authors.

Both auricles open into the 'left' (dorsal) part of the ventricle, so that to reach the 'right' (ventral) part, blood must pass across the free border of the interventricular septum. Much of the systemic venous blood from the right auricle does in fact follow

---

Fig. 3

A. Longitudinal section through brain of lizard. After Edinger (1908).

B, C. Heart, arterial arches, etc., of B, lizard and C, crocodile with heart structures shown diagrammatically in same plane from ventral side. Vessels carrying venous blood stippled, those carrying mixed blood stippled lightly; arrows in B show direction of blood flow in heart. The blood in the left aorta of the crocodile is normally oxygenated (see p. 43). Partly based on Hughes (1965).

D. Middle ear and ossicles of mammal.

E. Inner and middle ear of reptile, seen diagrammatically in partial cross-section.

F. Longitudinal section through skin of lizard with osteoderms.

aob, accessory olfactory bulb. *ar*, articular. *ca*, carotid-subclavian stem (left side). *ce*, cerebellum. *ch*, cerebral hemisphere. *coa*, coeliac artery. *cs*, corpus striatum. *da*, ductus arteriosus. *dao*, dorsal aorta. *dc*, ductus caroticus. *de*, ductus endolymphaticus. *der*, dermis. *dp*, dorsal process of extra-stapes. *eca*, external carotid artery. *eeo*, external ear opening. *ep*, epiphysial part of pineal complex. *epi*, epidermis. *est*, extrastapes. *eu*, eustachian tube. *fp*, foramen of Panizza. *h*, hinge of scale. *ica*, internal carotid artery. *in*, incus. *ivs*, main interventricular septum. *lag*, lagena. *lao*, left aorta (systemic arch). *lau*, left auricle. *lv*, left ventricle. *m*, malleus. *me*, melanophore. *mo*, medulla oblongata. *ob*, olfactory bulb. *oc*, otic capsule. *ola*, opening of left auricle into ventricle. *ora*, opening of right auricle. *ost*, osteoderm. *pe*, parietal eye. *ph*, pharynx. *pi*, pituitary. *pth*, parathyroid. *put*, pulmonary trunk. *pv*, opening of pulmonary vein into left auricle. *qu*, quadrate. *rao*, right aorta (systemic arch). *rau*, right auricle. *rv*, right ventricle. *sa*, saccule. *sb*, subclavian artery. *scc*, semicircular canal. *sco*, stratum corneum of epidermis. *ss*, secondary interventricular septum. st, stapes (= columella auris). *sv*, sinus venosus opening into right auricle. *te*, tectum of mid-brain. *th*, thyroid. *thal*, thalamus. *thy*, thymus bodies (shown on one side only). *tr*, trachea. *ty*, tympanic membrane (eardrum). *ut*, utricle. *v*, ventricle. *v4*, 4th ventricle of brain. Cranial nerves: I, olfactory; II, optic; III, oculomotor; VI, abducens; XII hypoglossal.

this path, so that the blood which reaches the 'right' of the ventricle is deoxygenated and is carried to the lungs in the pulmonary trunk. For this reason the 'right' part of the ventricle or cavum ventrale is also sometimes called the cavum pulmonale.

Owing to its smaller size, however, the 'right' part of the ventricle cannot hold all the systemic venous return and some of it remains (or flows back) into the 'left' side. From here most of it passes into the left aorta, which arises from a region nearly opposite, or slightly to one or other side of the free border of the incomplete interventricular septum. The composition of the blood in the left aorta is therefore much the same as that in the pulmonary trunk, and is therefore mixed or mainly venous.

The arterial blood in the left auricle will mostly enter the left side of the 'left' part of the ventricle and passes almost entirely into the right aorta for selective distribution to the head and forelimbs. This segregation of the bloodstreams to the left and right aortae is made more complete in certain lizards, at least, by the presence of another, secondary ventricular septum; the latter partly divides the 'left' side of the ventricle or cavum dorsale into two vertical halves and separates a left 'cavum arteriosum' related to the right aorta from a central 'cavum venosum' related to the left aorta. The difference in the composition of the blood flowing in the two aortae will disappear, however when they join to form the single dorsal aorta.

The secondary ventricular septum which has just been described may also be important from the evolutionary point of view, since it and not the main septum has apparently become the definitive interventricular septum of crocodiles and birds, where it divides the ventricle into two quite separate halves.

Some workers, who have studied other species of lizards, or certain snakes or chelonians, have obtained rather different results from those of Foxon *et al.*, outlined above. They have found that the blood in the left aorta is well oxygenated, resembling that in the right aorta rather than that in the pulmonary trunk. This discrepancy can be explained by the idea (for which there is some evidence) that the degree of oxygenation of the left aortic blood may vary in the same animal according to circumstances. It has been shown that during the phase of ventricular contraction, shunting of the blood from one side of the heart to the other may occur, as a response to changes in the balance between the resistances of the pulmonary and systemic circulations. Such shunts seem to be of special importance in amphibious reptiles such as terrapins. When these animals dive the resistance to the flow of blood through the lungs is apparently increased and the blood is shunted from the right to the left, sending more deoxygenated blood into the left aorta. This would tend to produce the condition observed by Foxon *et al.* in the green lizard. When the terrapin is breathing air, on the other hand, the direction of the shunt may be reversed so that the left aorta will carry oxygenated blood, like the right aorta. It is even possible that some of this arterial blood from the left side of the heart is shunted across into the 'right' main cavity (cavum ventrale or pulmonale) and re-circulated to the lungs (White, 1968).

In the completely partitioned heart of crocodiles, the right auricle leads into the right ventricle, the left auricle into the left ventricle (Fig. 3C). The right aorta arises from the left ventricle, the left aorta and pulmonary trunk from the right. It would seem from this arrangement that the left aorta, like the pulmonary trunk, must transmit entirely venous blood, since no mixing of the arterial and venous bloods can occur within the heart. The bases of the two aortae, however, communicate through a small opening known as the foramen of Panizza. It has been shown that as a rule oxygenated blood flows through this foramen from the right aorta to the left, so that the blood in the latter is arterial and not venous. As in terrapins, however, the pulmonary resistance is increased during diving and a right to left shunt is instituted. This may have the effect of forcing systemic venous blood into the left aorta so that any arterial blood entering it through the foramen of Panizza would be diluted; one would then expect the left aorta to carry mixed, or predominantly venous blood (see White, 1968).

It seems probably that in the ancestors of reptiles, as in modern amphibians and also in the embryos of higher vertebrates, the pattern of the systemic aortic arches was symmetrical. The retention of the left aorta in modern reptiles raises some very interesting problems; is it merely a useless and possibly undesirable relic, or does it have some real functional significance? One theory suggests that the left aorta has been retained as a kind of safety valve to lead away into the systemic circulation an excess of blood which could not be accommodated in the lungs—as, perhaps when the animal is indulging in strenuous activity. This idea has not met with general favour, and one can only suppose that the left aorta of reptiles has some value in allowing changes in the distribution of the blood to occur under different circumstances of the animal's life. It is possible that such circulatory changes may play some part in thermoregulation (V. A. Tucker in Milstead, 1967).

In both birds and mammals, at least in the post-natal state, the possibility of any mixing of the pulmonary and systemic circulations has been virtually eliminated, and only a single systemic aortic arch arises from the ventricle—the left ventricle. In birds the left aortic arch has been eliminated, whereas in mammals the right one has dropped out (except in so far as it contributes to the subclavian artery). This is only one piece of evidence which indicates that the birds and mammals arose from two distinct reptilian stocks which probably diverged from each other at a very ancient stage in reptilian history.

The heart will continue to beat for many hours after the 'death' of its owner; partly for this reason, the tortoise heart has been used quite extensively in studies of cardiac physiology. The normal rate of the heart beat is of course extremely variable, depending on such factors as temperature, activity and the time when food was last taken. Benedict (1932) found that the heart rate of a tortoise was around 10, 22 and 31–52 beats per minute at about 14, 20 and 30°C (57, 68 and 86°F) respectively. The heart rate of terrapins and alligators slows down when they dive; a similar bradycardia has been observed in aquatic mammals such as seals. The significance of this is not clear, but it may well be associated with changes in the distribution of the peripheral circulation, so that the blood flow is selectively distributed to the organs which most need it.

The red blood cells of adult reptiles are oval and nucleated. They are a great deal more numerous than the white cells. They vary in number from about $\frac{1}{4}$ to 2 million per cubic mm of blood, and in size from 14×8 microns to a maximum (in *Sphenodon*) of 23×14. The numbers of cells vary in individuals at different periods in the annual activity cycle. In mammals the red cells are considerably more numerous but individually smaller. The blood of reptiles is described by various authors in Gans *et al.*, 1970, v. 3.

Lymphatic vessels are present in reptiles and there are usually paired lymph hearts with contractile walls in the pelvic region. The aggregations of lymphoid tissue known as lymph nodes which are found in the mammalian body along the course of lymph vessels are only sparsely represented. Pharyngeal tonsils, present in some reptiles beneath the mucous membrane of the pharynx near the midline, are, however, bodies of this nature: so also, to some extent, are the thymus and the spleen. Some of these organs are probably concerned with the mechanism of immunity.

Respiratory system

In *Sphenodon* the lungs are simple sac-like organs, the cavities of which are directly continuous with the forked ends (bronchi) of the trachea (Fig. 4C). The lung walls contain small pockets or alveoli. In lizards the lung cavities are often split up by several incomplete partitions; in some lizards (notably the monitors) some turtles and in crocodiles the appearance is more like that in mammals, the whole lung consisting of a spongy mass of alveoli. (Fig. 4E, F) In these creatures the bronchi enter the lungs and traverse their substance, each main bronchus breaking up to form a number of smaller tubes into each of which a group of alveoli opens. In chameleons the lungs have air sacs which project like fingers from their surfaces (Fig. 4D).

The anterior part of the trachea is modified to form the larynx, which opens at the glottis at the back of the floor of the mouth. Special muscles open or close the laryngeal inlet and are involved in sound production. The epiglottis, a leaf-shaped cartilage which guards the glottis in mammals, is absent in most reptiles.

The intercostal muscles are the primary agents of respiration. Most reptiles breathe by moving their ribs with their intercostal muscles, expanding the thoracic cavity. As a result of the negative pressure so produced the lungs also expand, sucking in air at inspiration. Expiration is probably mainly brought about by contraction of the smooth muscle in the lung walls and by the transverse abdominal muscles. The respiration rate in reptiles, like the heart rate, is extremely variable and probably depends on similar factors such as temperature.

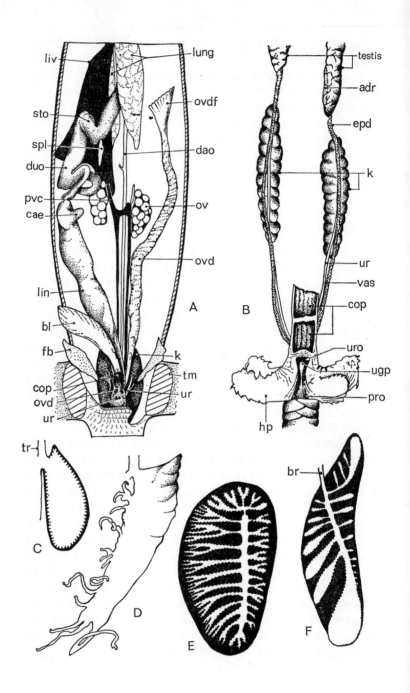

Alimentary canal and viscera

In reptiles the mouth characteristically extends back behind the eyes and the face is devoid of the fleshy muscular cheeks and lips of mammals. The tongue varies greatly in structure; it may be relatively immobile, as in turtles and crocodiles, or have a very wide range of movement, as in lizards and snakes (p. 208). Salivary glands of various kinds open on to the palate and around the margins of the mouth; in snakes some of these may be modified into venom glands.

The thyroid gland (Fig. 3B) lies in the midline of the neck across the trachea and just in front of the heart. Usually it is single but in a few lizards it consists of a pair of lateral lobes which may or may not be joined by an 'isthmus' across the midline. There is some inconclusive evidence that its secretions influence the periodicity of skin-shedding in addition to their other functions.

Thymus bodies are present on each side of the neck: two pairs, one anterior to the other in *Sphenodon*, snakes and lizards; and a single pair in most chelonians and in crocodiles where each thymus is much elongated. The thymus of lizards, like that of

---

Fig. 4

A. Contents of body cavity of female lizard (*Lacerta*). The viscera are turned over to the right side (of lizard) and the cloaca is cut open. The oviduct is shown on one side only. Modified from Saunders and Manton (1972).

B. Urogenital system of male adder (*Vipera berus*) seen from ventral aspect. After Voløse (1944).

C–F. Lungs of C, *Sphenodon;* D, *Chamaeleo,* showing air sacs; E, loggerhead turtle *Caretta;* F, the lizard *Varanus* showing saccular region at caudal extremity of lung. In C, E and F the lungs are shown diagrammatically in section, the connective tissue being in black. C, E and F after Wiedersheim (1909); D, after George and Shah (1965).

adr, adrenal. *bl*, bladder. *br*, bronchus. *cae*, caecum. *cop*, coprodaeum. *dao*, dorsal aorta. *duo*, duodenum. *epd*, epididymis. *fb*, fat body. *hp*, hemipenis. *k*, kidney. *lin*, large intestine. *liv*, liver. *ov*, ovary. *ovd*, oviduct and its opening. *ovdf*, oviduct funnel. *pro*, proctodaeum. *pvc*, posterior vena cava. *spl*, spleen. *sto*, stomach. *tm*, thigh muscles (cut). *tr*, trachea. *ugp*, urogenital papilla. *ur*, ureter and its opening. *uro*, urodaeum.

mammals, is known to undergo regression with age, but its function is obscure.

A series of small 'epithelial bodies', developed in the embryo like the thymus from the lining of the pharynx, are also found in the neck region near to the arterial arches. These probably correspond to the mammalian parathyroid glands, although in reptiles they are some distance from the thyroid; probably they have a similar physiological role (the regulation of calcium metabolism).

The alimentary canal seldom shows obvious specialization. A caecum is usually present, and most, perhaps all, reptiles possess a gall-bladder.

Little work has been done on the structure or function of the reptilian gut and herbivoruos forms such as tortoises in particular deserve further study. The rate of digestion and the passage of food through the gut varies greatly with temperature. Warm and active insectivorous lizards may fill their stomachs and pass the contents into the intestine at least once a day (Avery, 1973).

The terminal part of the gut, the cloaca, is a region of some complexity, and several chambers, partly separated by transverse partitions, can often be distinguished. Typically, there is an anterior chamber, the coprodaeum, which receives faeces from the rectum; a middle chamber, the urodaeum, into which the ureters and the ducts of the gonads open; and a final compartment, the proctodaeum, through which all the products of excretion and reproduction must pass before they reach the exterior (Figs. 4, 23I). Water is absorbed from the excretory products through the cloacal walls, which in some turtles also have a respiratory function (p. 75).

In many reptiles the peritoneal body cavity communicates with the pleural cavities through pleuro-peritoneal canals, there being, except in crocodiles (p. 124), no complete diaphragm separating the thoracic and abdominal cavities. As in mammals the peritoneal cavity usually contains a large peritoneal recess, the lesser sac, formed between the stomach and liver by the folding of the mesentery; this communicates with the main peritoneal cavity through the foramen of Winslow. The peritoneal membrane of some reptiles, for example the slow worm, is black, presumably owing to the presence of melanin pigment, but the significance of this is unknown. Paired masses of fatty tissue known as fat bodies (Fig. 4A) are present in most reptiles and may serve as food-reserve organs, being particularly important when females are laying down yolk in their eggs.

In the close vicinity of each gonad is the adrenal gland. This is composed of two quite distinct kinds of tissue, which in mammals are arranged into outer (cortical) and inner (medullary) zones, the latter secreting the hormone adrenalin. In reptiles, however, the 'medullary' cells are usually scattered about in groups throughout the 'cortical' tissue.

Excretory organs and excretion

The kidneys are partly developed from the posterior of the three kidney primordia in the embryo, the metanephros. In certain lizards and snakes the kidney tubules show an interesting sex difference: in the males each tubule has a swollen portion known as the 'sexual segment' which may undergo seasonal changes in cell structure. It is possible that the secretions of this may have some effect on the activity or the survival of the sperm. The kidney ducts or ureters open into the cloaca, often having a common opening with the vasa deferentia which may be raised up into a small urogenital papilla on the dorsal cloacal wall in the region of the midline (Fig. 23I, p. 200).

A urinary bladder is present in *Sphenodon*, turtles and some lizards. It usually opens into the ventral wall of the anterior part of the cloaca and has no direct connection with the ureters; the urine has to traverse the cloaca in order to enter or leave it.

Lizards and snakes were formerly believed to excrete the waste products of their nitrogenous metabolism almost entirely in the form of uric acid and its salts; it would seem, however, that substantial amounts of urea may also be produced, and in certain lizards this may actually predominate. The uric acid is passed as a whitish semi-solid mass, a characteristic reptilian 'dropping'.

Land tortoises, especially those from arid habitats, tend to excrete most of their nitrogen in the form of uric acid, but in some species the proportions of uric acid and urea may fluctuate even in the same individual. At times tortoises, like other chelonians, can produce a thin liquid urine. In marine and freshwater turtles and terrapins urea and ammonia in varying proportions are excreted, while ammonia is the principal nitrogenous excretory product of the alligator (Coulson and Hernandez, 1964; Cloudsley-Thompson, 1971).

In reptiles the products of urinary excretion may mingle in the cloaca with the faeces, derived mainly from the undigested remains of the food. However, urine and faeces may also be passed on separate occasions.

The excretion of the insoluble product uric acid (uricotelism) has the advantage over that of the soluble urea and ammonia in that very little water is needed for its elimination from the kidney. It is therefore not surprising that uric acid should be the principal end-product of nitrogen excretion in those reptiles which live under terrestrial, and especially under arid conditions. The value of uric acid excretion as a means of conserving water is enhanced by the ability of many reptiles to absorb fluid from their excreta through the walls of the cloaca. Such adaptations, like the relatively waterproof skin and the amniote egg, have served the reptiles well in their conquest of the dry land.

Marine reptiles have a special problem in ridding themselves of an excess of salt which they are likely to take in with their food. In sea turtles one of the orbital glands excretes the surplus salt which is washed away in the tears; in the marine iguana the nasal glands perform this function, while in sea snakes there is said to be a special 'natrial gland' at the front of the palate (see Bentley, 1971).

Reproduction and embryonic development

The gonads (testes or ovaries) are situated inside the abdominal cavity and may lie at different levels on the two sides of the body. Attached to each testis is the epididymis, through the tubules (vasa efferentia) of which the sperms pass before entering the vas deferens which carries them to the cloaca. In modern reptiles, except *Sphenodon*, the males always possess some form of intromittent organ, but its structure differs widely among different groups. It seems likely that such organs were absent in primitive reptiles and that different types of penis have subsequently been evolved independently, at least by crocodiles and turtles on the one hand and snakes and lizards on the other.

The oviducts in the female are always separate and do not

fuse caudally in the midline to form a single uterus and vagina as in most mammals. Fertilization takes place in the upper part of the oviduct.

One of the most interesting herpetological discoveries of recent years is that certain populations of lizards, notably of the rock lizard *Lacerta saxicola* in the Caucasus, of some North American species of *Cnemidophorus* (family Teiidae) and of some geckos, reproduce in the wild by parthenogenesis. The populations consist entirely of females and these (at least in the case of the Russian forms) produce greater numbers of eggs than 'normal' bisexual females of closely related species or races, and the incubation period of these eggs is shorter. As a rule, the eggs laid by the parthenogenetic females only give rise to female offspring. The chromosome complement of these lizards is either diploid or triploid and has been described by Darevski (1966) and by American workers (see Cuellar and Kluge, 1972).

Much interesting work has been done recently on the chromosomes of reptiles in general and the interested reader is referred to the books by Bellairs (1969), Goin and Goin (1971) and Porter (1972). It is worthy of note that in some reptiles the sex chromosomes are dissimilar in the female and similar in the male, the opposite of the mammalian condition (see Bücherl *et al.*, 1968 v. 1).

As in many other vertebrates, the reproductive organs go through a cycle of seasonal changes which are evoked by the activity of endocrine glands such as the pituitary and are also influenced by environmental factors such as temperature, light and possibly food supply. In temperate climes, at least, reptiles usually breed once a year, fertilization taking place in the spring and the young appearing towards the end of summer. Sometimes, however, a second, autumn mating may take place, the sperms probably living in the female's oviduct throughout the winter and fertilizing the eggs in the following spring. In some species, however, such as the adder (*Vipera berus*), females have a bi-annual cycle and any particular individual reproduces only once in every other year (or even less often)—at least in certain parts of the species' range (Prestt, 1971). Further accounts of the sexual cycle in Squamata are given by Fitch (1970) and Saint Girons and Pfeffer (1971). The ability of the sperms to live and survive for long periods in the female reproductive tract is demonstrated by instances of turtles and snakes laying fertile eggs after months or even years of solitary confinement. In some species special receptacles for sperm storage are present in the oviduct (see Cuellar, 1966). Such sperm storage should not be confused with parthenogenesis.

Most modern reptiles lay eggs and it may be supposed that this was the mode of reproduction in the earliest members of the class. Many snakes and lizards, however, are viviparous, retaining the eggs within the oviducts until the young are ready to be born. The term ovoviviparous is often applied to this type of reproduction in cases where the eggs are large and yolky, as in reptiles, to distinguish it from the viviparity of mammals where the eggs are small and the embryos are dependent on placental nutrition. In view of the fact that some snakes and lizards have a placenta (p. 214), however, the distinction between ovoviviparity and viviparity seems an artificial one.

The eggs of reptiles vary greatly in size, the range being from about 5×6 mm in small lizards, to 60×105mm in large pythons. In shape they may be nearly round, oval or elongated. They are usually whitish and are seldom if ever coloured, like many birds' eggs. They are laid on land in sheltered situations such as in crevices, among leaves or beneath sand. In some cases a simple nest is made, and in crocodilians and a few species of lizards and snakes the eggs are guarded or brooded by the mother (pp. 213, 214). The rate of development of the embryos is influenced considerably by fluctuations of the environmental temperature, even in viviparous forms. In temperate climes it may occasionally be retarded throughout the winter in some species.

The eggs are enclosed in a shell secreted by glands in the lower part of the oviduct. The degree to which the shell is impregnated with lime salts, and hence its hardness, varies considerably in different species. Beneath the shell is a shell-membrane within which is contained, at least in some reptiles, the egg-white or albumen secreted by the upper part of the oviduct. It provides a supply of water and probably also some food substances for the embryo. The reptile egg, unlike that of the hen, has no air space and lacks the twisted strands of dense albumen known as the chalazae which suspend the avian embryo and yolk within their albuminous covering. As in birds, the yolk is plentiful and provides the main source of food for the developing embryo; at first the embryo consists only of a tiny plate of cells, the blastoderm, on top of the great mass of yolk which is slowly used up as the embryo develops.

The embryos of reptiles, birds and mammals are distinguished by the fact that at an early stage they develop three special membranes, the amnion, chorion and allantois. Their presence in the embryos of all the three classes of higher vertebrates has led to the collective designation of these groups as the Amniota.

The amnion grows out at the sides of the embryo and soon comes to invest it almost completely in the form of a bag filled with fluid which bathes the surface of the embryo. The allantois develops as a saccular outgrowth from the hind part of the gut and in later embryonic life spreads out to surround the amniotic cavity and the embryo, as well as the greater part of the yolk sac. The chorion surrounds both the allantois and the amnion, and is closely applied to the inner surface of the shell membrane. In the early stages of embryonic life the chorion develops in close association with the amnion and is in continuity with it; the term amniochorion is therefore often used as a collective designation for the two membranes. The mode of development of the embryonic membranes is on the whole similar to that in birds.

The amnion serves to provide the embryo with an aquatic medium in which it can develop; the amniotic fluid, together with the albumen, helps to prevent the embryo and its yolk sac from adhering to the shell, a danger which is increased by the fact that the eggs of reptiles, unlike those of the hen, are seldom turned by their mothers. It may also afford some protection to the embryo against mechanical injury caused by disturbance of the eggs.

The allantois is a respiratory organ. Its outer surface is covered by vascular mesoderm, and as it grows out between the amnion and chorion its blood vessels are carried to the latter and brought close to the shell. Oxygen and carbon dioxide can pass through the shell into and from these vessels. It also serves another function as a reservoir for waste products during embryonic life. Both the allantois and the chorion may take part in the formation of a placenta and so may the yolk-sac.

The amniote eggs of reptiles and birds, with their tough shells and yolky food reserves are more or less self-contained, sheltering the embryos to a considerable extent from the hazards of the outside world. Eggs of this type have been called cleidoic or 'closed-box' eggs. However, few if any reptilian eggs, even those with hard shells, are completely impermeable to water; they probably take up some at least of the moisture required from their surroundings and thus often swell in size during development.

It is generally believed that the amniote type of egg was evolved by the immediate ancestors of reptiles as an essential adaptation to terrestrial life, an innovation which helped them greatly to become the first vertebrate colonists of dry regions. It has been suggested that many of the early reptiles lived under conditions of recurrent drought so that it was then safer to lay eggs in sheltered positions on land than to deposit them in a pool which might dry up—and where predators were likely to be more numerous. The necessity of laying eggs on land is certainly a basic reptilian character and even highly aquatic forms such as the sea turtles continue to do so. It would seem that the only way in which an aquatic reptile can avoid the necessity of returning to land in order to reproduce (a dangerous procedure for both adult and young) is by becoming viviparous, like the ichthyosaurs and the sea snakes.

Much information on the development of the different organs in reptile embryos has been gained from the study of preserved specimens by such methods as cutting them into serial sections for the microscope. Experimental work on living embryos has lagged behind that on amphibians and birds. Nevertheless, techniques for operating on the embryos of chelonians within their eggs have been devised, while the use of culture methods for raising the embryos of viviparous forms outside the mother have been ingeniously exploited by French workers, in particular by A. Raynaud. The eggs of the common lizard, *Lacerta vivipara,* are particularly easy to maintain in this way; if kept sterile, on a simple medium of saline and albumen, the embryos will develop in their membranes and hatch as normal young. Reviews of reptilian embryology are given by A. Bellairs (1969), in Grassé (1970), and by R. Bellairs (1971).

Temperature regulation and activity

Heat is produced as a by-product of many metabolic processes and it is largely by controlling the amount of this heat which is lost that mammals such as man are able to maintain their bodies at a constant temperature. To be able to do this is advantageous since alterations in the temperature of the internal environment may interfere with metabolic processes which must continue if the animal is to remain in a state of activity.

The metabolic rate of reptiles is lower than that of birds or mammals so that less heat is generated in their bodies. Indeed it has been shown that under resting conditions snakes may be often slightly colder than their surroundings: as the result of evaporation of moisture from their skins they lose more heat than their tissues produce. Not only do reptiles produce relatively less heat than birds or mammals, but what they do produce is more easily lost, since they have no insulating coat of fur or feathers, and do not seem able to raise their temperature by special expedients, such as shivering. Hence they are, to a very large extent, dependent on external sources of heat, such as may be provided by the sun's rays, or by the ground on which their bodies rest. For this reason typical reptiles are often known as ectothermic, in contradistinction to endothermic, the term applied to birds and mammals, which, mainly by virtue of their high metabolic rate, can generate all the heat they need within their own bodies. Some living reptiles, such as incubating pythons, monitor lizards and the leathery turtle may be partly endothermic and there is probably increasing evidence that certain extinct forms such as the advanced therapsids (p. 102), dinosaurs and pterosaurs were more or less endothermic too. Following a common practice in modern herpetology, we have used the term ectothermic as synonymous with the more familiar poikilothermic (having a variable temperature) or 'cold-blooded', and the term endothermic as more or less equivalent to homoiothermic (having a stable temperature) or 'warm-blooded'. Specialists may prefer to draw finer distinctions, however, and our procedure could be usefully criticized on semantic grounds.

While reptiles may require a fairly high environmental temperature to maintain them in an active state, they are very susceptible to overheating and may be killed when their body temperatures rise to a level only a few degrees above that brought about by conditions to which they voluntarily expose themselves. It has been found, for example, that a body temperature of about 46°C (115°F), is potentially lethal to certain desert lizards, whereas one of about 40°C (104°F) is tolerated without distress. It is also possible that the germ cells have a greater heat sensitivity than the body as a whole, since male lizards (*Xantusia*) are known to become sterile at temperatures which seem to cause no discomfort. The susceptibility of reptiles to heat is probably at least partly due to the fact that they have no rapid cooling device comparable to the sweat glands which many mammals possess.

Although reptiles have little power of maintaining their bodies over long periods at temperatures which differ greatly from those of their surroundings, it must not be supposed that they are entirely devoid of any means of temperature control. In an important series of pioneer studies, C. M. Bogert, R. B. Cowles and their collaborators have shown that under natural conditions reptiles tend to behave in such a way as to ensure that their body temperatures remain within a certain optimum range.

Different species of reptiles tend to have their own preferred ranges of body temperature; the mean figure is called the 'eccritic' temperature. As might be expected, this is higher in diurnal than in nocturnal or burrowing forms. The alligator has a mean preferred temperature of about 33°C (91°F); in many diurnal desert lizards the figure ranges between 37 and 40°C (99 and 104°F) or even more; the agamid *Uromastyx,* the desert iguana *Dipsosaurus* and the teiid genus *Cnemidophorus* are at the top of the range. Secretive or nocturnal lizards, such as many skinks and geckos, and arboreal forms such as *Anolis* have ranges of the order of 27–33°C (81–91°F), and similar figures have been obtained for various chelonians and snakes. *Lacerta vivipara,* the common lizard found in England, which ranges as far north as the Arctic Circle, seem to prefer a body temperature as warm as 30°C (86°F), but in our climate it can seldom maintain this for long and must frequently stop hunting and retreat when the sun goes in. Some reptiles, such as the tuatara and the sea turtles seem to have their activity geared to low temperature levels; turtles usually have body temperatures of the same order as that of the surrounding water, but they can raise them to some extent by basking on the surface, or perhaps even by retaining metabolic heat (p. 82).

In some reptiles at least the optimal body temperature may vary under different conditions. Thus, certain geckos have low temperatures at night when they are actively searching for food, but high ones when they are digesting it in diurnal concealment. Marine iguanas swimming in the cool Galapagos waters have a lower body temperature than those basking on the lava boulders along the shore.

The methods of temperature control available to reptiles largely depend upon their ability to seek or shun the external sources of heat which are available in their natural habitats. Basking in the direct rays of the sun or resting on warm rock surfaces are obvious ways of raising the body temperature. Some lizards, such as *Phrynosoma*, adjust their posture, or the angle which their bodies make with the sun's rays in such a manner as to increase or decrease the exposed surface area as required. Nocturnal reptiles probably obtain most of their heat from the substratum. By such methods a reptile may be able to maintain its body temperature several degrees above that of the surrounding air.

To avoid overheating, reptiles take shelter in protected situations, in water, or by burrowing. They can make short sallies into regions where the temperature is far above the optimum, such as across rocks or sand too hot for the hand to touch, especially if, like many lizards, they are fleet-footed and able to run to cover before their temperature approaches a critical level. Under prolonged conditions of great heat reptiles may undergo a dormant period of aestivation, as do some crocodiles and tortoises which bury themselves in the hot season.

Some further methods of temperature control involving physiological rather than behavioural responses should be mentioned, although they are probably only of subsidiary importance.

In large and active lizards (some agamids, iguanids, monitors), the rate of absorption or loss of heat from or to the surroundings can be influenced by changes in the distribution of the circulating blood—as for instance between the superficial and deep tissues of the body. It is possible that shunting of the blood from the pulmonary trunk to the left aorta may be a device involved in this mechanism. Such a shunt would have the effect of reducing the blood flow to the lungs and increasing that in the systemic circulation, where it would be more readily available for the enchange and transport of heat.

Colour change (p. 218) is another method of temperature control practised by certain reptiles, since the amount of heat absorbed by an object depends to some extent on its coloration. The African lizard *Uromastyx* is said to grow darker when first exposed to the sun, presumably in order to increase heat absorption, but subsequently to grow lighter in order to retard a further temperature rise. Finally, in excessive heat, reptiles, like mammals, are able to cool themselves by panting, losing water through the mucous membrane of the mouth and respiratory tract. This is a desperate remedy since it helps to exhaust the animal's supply of water.

Reptiles are more resistant to extremes of cold than of heat, at least in so far as danger to life is concerned. Prolonged temperatures below freezing point are probably lethal, but above this level they can exist in a state of suspended activity for long periods. In temperate zones seasonal hibernation is always a feature of reptile life; the animals take refuge from the frost, often beneath the ground, in the autumn and emerge from their retreats in the spring. It is possible that protracted exposure to temperatures below those necessary for normal activity but not sufficiently low to cause the animals to hibernate is a special source of danger. Under such circumstances reptiles may move about, but will often refuse to feed. Moreover there is some evidence that the peristaltic activity of the gut and defaecation may be inhibited at temperatures which are still high enough for feeding to occur. Such considerations may explain why it is difficult to keep continental reptiles alive through the early spring in outdoor vivaria in this country, even though they have managed to survive the cold months of the winter.

The fact that reptiles depend so largely on their behaviour for thermoregulation suggests that they possess some rather precise mechanism for detecting temperature changes. There is, in fact, evidence that such a mechanism exists in the hypothalmic region of the brain, which has been shown in turtles to be sensitive to small temperature changes.

The reactions of reptiles to heat are in part determined by their size. Large animals, by virtue of their greater ratio of volume to surface area, lose and absorb heat more slowly than small ones. While they run less risk of damage from short exposures to extreme heat, they also require fairly long periods of warmth to bring their bodies to an activity level of temperature. It is perhaps for this reason that the largest reptiles are found in warm, stable climates. The possible relevance of body size to the extinction of the dinosaurs is discussed on p. 143.

There can be little doubt that the thermal requirements and tolerances of reptiles have been important in influencing their geographical distribution and adaptive radiation. Despite their basic limitations as ectothermic animals, however, the modern reptiles as a group show quite an impressive degree of thermal adaptability. To withstand conditions as diverse as those of a tropical forest from those of a Scottish moorland, the tissues in different species must have become adjusted to widely differing temperature ranges; different patterns of behaviour, appropriate to each environment, must have been evolved to ensure that these temperatures were kept within the limits necessary for survival.

Temperature conditions tend to impose on reptiles a daily (circadian) rhythm of activity. Diurnal forms may be potentially active throughout the warmer part of the day. Other species, or perhaps different populations of the same species living in a different climate, show a bimodal rhythm. They have a peak of activity in the morning and another in the later afternoon, but shelter during the hottest hours of the day.

When watching reptiles one is often struck by the spasmodic nature of their behaviour. This impression can be exaggerated, especially if it is based on captive individuals which are often kept under unsuitable temperature conditions and have no need (or perhaps, urge) to search for food and mates. In the wild, some lizards such as monitors are often very active and can run for considerable distances with great speed. Turtles make long voyages across the oceans, and the leathery turtle is said to be one of the fastest swimmers afloat. Nevertheless, it is probably true to say that reptiles in general are inferior to birds and mammals in their power of sustained effort, and this may be ascribed to their poorer capacity for internal homeostasis. Factors involving many aspects of reptilian organization are implicated here, e.g. their relatively inefficient method of temperature control. Inefficiencies of the respiratory and circulatory systems may also be important, especially—and despite the possibility of physiological adjustment (p. 43)—the incomplete separation of the arterial and venous bloodstreams.

Temperature regulation in reptiles has been described by Bellairs (1969), Templeton (1970, 1972), Cloudsley-Thompson (1971, 1972), and Spellerberg (1972), who is particularly concerned with its relationship to habitat distribution.

A reptile's activity is also influenced by other environmental factors beside temperature, such as light ('photoperiod') and humidity, but much less is known about their importance. All these factors are significant, too, in the determination of long-term rhythms, such as the maturation of the gonads during the sexual cycle, and here again the role of temperature may be predominant (Licht *et al.*, 1969). The situation is complicated by the fact that in some reptiles at least there appear to be intrinsic or endogenous rhythms which operate independently from the environment (like the menstrual cycle of the human female), but upon which rhythms induced by the environment are superimposed.

Ecology and ethology

During recent years many important studies have been made on the ecology and ethology of reptiles, and embrace such aspects of reptile life as the number of eggs and young produced, the rates of post-natal growth; the diet; activity cycles; social and reproductive behaviour; population density and population structure in terms of sex and age groups; enemies; and life-span. Much of this work has been done in the United States and some of it is reviewed in the books on general herpetology by Goin and Goin (1971) and Porter (1972). Here we would like to mention the work by Moll and Legler (1971) and Grubb (1971) on chelonians; by Cott (1961) on crocodiles; by Bustard (1970; 1972; 1973) on turtles and lizards; by Harris (1964), Milstead (1967) and Tinkle (1967) on lizards; and by Fitch (1963) on snakes. Such work has done much to raise the natural history of reptiles from the realm of anecdote to that of scientific observation, often controlled and amplified by the use of quantitative methods.

Reptiles in captivity

Given adequate care reptiles will survive in captivity for long periods, even when little attempt is made to reproduce their natural surroundings in the cages. Under such conditions, however, their behaviour tends to become a travesty of that in nature. Although some species usually feed readily others, particularly certain snakes, are liable to go on hunger-strike, eventually dying of inanition. Courtship and breeding seldom take place, although females impregnated prior to capture may of course lay eggs or bear their young. The ease with which captive reptiles are deflected from many natural, even vital, activities, is well known. It is probably due in part to their lack of behavioural adaptability and in part to their sensitivity to such factors as light, temperature and humidity, and their need for a more varied diet than it is easy to give them. Furthermore, captivity may upset intrinsic physiological rhythms which underly such activities as mating, skin-shedding and hibernation and are still very incompletely understood.

To attempt to reproduce conditions under which reptiles, especially foreign species, can pursue a more or less natural existence may, for obvious reasons, involve the expenditure of much time and money. Artificial heating which allows a temperature gradient in a cage so that the animal can control its own body temperature may be difficult to arrange, and space requirements present a further problem. Many reptiles in the wild show some form of territory behaviour and it is impossible for individuals or breeding pairs to segregate if large numbers are crowded together. Experiments in keeping selected, especially native, reptiles in large outdoor enclosures where some natural food, soil and vegetation can be made available, might, however, produce encouraging results and throw much light on different aspects of their behaviour. Methods of keeping reptiles in captivity are described by Ball and Bellairs (1972).

Diseases and abnormalities

It is possible to touch on only a few of the more important and interesting disorders with which reptiles are liable to be afflicted. Although comparative pathology (outside veterinary work) is still in its infancy, some idea of the range of diseases from which reptiles may suffer can be gained from the Pathologist's Reports published in the Proceedings of the Zoological Society of London and the book by Reichenbach-Klinke and Elkan (1965).

Infections due to bacteria of *Pseudomonas* and *Pasteurella* type are common and in captivity may be responsible for a kind of 'mouth-rot' or canker to which snakes are especially prone. Such conditions are often the result of the secondary infection of injuries. Bone infections (osteomyelitis) occur, and their manifestations have been seen in the fossilized skeletons of dinosaurs. Various kinds of pneumonia and tuberculosis are not uncommon. Infections by protozoal parasites such as amoebae are very dangerous in collections, causing abscesses and a virulent type of enteritis. *Entamoeba invadens,* which occurs in snakes, is almost identical with *E. histolytica,* the organism responsible for amoebic dysentery in man.

Multicellular parasites of reptiles include a variety of flat- round- and tape-worms, and arthropods such as mites, ticks and pentastomids or 'tongue-worms' (e.g. *Porocephalus*) which live as blood-suckers in the lungs of their hosts (see M. A. Smith, 1973).

Diseases apparently due to vitamin deficiency are common in captivity, especially a form of rickets (p. 77). Cancers of malignant and non-malignant type are known in most groups or reptiles.

Partial or Siamese twinning has been observed in turtles, lizards and snakes; the occurrence of serpents with double heads or tails is sufficiently common to have provoked a considerable literature on the subject going back to Aristotle. The anomaly of cleft palate (Fig. 22C) has been seen in late embryos of snakes; it is essentially similar to the well known condition in mammals, except that the cleft passes through the septomaxillary bone in the floor of the nose. Doubtless further research would reveal as extensive a range of congenital abnormalities as occurs in mammals (see Bellairs, 1969).

3 | Origin, radiation and classification of reptiles

Class AMPHIBIA
Subclass LABYRINTHODONTIA
  Contains various extinct groups including the order Anthracosauria
  from which the reptiles were descended and of which *Seymouria*
  (L. Perm.) was a late representative
Subclass LEPOSPONDYLI
Subclass LISSAMPHIBIA
  Includes Anura (frogs, etc.), Urodela (newts, etc.) and Apoda

Class REPTILIA
Subclass ANAPSIDA
  Order Cotylosauria (U. Carb.–U. Trias., W.w.)
    Suborder Captorhinomorpha: *Hylonomus* (U. Carb., N.Am.),
      Captorhinus (L. Perm., S.Af.), *Eunotosaurus* (M. Perm., S.Af.),
      Limnoscelis (L. Perm., N.Am.)
    Suborder Procolophonia: *Milleretta* (U. Perm., S.Af.), *Pareia-*
      saurus (U. Perm., S.Af.), *Procolophon* (L. Trias., S.Af.)

Labyrinthodonts and reptile origins

During the Carboniferous period, between about 280 and 340
million years ago, much of the earth was covered by swampy
forests of giant tree-ferns which have become fossilized as coal.
The coal forest pools were inhabited by a variety of amphibians,
the earliest kinds of vertebrates which were able to live partly
on land. The class Amphibia had originated during the previous
Devonian period from a group of bony fishes, the Crossopterygii
(lobe-finned fishes), whose closest living relatives are the coela-
canth (*Latimeria*) and the lung fishes (Dipnoi).

  The majority of the early amphibians belonged to a large and
important group, known, because of the folded structure of
their teeth, as the Labyrinthodontia. These animals varied

considerably in size and appearance; some were large creatures of rather crocodilian proportions, while others were small and superficially like newts or salamanders. A few of them became quite well adapted for terrestrial life, but the majority seem to have been mainly aquatic in habits, probably living on fish and smaller amphibians, and leaving the water only to move from one pool to another.

The labyrinthodonts flourished during the Carboniferous and early Permian periods, becoming extinct at the end of the Triassic. Possibly they were unable to compete with the various types of water-living reptiles which had appeared by this time. Long before they disappeared however, they gave rise to descendants, the reptiles, which were destined to have a long and successful career and from which the birds and mammals originated in their turn. The origins of the modern groups of Amphibia (frogs, salamanders, etc.) are still obscure.

In early Permian are found the remains of a creature known as *Seymouria* (Fig. 8, p. 90) which must have looked rather like a massively built salamander about 50cm (20in) long. It was clearly near the dividing line between amphibians and reptiles, and many workers have regarded it as the most primitive known member of the reptilian class. A good case can be made, however, for the view that it was an amphibian and not a reptile, for it shows some characteristically amphibian features, such as faint traces of lateral line sensory canals upon the skull. It existed, in any case, too late in time to have been ancestral to reptiles, since these had already appeared before the end of the Carboniferous. Moreover, its relatives had external gills.

Now that *Seymouria* seems no longer to occupy the position which it has often graced in textbooks as the ideal primitive reptile, another creature, *Limnoscelis* (Figs. 5, 8), has special claims to attention. This was a genuine reptile from the late Carboniferous or early Permian of New Mexico; apart from other considerations it was also too late an arrival on the geological scene to have been the actual prototype of the reptilian class. Judged on anatomical criteria, however, it illustrates many, though perhaps not all the conditions which one might expect to find in a member of the primitive reptilian stock.

Limnoscelis was about 1.5m (5ft) in length, some half of which was made up by tail, with an elongated body low-slung on

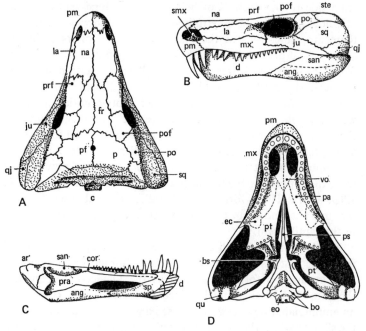

Fig. 5

A–D. Skull of the cotylosaur *Limnoscelis*; C, inner view of lower jaw. After Romer (1946).

Membrane bones
ang. angular. *cor,* coronoid. *d,* dentary. *ec,* ectopterygoid (= trans-palatine). *fr,* frontal. *ju,* jugal. *la,* lachrymal. *mx,* maxilla. *na,* nasal. *p,* parietal. *pa,* palatine. *pm,* premaxilla. *po,* postorbital. *pof,* postfrontal. *pra,* prearticular. *prf,* prefrontal. *ps,* parasphenoid. *pt,* pterygoid. *qj,* quadratojugal. *san,* surangular. *smx,* septomaxilla. *sp,* splenial. *sq,* squamosal. *ste,* supratemporal. *vo,* vomer.

Cartilage bones and other structures
ar, articular. *bo,* basioccipital. *bs,* basisphenoid. *c,* occipital condyle formed from *bo* + *eo*. *eo,* exoccipital. *pf,* pineal foramen. *qu,* quadrate.

short stubby legs which sprawled outwards from its sides. Like *Seymouria,* it was probably partly aquatic in habits.

In only a few characters does *Limnoscelis* differ significantly from *Seymouria,* but these are mostly features which connect it with later reptiles and indicate its essentially reptilian nature. The skull was of the anapsid type, but was somewhat compressed

C

from side to side instead of being flattened dorsi-ventrally. The otic notch, present in labyrinthodonts, had disappeared, though there are indications at the back of the skull of its region of closure. The premaxillary teeth were enlarged and overhung the front teeth in the lower jaw, a small specialization common among early reptiles but seldom seen in amphibians.

Limnoscelis is placed in the order Cotylosauria, a group which, as its popular name 'stem-reptile' suggests, contained the most primitive members of the class. Some related forms such as *Captorhinus* also occur in the early Permian and remains of even more ancient reptiles such as *Hylonomus* are now known from the Upper Carboniferous (see R. L. Carroll in Gans *et al.*, 1969, v. 1). These forms are placed in the suborder Captorhinomorpha and seem to lie closer than any others to the base of the reptile stem.

Another, more specialized line of cotylosaurs, perhaps derived from the last, is represented by the suborder Procolophonia. This group was formerly known as the Diadectomorpha, but the name has become invalid since *Diadectes* is now considered an amphibian. Some forms possessed an otic notch at the back of the skull to which the tympanic membrane is thought to have been attached; this notch was, however, of a different type to that found in labyrinthodont amphibians.

Some of the Procolophonia were small agile reptiles of lizard-like build such as *Procolophon* itself, which survived until the close of the Triassic. Others, the pareiasaurs of the later Permian (Fig. 9) were lumbering creatures and among the first really large reptiles to make their appearance. Many of them developed spiny excrescences on the head and a heavy armour of bony plates along the back, presumably a defence against carnivorous mammal-like reptiles (Ch. 5). The millerettids (p. 154) were another interesting but very different group which is provisionally classi-fied here.

It is likely that at some early period the reptiles split into two divergent evolutionary lines, one (sometimes called the 'Theropsida') leading to the mammal-like reptiles and mammals, while the other (the 'Sauropsida') led to the remaining reptiles and the birds. It is quite likely that most, if not all, later reptiles, both theropsid and sauropsid, have been derived directly or in-directly from the captorhinomorph cotylosaurs, of which group

Limnoscelis was a fairly primitive member. The position of the ichthyosaurs and plesiosaurs (p. 105) is problematical, however. Moreover, it is likely that the Chelonia, though perhaps derived from the common captorhinomorph stock, are not at all closely related to the other groups of modern reptiles (see Parrington, 1958; Romer, 1966, 1968; R. L. Carroll, in Gans *et al.*, 1969).

Although authorities are not yet agreed as to the precise stage in evolution at which the 'theropsid' and 'sauropsid' lines split off from one another, there is good evidence that such a dichotomy must have taken place. The brain of a mammal, for instance, is in some ways (p. 32) fundamentally different from that of a modern reptile and could not have been evolved from the latter. The same observation applies to the mode of origin of the great arteries from the heart.

It seems clear, therefore, that the modern reptiles are not intermediate in the evolutionary sense between the amphibians and the mammals, and that to find a common ancestor for a creature such as a lizard and a mammal one would have to go back to a very ancient reptilian stage in evolution.

Radiations of reptiles

In the history of most vertebrate classes there is a constant pattern. The earliest members are comparatively scarce, but give rise to more numerous descendants which branch off along divergent lines, some closer together than others. The members of each line evolve a characteristic type of specialization, often for some new mode of life, which enables them to become rapidly successful and abundant. This process is known as adaptive radiation.

After a time a new and more advanced group of animals makes its appearance; usually it originates from some of the less specialized members of one of the earlier branches. This group in turn undergoes a new cycle of adaptive radiation; since its members generally embody certain 'improvements' on the previous types, they tend to replace them in any spheres of activity where they compete. Others again will probably follow ways of life which are quite new and become adapted for conditions of environment which have not been previously exploited.

These successive radiations, each largely replacing the last, may be repeated several times in the history of a class. Sometimes a few representatives of the earlier cycles or even of the primitive ancestors of the whole group survive in almost unmodified form long beyond their time; *Sphenodon* (p. 155) is an example of 'such living fossils'.

The importance of the cotylosaurs is not merely due to the fact that they gave rise to other more advanced groups. As Romer has pointed out, animals cannot spend their time being diagrammatic ancestors; with some exceptions, like those noted above, they must become specialized and undergo adaptive radiation in order to survive and get their livings. The cotylosaurs represent the earliest radiation of the reptilian class.

While the cotylosaurs were in some respects hardly beyond the amphibian grade of organization, they must also have acquired some new specializations and abilities which the amphibians did not possess. One of the most important of these may have been the capacity to lay eggs on land and to dispense with an aquatic tadpole stage; we know that eggs of reptilian type were being laid in early Permian times. Romer (1966) has in fact suggested that in the evolution of amniotes the egg anticipated the adult in adaptation to terrestrial life, the parents coming ashore to breed but still spending much of their time in the water. However, this view is not entirely supported by recent work on *Hylonomus* and other very early reptiles from the Upper Carboniferous, which seem to have lived in a terrestrial environment (R. L. Carroll in Gans *et al., 1969,* v.1).

Cotylosaurs such as *Limnoscelis* and *Captorhinus* must, from the simple nature of their teeth, have been eaters of fish, flesh or insects, but there can be little doubt that the pareiasaurs were herbivorous. In fact, they were probably the earliest land vertebrates to exploit successfully the vast supplies of vegetable food available on the earth. The pareiasaurs were among the first of a series of herbivores whose bodies ran to bulk, armour and spinescence. They disappeared by the beginning of the Triassic.

The first cycle of reptilian radiation was already under way by the end of the Carboniferous, for not only cotylosaurs but members of other groups also occur in deposits of this time. It would seem, therefore, that the class itself must have originated about the middle of this period although only a few reptilian remains approaching this antiquity have been discovered.

The rise of the reptiles may be correlated with the widespread climatic, geological and floral changes which took place at the end of the Carboniferous. This was a time of great mountain building. The climate seems to have been variable; in some regions it was glacial, while in others it apparently became hot and dry, and deserts were formed. In many places the forests of tree-ferns and giant horsetails were superseded by plants such as conifers and seed ferns more suited to dry conditions. The appearance of such new types of environment may well have favoured the radiation of the reptiles as a terrestrial group. Another and more impressive radiation occurred towards the end of the Triassic and gave rise to many important groups of the past and present. The Chelonia, the crocodiles, the dinosaurs, the flying reptiles, the ichthyosaurs and the earliest mammals all came into being around this time.

Major classification

The early divergence of the reptilian stock into two main groups has been emphasized by such authorities as E. S. Goodrich and D. M. S. Watson. It might therefore be logical to divide the class Reptilia into two subclasses, the 'Theropsida' and 'Sauropsida', giving the various subordinate groups of reptiles a lower taxonomic rank. This view is not followed, however, by the majority of modern workers, and in a book of this kind there is much to be said for conservative classification. The following scheme, which like all classifications is provisional, is based on that given by Romer (1966), in his textbook *Vertebrate paleontology*.

The whole group of cotylosaurs, together with the Chelonia (turtles, etc.), being the only reptiles to retain the primitive closed-in type of skull, are placed in the subclass Anapsida. Reptiles having a single opening in the temporal region of the skull with the postorbital and squamosal often meeting above it comprise the subclass Synapsida; this group contained the ancestors of mammals and flourished during the Permian and Triassic.

Two more subclasses, the Ichthyopterygia and the Euryapsida, contained the ichthyosaurs and pleisosaurs, two groups of reptiles which had reverted to a thoroughgoing aquatic mode of life and which were very common in the seas of the middle and later Mesozoic. These both possessed a single temporal opening or fenestra (p. 105), although they were not closely related.

Finally we come to two subclasses of diapsid reptiles whose primitive members have two openings in the cheek region of the skull. One of these, the Archosauria, includes the dinosaurs, crocodiles and flying reptiles, and predominated in the later Mesozoic when its members replaced those of the earlier synapsid radiation. The other subclass, the Lepidosauria, contains *Sphenodon*, and the most successful of present-day reptiles, the snakes and lizards (order Squamata).

4 | Tortoises and turtles

Subclass ANAPSIDA
Order Chelonia [= Testudinata] (since U. Trias., W.w.)
  Suborder Proganochelyoidea (U. Trias.): *Proganochelys* [= *Triassochelys*] (Eur.)
  Suborder Amphichelydia (Jur.–Tert.): *Meiolania* (Tert., Aus.)
  Suborder Pleurodira
    Family Pelomedusidae (Af., Mad., Sn.Am.): *Pelomedusa* (Af., Mad.), *Podocnemis* (Sn.Am., Mad.)
    Family Chelidae (Aus., Sn.Am.): *Chelus* (Sn.Am.), *Chelodina* (Aus.)
  Suborder Cryptodira (some extinct families omitted)
    Family Chelydridae (N.Am.): *Chelydra, Macroclemys*
    Family Kinosternidae (N.Am., Sn.Am.): *Kinosternon*
    Family Dermatemydidae (Sn.Am.): *Dermatemys*
    Family Platysternidae (As.): *Platysternon*
    Family Emydidae (W.w. except Aus. and S.Af.): *Chrysemys* (N.Am.), *Emys* (As., Eur., N.Af., N.Am.), *Graptemys* (N.Am.), *Malaclemys* (N.Am.), *Pseudemys* (N.Am., Sn.Am., W.I.), *Terrapene* (N.Am.)
    Family Testudinidae (W.w. except Aus.): *Geochelone* (Af., Aldabra, As., Mad., Sn.Am., Gal.), *Gopherus* (N.Am.), *Kinixys* (Af.), *Malacochersus* (Af.), *Testudo* (Eur., As., N.Af.)
    Family Prostegidae: (U. Cret.): *Archelon* (N.Am.)
    Family Dermochelyidae: *Dermochelys* (oceanic)
    Family Cheloniidae: *Caretta, Chelonia, Eretmochelys* (oceanic), *Lepidochelys* (parts of Atlantic and Pacific)
    Family Carettochelyidae (New Guinea): *Carettochelys*
    Family Trionychidae (Af., As., N.Am.): *Trionyx* (Af., As., N.Am.)

Many groups of reptiles have found a pattern for survival in the evolution of a massive body armour as a protection from their enemies. Perhaps no other reptiles, however, have armoured themselves so completely as the chelonians and, as we shall see, the development of a rigid box-like shell in these creatures has necessitated some remarkable changes in the skeleton and internal organs.

The chelonian shell consists of two main pieces, the carapace above and the plastron below. These are usually joined by a bridge in the middle region of each side, leaving apertures in front and behind for the head, legs and tail. In some species parts of the plastron are movable at transverse hinges and can be pulled up against the carapace, giving a better protection for the body. There may be two hinges, one towards each end of the plastron, as in *Kinosternon*, or a single one in the middle, as in *Emys* and *Terrapene*. In one genus of tortoises, *Kinixys*, the back of the carapace is hinged and the plastron projects in front to form a ram-like structure. The curious East African tortoise *Malacochersus* has a flat, flexible shell which may help it to squeeze into crevices in its rocky habitat.

The shell is made up of two materials, an outer layer of horny scutes or laminae, and an inner layer of bony plates. The scutes do not conform with the bones beneath them either in position or number; their arrangement shows certain similarities, however, for in both cases there is on the carapace a single row of elements down the midline, a row of wider ones on each side of the latter and a series of small ones around the margins of the shell. The bony plastron may in part have been evolved from an abdominal rib system.

The horny scutes grow by the increment of new substance to their lower surfaces, each newly formed layer being larger than, and so visible round the periphery of the last. In many species, at least in those which inhabit temperate zones, there is a seasonal growth cycle. During each winter the growth of the scutes is arrested and this dormant period is marked by the appearance of a line around the edge of each scute. The number of these lines should therefore represent the number of years of the animal's life, but unfortunately simple counts are often invalidated by such factors as wear and disease which may cause irregularity in the normal growth cycle. When critically interpreted, however, they may give valuable information on the growth of some species.

Casual inspection of the skeleton of a tortoise (Fig. 6) suggests that there has been drastic reduction of the axial skeleton. The backbone is much shorter than in other reptiles and all but the first of the ten trunk vertebrae have become firmly attached to the median row of shell bones, the neurals. The dorsal ribs are more or less fused with the lateral rows of shell bones, the pleurals, but the two sacral ribs are free. There is no sternum, and the clavicles and interclavicle have probably been absorbed into the epiplastral and entoplastral parts of the plastron. In many chelonians the vertical blade of each scapula makes a kind of joint with the inside of the carapace, and in some (the Pleurodira) the ventral part of the pelvic girdle is fused with the plastron.

The strange position of the limb girdles in chelonians has aroused much interest, for they lie partly inside the rib elements. Embryological studies show that this condition is reached as a result of the developing ribs becoming associated with the carapace and being carried out over the girdles by the growth of the shell (see Gregory, 1951). The incorporation of much of the skeleton into the shell is associated with the disappearance of most of the back muscles, apart from those which move the neck and tail. Limb morphology and locomotor patterns are described by W. F. Walker in Gans *et al.* (1973).

To compensate for the rigidity of the trunk the neck is long and mobile, and in most species the head can be drawn back until it is almost hidden by the carapace. The joint surfaces of the eight or so neck vertebrae are specially constructed to allow the neck to kink in two or three places as it is retracted (Williams, 1950).

The skull in many forms, including the most ancient ones, is devoid of openings in the temporal region (Fig. 6G); consequently the Chelonia are placed with the cotylosaurs in the subclass Anapsida. In some species, however, the membrane bones at the back of the skull are 'eaten away' in a long wide notch (Fig. 6F). This condition occurs, for instance, in the snapping turtles (Chelydridae), where the supraoccipital bone is drawn out into a sagittal crest, giving attachment to the jaw muscles. This eating away or emargination of the skull roof is regarded by most workers as not representing a true temporal vacuity, although its function, to allow the jaw muscles to expand, is analogous. Hence it does not affect the anapsid status of the Chelonia as a group.

A few of the earliest chelonians had palatal teeth, but all

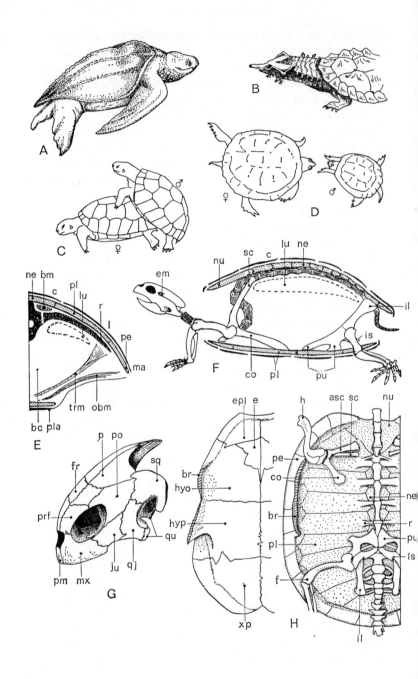

recent forms have a horny beak instead of teeth. In some sea-turtles there are horny papillae on the lining of the gullet.

The lungs lie beneath the carapace and dorsal to the viscera so that they will be affected by any pressure changes which occur within the main visceral cavity. Such changes are mainly brought about by certain abdominal muscles (Fig. 6E) which have an important respiratory function; movements of the limbs and particularly of their girdles are also involved (see Gans, 1970). In some chelonians, at least, inspiration is brought about mainly by contraction of the oblique abdominal muscles at the hind-leg pockets; this decreases the pressure of the viscera. Expiration is produced by contraction of the transversus muscles which push the viscera against the lungs and deflate them.

Some freshwater turtles have accessory respiratory mechanisms, the vascular mucous membrane of the pharyngeal or the cloacal membrane being used as a gill through which water can be pump-ed. Soft-shelled turtles (*Trionyx*) take up oxygen from the water

---

Fig. 6

A, leathery turtle (*Dermochelys*). B, matamata (*Chelus*). C, mating of tortoises (*Gopherus*). D, courtship of red-eared terrapin (*Pseudemys scripta elegans*). E. diagrammatic cross-section of chelonian through hind-limb pocket. The rib is shown slightly separated from the bony plates with which it is actually fused. F, diagrammatic longitudinal section through parts of chelonian skeleton. G, skull of green turtle (*Chelonia*). H, bony shell and parts of skeleton of terrapin (*Emys*). The plastron is seen from above and the extremities are not shown.

A and F, after Deraniyagala (1939). C, after Auffenberg (1966). D, after Oliver (1955). H, after Zittel (1932).

asc, acromion process of scapula. *bc*, body cavity. *bm*, back muscles. *br*, bridge (cut) joining carapace with plastron. *co*, coracoid. *em*, emargination of skull roof. *f*, femur. *fr*, frontal. *h*. humerus. *il*, ilium. *is*, ischium. *ju*, jugal. *lu*, lung. *mx*, maxilla. *obm*, oblique abdominal muscle. *p*, parietal. *pla*, plastron. *pm*, premaxilla. *po*, postorbital. *prf*, prefrontal. *pu*, pubis. *qj*, quadratojugal. *qu*, quadrate (forms a kind of otic notch). *r*, rib. *sc*, scapula. *sq*, squamosal. *trm*, transverse abdominal muscle.

Epidermal scutes or laminae (in black): *c*, centrals. *l*, laterals. *ma*, marginals. Bony plates: *e*, entoplastron. *epl*, epiplastron. *hyo*, hyo-plastron. *hyp*, hypoplastron. *ne*, neurals. *nu*, nuchal (proneural). *pe*, peripherals. *pl*, pleurals. *xp*, xiphiplastron.

The nomenclature of the various shell elements follows that given by Carr (1952); other systems are listed by R. Zangerl in Gans *et al.*, 1969, v.l. Older authors often give the same names (e.g. neurals, costals, marginals) to the horny and bony elements alike.

both through the skin and through special papillae in the pharynx. Aquatic respiration seems to be of particular importance in these turtles; they are sometimes killed when lakes are poisoned with derris (a respiratory poison for fishes), although other turtles living in the same water are unscathed. Some freshwater chelonians also appear to have an inherent physiological mechanism for coping with oxygen lack; they can survive in an atmosphere of almost pure nitrogen for eight hours or more, and it is thought that they are able to practise some form of anaerobic respiration (Belkin, 1963). By such methods certain species are able to remain submerged for long periods, especially if they are inactive, and may perhaps even hibernate at the bottom of a pool throughout the winter.

The sight of chelonians seems to be fairly good and some are known to be receptive to infra-red radiation. The sense of smell is probably keen, since the olfactory parts of the brain are well developed. Touch sensibility on both the extremities and the shell, and vibration sense are delicate.

The ear of chelonians, like that of many other reptiles, seems to be efficient only as a recorder for sounds of rather low frequency, i.e. for low notes. Studies by Wever and others of the electrical activity in the auditory nerve show that the green turtle, for example, can perceive sounds of between 60 and 1000 Hz fairly well; this range is wide enough to enable the animal to register important signals both on land and in the sea. Although chelonians are not particularly vocal creatures, some species emit various crying, grunting and even roaring sounds during courtship and mating. When attacked, the leathery turtle may utter 'pathetic wails, groans, roars and bellows' (Carr, 1952).

The two sexes are much alike, although males usually have a longer, thicker tail, inside the base of which the penis is housed, and a somewhat concave plastron to fit over the female's carapace during mating. The cloaca is essentially similar to that of crocodiles. In some species the male is furnished with special devices for clasping the female in copulation, such as an enlarged scale on the tail tip or long claws on the front feet. There may be differences in the colour or size of the head or body, which is sometimes larger in one sex, sometimes in the other. In *Graptemys* the females may be twice as big as the males.

In copulation the male mounts the female's back, curving

round his cloacal region until it approaches that of the female, beneath the back of her carapace (Fig. 6C). It may be preceded by courtship activities in which the male butts and bites the female. Some species have a more elaborate courtship; in certain *Chrysemys* and *Pseudemys* the male swims backwards in front of the female, stroking her face with his elongated front claws (Fig. 6D). In aquatic chelonians both courtship and copulation occur in the water. The mating of tortoises has been described in poems by D. H. Lawrence (in *Birds, beasts and flowers*), which are of zoological as well as literary interest.

The eggs of tortoises are hard-shelled, much like those of birds, but in turtles and many terrapins the shells are fairly soft. They are usually laid in nests excavated by the feet of the mother in sand, in earth or among rotting vegetation. The parent often urinates on them after laying, a procedure which may provide fluid for the developing embryo, but perhaps more probably is only a device for softening the ground. The number of eggs laid at a time varies from one (in *Malacochersus*) to over 100; some turtles lay several times a year. Young chelonians, like crocodiles, have a horny egg-caruncle for rupturing the eggshell.

Despite their longevity, chelonians become sexually mature fairly quickly, often in 3–9 years. Reliable age records for the longer-lived species are hard to come by, but it would seem that some small species like *Testudo graeca,* as well as giant tortoises, may live for over 100 years, possibly for much longer periods. A specimen of the big Madagascar tortoise *Geochelone radiata,* reputedly presented by Captain Cook to the Queen of Tonga in 1773 or 1777, may hold the record for longevity, for it died, battered and blind, in 1966 (Pritchard, 1967).

Tortoises and terrapins are often sold in pet-shops, but they require more care than they generally receive. Young individuals are prone to deficiency diseases which lead to defective ossification of the shell (which is soft in hatchlings) and of the limb bones. These can often be remedied by giving fish-liver oils and bone-meal smeared on the food, together with access to sunlight. Directions for looking after chelonians (and other reptiles) in captivity are given by Ball and Bellairs (1972).

The Chelonia were presumably derived from some branch of the cotylosaurian stock but their origin remains obscure. A small reptile, *Eunotosaurus,* from the Permian showed some interesting resemblances; it had a short back and flat leaf-shaped ribs which made up a sort of carapace, although there was no dermal armour resembling the modern tortoise's shell. The creature was once regarded as a likely chelonian ancestor, but this is now considered unlikely (Cox, 1969).

The earliest true chelonians (Proganochelyidae) appeared in the later Triassic and differed little in essentials from those alive today. They were superseded by another primitive group, the Amphichelydia, from which the two existing suborders (Pleurodira and Cryptodira) were probably derived. The majority of the amphichelydians became extinct in the Mesozoic, but some strange types with horned skulls such as *Meiolania* survived in Australia until the late Tertiary.

Living chelonians have a wide geographical distribution and occur in most warm and some temperate parts of both hemispheres. They number about a dozen families, 60 genera and over 200 species. Considering how conservative they are in basic structure, they show a fair range of adaptive radiation and fall into three main categories: highly aquatic, amphibious and terrestrial. In England it is the custom to call the marine and some of the more highly aquatic freshwater forms turtles, the smaller amphibious ones terrapins or water-tortoises, and the terrestrial ones tortoises, but many American workers refer to all chelonians as 'turtles'—as we have done in Chapter 2. Carr (1952) has produced an excellent handbook on the American forms, and Pritchard's book (1967) which deals with all the living species can be highly recommended. The classification used here for the living forms is based on the invaluable key by Wermuth and Mertens (1961) which includes the tuatara and crocodilians.

The members of the suborder Pleurodira are distinguished by the fact that they retract their necks sideways, instead of vertically, into their shells. These rather primitive turtles comprise two families and are found in the warmer parts of America, Africa and Australasia; during geologically recent times they have been virtually restricted to the southern hemisphere.

Side-necked turtles are all more or less aquatic. A large form, *Podocnemis,* found mainly in South America, differs from most other freshwater chelonians in being herbivorous. Its eggs are taken in enormous numbers by Amazon Indians, both for food and for the oil which can be extracted from them. Other notable types are the Australasian snake-necked turtles (*Chelodina*) in which the head and neck may be as long as the carapace, and the remarkable matamata (*Chelus*) from South America (Fig. 6B). This big turtle has a rough knobby back and a long thin proboscis through which it can breathe when lying almost submerged. Its neck and the edges of its enormously wide mouth are furnished with curious filaments; these act as a lure to attract small fishes which are sucked in when the jaws are suddenly opened.

In the suborder Cryptodira the neck is retracted in an S-shaped vertical loop. This group contains the majority of living and many fossil species; of the numerous freshwater types it is only possible to mention a few individually.

The snapping turtle (*Chelydra serpentina*) and the alligator snapper (*Macroclemys temmincki*) are large aggressive turtles inhabiting North America, the latter being one of the biggest freshwater chelonians and reaching a weight of 91kg (200lb).

The heads of these creatures are too large to be drawn into the shell and the plastron is reduced. They capture prey, aquatic animals including waterfowl, by lunges of the head, but also take a fair amount of plant food. Their jaws are certainly strong but their power has been exaggerated. It is often stated, for instance, that an alligator snapper can sever a broomstick; in fact specimens of up to 18kg (40lb) can scarcely bite through a pencil (Carr, 1952)! The prey is eaten under water and as in other freshwater turtles the front feet may be used to assist the jaws in tearing it apart. *Macroclemys* is remarkable in that the tongue is provided with a bifurcated worm-like appendage which is said to lure fish into the gaping mouth, another example of an angling device used by turtles.

The family Emydidae contains many small and medium-sized terrapins such as the brightly marked painted and red-eared terrapins (*Chrysemys* and *Pseudemys*); the edible diamond-back terrapins (*Malaclemys*), also from North America; the European pond-tortoise (*Emys orbicularis*) which inhabited England in post- or inter-glacial times; and the American box turtles (*Terrapene*), so called because they can box themselves up very tightly with their hinged plastral lobes. Unlike the other forms mentioned above, the box turtles have high domed shells, live mainly out of water and have taken to a more or less herbivorous diet. The American musk turtles (Kinosternidae) are another group of smallish amphibious species which owe their name to the fact that they produce a strong odour from glands in the groin.

The soft-shelled turtles (family Trionychidae) of the New and Old World are distinctive forms in which the shell is flattened and much reduced. It lacks horny scutes and is covered with a leathery skin. The snout is drawn out into a proboscis and the jaws have fleshy lips, an unusual feature in reptiles.

These turtles are highly aquatic, spending much time buried in the mud beneath the water with only the front of the head exposed. Some are quite large, an Indian species having a shell 61cm (2ft) in length. They are ferocious creatures, and can strike almost with the speed of a snake, inflicting severe bites. They feed on aquatic vertebrates and molluscs; in individuals addicted to the latter diet the back part of the beak has a broad crushing surface. Soft-shelled turtles are very susceptible to kyphosis, a deformity of the back which gives them a curious humped appearance. It is perhaps due to differences in relative growth between the backbone and the overlying shell. The curious New Guinea turtle *Carrettochelys* is also devoid of horny scutes and may be related to the trionychids; this large turtle is the only freshwater chelonian with really paddle-like limbs.

The family Testudinidae contains the land tortoises which have for the most part become adapted for life in dry surroundings such as prairies, rocky uplands and deserts. The shell is usually domed; the legs are massive and furnished with strong claws. Tortoises are mainly herbivorous, eating a variety of plants including grasses and cacti; some species are partial to clover and bright-coloured flowers. However, they may also take carrion occasionally and should be offered meat from time to time in captivity. Some tortoises are alleged to store water in their bladders or in accessory cloacal diverticula, but it is not known how far this water can actually be reabsorbed into the bloodstream. The significance of uric acid excretion in the conservation of water by tortoises is discussed on p. 49.

Various species of the genus *Testudo* are found in southern Europe, North Africa and Asia. *T. graeca* occurs on both sides of the Mediterranean (though not actually in Greece) and can be distinguished from its relatives by the presence in both sexes of a large spur on the inside of each thigh. This is probably the species most commonly imported for sale in pet-shops in this country.

Most of the land tortoises which live outside the Mediterranean region are now placed in the genus *Geochelone*, though they were formerly classified under *Testudo* (Pritchard, 1967). Some of the species found on continental mainlands reach a substantial size; *Geochelone radiata* from Madagascar may have a shell 46cm (18in) long. The individual scutes are beautifully marked with radiating bands of brown and orange; as in other, similarly marked forms, this pattern probably has a disruptive effect, assisting in concealment.

In recent times the real giants have been confined to certain isolated island habitats in the Indian Ocean, and to the Galapagos Islands in the Pacific, 600 miles (966km) off the coast of Ecuador. These tortoises may reach weights of over 250kg (553lb) and lengths over the curve of the carapace of over 1.5m (5ft). They are much exceeded, however, by the extinct *Testudo atlas* from North India which had a shell nearly 1.8m (6ft) long.

During the last three centuries giant tortoises have been subject to the depredations of buccaneers, whalers and other mariners who carried them away alive on board ship for food; their ability to survive for a year or more without food or water made them particularly valuable as a 'living larder'. The Indian Ocean tortoises were exterminated on some of their island habitats but one form (*Geochelone gigantea*) is still very abundant on Aldabra, where its ecology has recently been studied by Grubb (1971). It may be remembered that a few years ago this island was saved (partly by an economic crisis) from becoming a base for military aircraft; this would most probably have had a disastrous effect on the tortoises. An introduced population of this species exists on the Seychelles.

The famous Galapagos tortoises attracted the attention of Charles Darwin on his voyage of HMS *Beagle*. They provide classical examples of the effect of geographical isolation since each island has tended to develop a race, or races, of its own. In the 'saddle-back' forms, for example, the front of the carapace is flared up in a striking fashion; this appears to be an adaptation to browsing on higher vegetation since it facilitates dorsal extension of the neck.

Some of the races or subspecies of the Galapagos tortoises (now regarded as comprising the single species *Geochelone elephantopus*) have also been exterminated (Thornton, 1971). Some of the remaining populations are still threatened by feral domestic animals such as dogs, pigs and goats, which kill the young or compete with the adults for food. The tortoises are, however, now highly protected by the Govermnent of Ecuador which has designated nearly all the island territory as a reserve. In recent years the conservation and study of the Galapagos fauna has been greatly assisted by the establishment of the Charles Darwin Research Station on the island of Santa Cruz (or Indefatigable) and there are good grounds for hoping that the future of these magnificent tortoises will be assured; such at any rate is the optimistic view of one of the authors who visited the islands in 1973.

Another interesting group of tortoises is the American genus *Gopherus*, desert tortoises in which the fore-limbs are flattened as a burrowing adaptation. They make long burrows which are shared by a variety of animals including foxes, opossums, snakes and frogs. Some species of these tortoises retire to communal dens in the winter, travelling between them and their feeding grounds in the spring and autumn, and wandering in the course of their migrations over areas of 4–40 hectares (10–100 acres).

The marine turtles are perhaps the most fascinating of all chelonians; they pursue a way of life—at least when permitted by man—which can have changed little since their forbears swam in Mesozoic seas. Among living forms the leathery turtle (*Dermochelys coriacea*) (Fig. 6A) deserves a special place. It is the swiftest of all sea turtles and the most thoroughly adapted to oceanic life. It quite often appears in relatively northern waters and there is some evidence that it may be partly endothermic. Its great bulk perhaps enables it to conserve some of the heat produced by its muscular activity (Frair *et al.*, 1972). Exceptionally it reaches a shell-length of 1.8m (over 6ft) and a weight of at least 550kg (1200lb). The Cretaceous sea turtle *Archelon*, however, had a shell-length of over 3m (10ft).

Dermochelys has no typical bony shell, its armour consisting mainly of a mosaic of small bony platelets, sutured together to form a kind of carapace and a ring of reduced, but true plastral bones on the belly. Some of the bigger platelets on the back are raised up to form longitudinal ridges which give the animal a streamlined appearance. The dorsal platelets are sometimes referred to as epithecals and probably correspond with the osteoderms of other reptiles rather than with the large bony (thecal) plates of the typical chelonian shell. As in the soft-shelled freshwater turtles, there are no horny scutes. In the adult the shell and paddles are covered with dark scaleless leathery skin; in the young, however, these areas are furnished with small scales which are subsequently shed. In contrast with other living chelonians, the backbone and ribs are not attached to the shell.

The leatherback was formerly regarded as very distinct from other turtles but today it is thought of as an aberrant descendant of the common sea turtle stock which has reduced its horny shell and typical bony armour and (for some quite obscure reason) has secondarily evolved an armour of small dermal platelets. We may note here that reduction of armour is characteristic of many aquatic chelonians, especially of the bigger less vulnerable forms and helps to cut down the specific gravity of the animal. Among freshwater turtles this reduction is particularly evident in the trionychids. In these, as in the typical sea turtles described below, there are gaps between the ends of the ribs and the peripheral bony plates, the bridge is absent and there may be conspicuous vacuities in the bony plastron.

The remaining marine turtles, apart from *Dermochelys,* are placed in the family Cheloniidae. They comprise the green turtle (*Chelonia mydas*); the flatback (*C. depressa*) confined to northern Australian waters; the hawksbill (*Eretmochelys imbricata*); and the Pacific and Atlantic ridleys (*Lepidochelys olivacea* and *L. kempi*). Like the leathery turtle they are typically inhabitants of the warm oceans but sometimes stray into colder regions; some species appear from time to time off the shores of Britain.

The limbs of all marine turtles have been converted into paddles, the front pair being considerably longer than the back. The distal segment of the paddle is fairly stiff and bending movements take place mainly at the elbow and knee. Except in *Dermochelys*, each paddle carries one or two claws. In swimming the paddles sweep gracefully up and down with a motion which has been compared with a bird's wings. The mode of swimming is unlike that of most freshwater species which kick their way clumsily through the water, the diagonal pairs of webbed feet often working synchronously, each diagonal pair alternating with the other. On land marine turtles are very clumsy and like other chelonians may have great difficulty in righting themselves when turned on their backs.

The breeding habits of the various marine turtles are basically similar; the following account is based on the green turtle which has been more thoroughly studied than the other species. The males and females arrive together at the nesting beaches and mate in the water, which the males hardly ever leave. Individual females are believed to reproduce only once in every two or three years, and it is likely that the eggs laid in any given season are fertilized by sperms which have been previously stored for a year or more. Each female comes ashore several times, laying a clutch of 100 or more spherical, rubbery-shelled eggs each time; about twelve days elapse between each nesting, which usually occurs at night. The female first digs a wide pit in the sand to conceal her body and then excavates a smaller flask-like chamber in its floor in which the eggs are actually laid (Fig. 7). The nest is finally covered over with apparent care before she returns to the sea.

In some parts of the world, at least, green turtles appear to migrate for long distances to their breeding grounds. Tagging experiments by Carr and his collaborators have shown, for instance, that turtles may travel from the coast of Brazil to Ascension Island in the South Atlantic in order to nest, a distance of

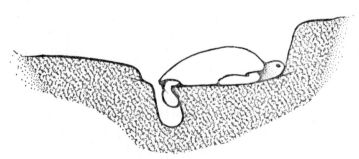

Fig. 7

Nest of green turtle (*Chelonia*) in profile. The turtle is in the main pit. about to lay into the egg-chamber. After Hendrickson (1958).

some 2254km (1400 miles). Their ability to navigate was known to the seventeenth-century buccaneers, but the method still largely remains a mystery. It is possible that they are able to use the sun as a compass and that responses to illumination similar to those of the hatchlings are involved. Other species of sea turtle also appear to be migratory, while certain land and fresh-water chelonians are known to have homing ability, often returning at intervals to a particular area (see Moll and Legler, 1971).

The hatching and emergence of the young sea turtle is also fraught with biological problems of great interest. The sheer number of the eggs is an important factor in survival, for each baby as it hatches pulls down sand from the walls of the egg chamber, raising its floor and making it easier for later hatchlings to climb out. Moreover, the struggling of the first hatchlings is transmitted through the mass of eggs and stimulates the tardy ones to break out of their shells. The perilous journey down to the sea is also facilitated by social activity, for each little turtle, bumping into the next, seems to stimulate the mass migration of the whole group down to the water. Much thought has been devoted to the problem of how the babies find their way over a distance of about 50m (164ft) when the sea is often concealed by intervening sand dunes. Responses to light seem to be over-whelmingly important, the turtles being attracted towards a broad open horizon such as the sky over the sea. Mrosovsky (1972) has made many interesting investigations of these light responses, which are important in freshwater as well as marine chelonians.

The compulsion to lay eggs on land is the weak link in the life-history of most aquatic reptiles, and it is bad luck for turtles and crocodiles that they have not been able to make the necessary physiological adaptations to viviparity. The nesting adults are relatively safe against the majority of predators apart from man. The young, however, are exceptionally vulnerable and are preyed on by a wide variety of animals: crabs, monitor lizards, birds and mammals. Even when they have reached the water they may be attacked by fish until they can reach some shelter such as rocks or seaweed.

The flesh of the green turtle is esteemed in many countries and the eggs of all marine turtles are widely used as human food.

The scutes of the hawksbill are the source of tortoiseshell, employed for a variety of decorative purposes. These turtles, like the giant tortoises, have been ruthlessly persecuted by man; Bustard (1972) has pointed out that nearly all early nautical and colonial activity in the New World tropics was in some way dependent on these luckless creatures. Their numbers have been greatly depleted, especially in the Caribbean, and some species, including the unique leatherback, appear to be seriously threatened. Luckily, during recent years, a group of able and dedicated men have made tremendous efforts to promote the conservation of sea turtles and have also contributed much to our knowledge of turtle biology. The labours of Archie Carr and P. C. H. Pritchard in America, of Tom Harrisson (who has also studied the remarkable lizard, *Lanthanotus,* p. 172), in Sarawak), of J. E. Hendrickson in Malaya and of H. R. Bustard (also a leading figure in crocodile conservation) in Australia, deserve special mention. This work is surveyed in the books by Carr (1968) and Bustard (1972, 1973), and is supported by the International Union for Nature and Natural Resources (IUCN).

Legislation to protect sea turtles is essential, but its efficacy depends on both the will and power of governments to check poaching and interference with the nesting beaches. The collection of eggs and subsequent rearing and release of the young after they have passed through their vulnerable early life is a valuable measure. One must admit, however, that turtles, in particular the green turtle, are great potential assets to man, especially to the protein-hungry peoples of underdeveloped countries. Controlled farming, if possible from stock which has been bred and reared in captivity, offers great possibilities. We may hope that a combined policy of protection and rational exploitation may do much to safeguard the future of these appealing and valuable reptiles.

5 | The ancestors
of mammals

Subclass SYNAPSIDA
Order Pelycosauria (U. Carb.–M. Perm., W.w.).
  Suborder Ophiacodontia: *Ophiacodon* (L. Perm., N.Am.), *Varano-
  saurus* (L. Perm., N.Am.)
  Suborder Sphenacodontia: *Dimetrodon* (L.–M. Perm., N.Am.),
  Sphenacodon (L. Perm., N.Am.)
  Suborder Edaphosauria: *Edaphosaurus* (U. Carb.–L. Perm., Eur.,
  N.Am.)
Order Therapsida (M. Perm.–M. Jur., W.w.)
  Suborder Phthinosuchia: *Phthinosuchus* (M. Perm., Russia)
  Suborder Anomodontia
    Infraorder Dinocephalia: *Jonkeria* (M. Perm., S.Af.), *Moschops*
    (M. Perm., S.Af.)
    Infraorder Dicynodontia: *Dicynodon* (M.–U. Perm., S.Af.),
    Kingoria (U. Perm., S.Af.), *Kannemeyeria* (L. Trias., S.Af.),
    Lystrosaurus (L. Trias., S.Af., As., Antarctic)
  Suborder Theriodontia
    Infraorder Gorgonopsia: *Lycaenops* (U. Perm., S.Af.), *Rubidgea*
    (U. Perm., S.Af.)
    Infraorder Therocephalia: *Whaitsia* (U. Perm., S.Af.)
    Infraorder Cynodontia: *Cynognathus* (L.–M. Trias., S.Af.), *Dia-
    demodon* (L. Trias., S.Af.), *Thrinaxodon* (L. Trias, S.Af.)
    Infraorder Bauriamorpha: *Bauria* (L. Trias., S.Af.)
    Infraorder Tritylodontoidea: *Tritylodon* (U. Trias., S.Af., N.Am.,
    Eur.)
    Infraorder Ictidosauria: *Diarthrognathus* (U. Trias, S.Af.)

The origin of mammals is one of the most fascinating and well
documented chapters in the history of the vertebrates. It begins
in the late Carboniferous, for the earliest reptile faunas yet discovered include forms with incipient mammalian characters,
and ends towards the close of the Triassic with the appearance of

small animals which, on the evidence of their skeletal remains, must be considered as true mammals. The Triassic was clearly a critical time in the evolution of land vertebrates for it marks the appearance, from quite separate ancestral groups, of both the mammals and the dinosaurs. Whereas the dinosaurs were to dominate the scene for the remainder of the Mesozoic, the mammals were to remain relatively insignificant until the beginning of the Tertiary (Attridge and Charrig, 1967).

The two extinct reptilian orders, Pelycosauria and Therapsida, are collectively known as the mammal-like reptiles; therapsids evolved from and replaced the pelycosaurs and together these fascinating reptiles bridge the gap between reptile and mammal. As a result of intensive study by palaeontologists past and present, many of the structural and, by implication, the physiological stages involved in this transition are known in surprising detail. Such is the gradation that in the case of some of the late Triassic forms it is difficult to decide whether to place them in the reptilian or mammalian class.

In addition to containing the ancestors of mammals, the group of mammal-like reptiles was important in its own right. During the late Palaeozoic and early Triassic mammal-like reptiles were the dominant land vertebrates and radiated into a host of herbivorous and carnivorous types (Figs. 8–10). However, by later Triassic times they were in marked decline and only one or two forms lingered on into the Jurassic; it is likely that the emergence of the archosaurs was the major factor in their extinction.

Pelycosaurs

The most ancient mammal-like reptiles, the pelycosaurs, appeared towards the end of the Carboniferous. In some respects they were like the stem reptiles of *Captorhinus* type from which they were descended and which still existed, like surviving grandparents, alongside them. Even the earliest pelycosaurs had, however, developed one important innovation, a feature which is diagnostic of the whole subclass of the mammal-like reptiles and of the mammals also. The skull roof of dermal bones behind the eye had become perforated by a single opening in a lateral position (Figs. 2B, 10B) allowing some of the jaw muscles to bulge outwards on contraction thus increasing the efficiency of the bite. It is this feature which gives the whole group of mammal-like reptiles its name: the subclass Synapsida. In typical synapsids the postorbital and squamosal bones meet above the temporal fossa but the artificiality of a classification based upon a single character is shown by the fact that in the much figured therapsid *Cynognathus* the euryapsid condition is found with these two bones meeting below the opening.

Primitive pelycosaurs, such as *Ophiacodon* (Fig. 8D) and *Varanosaurus* (Fig. 8B), were long-bodied beasts which still lived partly in the water and had teeth well adapted for their diet of fish. More enterprising types of pelycosaurs soon made their appearance. *Sphenacodon* and *Dimetrodon,* for example, were powerful land-dwelling carnivores up to 3m (10ft) long. *Dimetrodon* (Fig. 8E) must have been a remarkable looking creature, for the spines of its back vertebrae were elongated to form a sail-like structure 60–90cm (2–3ft) tall. The function of the 'sail' is problematical. It could hardly have served a protective function and in any event the dimetrodonts were the dominant carnivores of the age; nor was it a secondary sexual character present in only the males or the females. The numerous grooves in the spines suggest that the skin covering it was well supplied with blood vessels. Romer (1966) and more recently Bramwell and Fellgett (1973), have offered the most plausible suggestion that the 'sail' was concerned with temperature regulation, absorbing heat in the Permian mornings and radiating it when the animal got overheated. Predators such as *Dimetrodon* would therefore be able to reach an active state in the early part of the day and attack their prey when these were still sluggish. The evidence favours a dimetrodont ancestry for the later therapsid groups; at first sight the exotic character of the vertebral column, which is not seen in any therapsid, presents a difficulty but, fortunately, in the closely related *Sphenacodon* the vertebrae were conventional, with spines but a few centimetres in length.

Another group of pelycosaurs became specialized for eating plants, and of those *Edaphosaurus* (Fig. 8A) also developed a 'sail' of slightly different construction with short cross-pieces projecting transversely from the spines.

Fig. 8

Diorama. The Lower Permian Redbeds fauna and flora of S.W. U.S.A.
A, *Edaphosaurus* (herbivorous pelycosaur). B, *Varanosaurus* (pelycosaur). C, *Limnoscelis* (cotylosaur) [middle right]. D, *Ophiacodon*
(pelycosaur). E, *Dimetrodon* (pelycosaur). F, *Seymouria* (advanced
amphibian, close to reptiles). Not to scale.

Later mammal-like reptiles

Although the pelycosaurs seem to have had an almost world-wide distribution, their remains are commonest in the Redbeds deposits of the southern USA. They have been studied mainly by American palaeontologists, particularly by Romer and Olson.

Around the middle of the Permian, pelycosaurs disappear from the American rocks and the thread of pre-mammalian evolution is picked up in the Old World where there is evidence that a new and more ambitious radiation had commenced. These new forms, which make up the order Therapsida, seem to have originated from sail-less pelycosaurs of the sphenacodont type. During Middle Permian times the therapsids were common in the south of Russia and in Africa, and their remains are very abundant in the Karroo of southern Africa which was then a well watered plain, although now it is an arid area. Our knowledge of the therapsids of the Upper Permian and Triassic is mainly based on South African material but important Triassic faunas have been found in Brazil and China and, very recently, in Argentina (see Romer, 1973). It is likely that the therapsid group was even more widespread than the geological record suggests. Its evolution seems to have taken the form of a series of successive radiations each of which, broadly speaking, made a closer approach to the mammalian condition than its predecessor.

The discovery and study of the South African fossils began over a hundred years ago and has been one of the most exciting episodes in the history of palaeontology. Of the many zoologists who have studied the therapsids, perhaps the greatest contribution has been made by the late Dr. Robert Broom, also renowned for his discoveries of South African fossil ape-men. It would be quite misleading, however, to give the impression that the greater part of the work has been done and that the record is complete. Many significant discoveries have been made in the last decade, field exploration continues, and there are important gaps to be filled.

The earliest radiation of the therapsida is represented by the Dinocephalia ('terrible heads') which for some obscure reason had a tendency to develop a massive thickening of bone on the roof of the skull. They were mostly large clumsy creatures and some were the biggest of all mammal-like reptiles. *Jonkeria*, a carnivore with powerful canine tusks, was 4.3m (14ft) in length; the large and heavily armoured pareiasaurs were probably its main prey. In some dinocephalians there was a trend for the reduction of teeth suited for predation and their replacement by a more herbivorous dentition; *Moschops* (Fig. 10C) was a herbivorous dinocephalian with sloping hindquarters and a build suggestive of certain antelopes.

In detailed anatomy the dinocephalians and their allies, especially some of the primitive Russian forms like *Phthinosuchus*, were not far removed from their ancestors, the pelycosaurs. Despite their ungainly build, however, the dinocephalians had begun to lengthen their limbs and pull them in beneath the body, raising it off the ground in semi-mammalian fashion, instead of sprawling lizard-wise as the pelycosaurs must have done.

The clumsy dinocephalians were extinct by the end of the Middle Permian and were replaced by the herbivorous anomodonts and carnivorous theriodonts. Both groups had improved powers of locomotion and a more efficient masticatory apparatus.

The plant-eating anomodonts were extraordinarily successful and wandered the late Permian plains of Africa in great herds, much as the herbivorous mammals do today. Their jaw adaptations were quite distinctive and preclude them from any role as mammalian ancestors. One diagnostic feature was a loose jaw articulation which allowed considerable fore and aft movements of the mandible during feeding; another was a reduction in tooth number and the development of turtle-like horny jaw pads. These specializations were taken to the extreme in the largest anomodont group, the dicynodonts (Figs. 9C, E). In primitive dicynodonts the upper jaw was toothless apart from a pair of canine tusks which held the food, and the lower jaw was set with a few serrated teeth which sliced the food as the mandible was retracted. In later dicynodonts, such as *Kingoria* (Fig. 10A), only the canine tusks were retained and the horny beaks were entirely responsible for the maceration of the food. Species which have been included in the genus *Dicynodon* range in size from that of a rat to that of an ox. Some of the big dicynodonts were probably marsh-dwellers, but one member of the group, *Lystrosaurus* (Fig. 10D), was quite well adapted for aquatic life and had paddle-like limbs, dorsally placed eyes and nostrils,

Fig. 9

Diorama. Upper Permian–Lower Triassic fauna and flora of the Karroo of South Africa.
A, *Pareiasaurus* (specialized cotylosaur; Procolophonia). B, *Thrinaxodon* (small cynodont). C,
Kannemeyeria (large dicynodont). D, *Lycaenops* (gorgonopsian). E, *Dicynodon* (small dicynodont).
A, D and E from U. Perm., B and C from L. Trias. Not to scale.

and a down-turned snout probably for grubbing at the water-bottom. The recent discovery of *Lystrosaurus* in Antarctica is of great interest to students of palaeozoogeography. The dicynodonts dwindled towards the end of the Lower Triassic but a few forms lingered on into the Upper Triassic. No doubt the dicynodonts fell easy prey to the archosaurs.

The carnivorous members of the Therapsida, the theriodonts, are in some ways of greater interest to us than the herbivores for they include the ancestors of the mammals. The most cursory glance at even the more primitive forms, such as the gorgonopsians of the later Permian (Fig. 9D), calls up the likeness of an active hunting mammal, a creature resembling a dog with prominent canine teeth, a large head and a fairly long tail. These animals had much the same size range as carnivorous mammals today; some of the gorgonopsians reached the size of a lion or even larger. The fossils of these predators are rare compared with the abundant herbivorous members of the fauna, an ecological balance which is, of course, true for Africa today. In certain gorgonopsian genera, notably the huge *Rubidgea*, which had a skull about 46cm (18in) long, the canine teeth, particularly the uppers, were enormous and the jaws must have had an immense gape to clear their tips.

The jaw adaptations of the theriodonts were quite different to those seen in the dicynodonts for the jaw joint was tight and allowed no sliding fore and aft movement of the mandible. Some theriodonts, however, developed a movable (streptostylic) quadrate hinged to the skull at its upper end. This effectively increased the jaw gape and on jaw closure allowed the anterior teeth of the lower jaw to bite against the posterior surfaces of the upper teeth, to give a shearing action useful in the dismemberment of a carcass.

Around the beginning of the Triassic many of these carnivores died out and were replaced by similar but even more mammal-like types such as the advanced therocephalians and the cynodonts. The latter were almost certainly ancestral to the mammals. *Cynognathus* (Fig. 10E) was a rather large cynodont, the size of a wolf, which it resembled in build, and one can envisage it in packs pursuing its prey along the edges of the Karroo marshes. The much smaller cynodont *Thrinaxodon* of the early Triassic (Fig. 9B) is noted for its dentition, which in many detailed res-

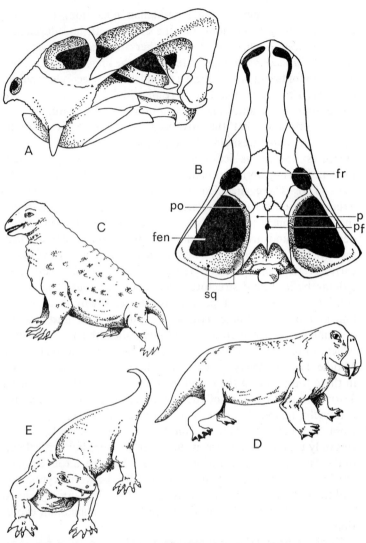

Fig. 10

A, skull of the dicynodont *Kingoria* (U. Perm.). B, skull roof of a gorgonopsian showing synapsid fenestra. C, the dinocephalian, *Moschops* (M. Perm.). D, the amphibious dicynodont, *Lystrosaurus* (L. Trias.). E, the carnivorous therapsid, *Cynognathus* (L. Trias.). C, after Špinar and Burian (1972); A, E, after Cox (1969).

fen, synapsid fenestra. *fr*, frontal. *p*, parietal. *pf*, pineal foramen. *po*, postorbital. *sq*, squamosal.

pects ideally anticipates the mammalian condition. The tooth row was clearly heterodont and the cheek teeth had developed a cusp pattern which, coupled with rather complex jaw movements enabled *Thrinaxodon* to masticate food in the mammalian fashion. The cynodonts had also evolved a complete bony secondary palate (Fig. 11F) to allow continuous respiration via the nasal route while food was retained and broken down in the mouth.

It is probable that the advanced cynodonts were close to the mammalian threshold. Another interesting group of small creatures known as ictidosaurs had evolved a type of jaw joint possessing both reptilian and mammalian features (p. 98, Fig. 11D). These included *Diarthrognathus* from the Upper Triassic of South Africa and certain related genera from Europe; they are variously considered as advanced cynodonts or cynodont derivatives, and are usually classified in an infraorder of their own (p. 87). The cynodonts were a varied group and even in the early Triassic another line represented by *Diademodon* had, judging by its dental structure, become omnivorous. This group continued its evolution parallel to the carnivorous cynodont line and by the Middle Triassic it had radiated into a large assemblage of herbivorous cynodonts called the traversodonts which, in terms of numbers, dominated the therapsid scene. The Middle Triassic deposits of South America are particularly rich in these forms. From the transversodonts evolved the specialized *Tritylodon* and its allies of the Upper Triassic, which were also extremely mammal-like in many ways. Nevertheless, it was from the carnivorous cynodonts that the mammals almost certainly took origin. There is, however, a short but critical gap in the Triassic record, for as yet no fossils have been found which are clearly intermediate morphologically between cynodonts and the first undoubted mammals; even the ictidosaurs appear to be somewhat removed from the main line of mammalian evolution.

In the Upper Triassic typical mammal-like reptiles are rare; almost at the end of this period the first mammals are found. About the same time the dinosaurs, both saurischian and orni-thischian, achieved a world-wide distribution. The extinction of so many of the synapsid types, until then such prominent members of the reptilian fauna since early Permian times, may be attributed to competition from the early dinosaurs and other

ascendant types of archosaurs, the ruling reptiles of the Mesozoic.

The complete transition from an early pelycosaur to the first
mammal occupied some 100 million years of the earth's history,
and it was to be another 120 million years before the mammals
were to radiate into the variety of forms found in the early
Tertiary. Upper Triassic mammals have been found in Asia,
southern Africa and the British Isles. Without exception, these are
minute shrew-like creatures, and in nearly all cases their remains
consist only of isolated skulls, jaws and post-cranial fragments.
However, in *Megazostrodon rudnerae* from the Upper Triassic
of Lesotho, we have one nearly complete skull in articulation
with the skeleton (Crompton and Jenkins, 1968). Early mammals
are described by Parrington (1971), by various authors in a
symposium (ed. Kermack and Kermack, 1971), and by Crompton
and Jenkins (1973).

From reptile into mammal

In general terms the mammal-like reptiles can be seen as a
varied group with a number of lines independently approaching
the mammalian threshold. The evidence favours a cynodont
ancestry for the therian mammals, including the marsupials
and placentals, and a separate, and as yet unknown, origin for
the prototherians, including the egg-laying monotremes. The
picture is complicated by a pattern of 'mosaic' evolution in which,
in certain lines, the characters of skull and skeleton do not
necessarily show a similar level of approach to the mammalian
condition. What is true for some therapsids is also seen in the
monotremes today. Whereas the monotreme skull is thoroughly
mammalian, many primitive characters persist in the post-
cranial skeleton; the shoulder girdle, for example, is quite
therapsid in structure although the pelvic girdle is like that of
any other mammal—a cautionary tale for the palaeontologist
working on fragmentary and dissociated material!

A mammal is an active warm-blooded furry beast with milk
glands and a high metabolic rate, distinguishable at a glance
from any living reptile by a host of anatomical and physiological
characters. Many of these characters cannot be directly observed
in fossil material, and to distinguish between mammal-like

D

reptiles and mammals (which must, of course, have formed a continuous evolutionary series), it is necessary as a first step to select some visible features in the hard tissues as the criteria for reptilian or mammalian status. The nature of the jaw joint has been conventionally established as the most important criterion. If the joint is formed by the quadrate and articular bones the creature is said to be a reptile; if it is formed by the squamosal and dentary bones, we are dealing with a mammal. Virtually all the stages in the remarkable process by which one type of jaw was converted into the other are shown in the later mammal-like reptiles, and it is of great interest that they are to some extent recapitulated in the development of the mammalian embryo (Fig. 11D).

In reptiles generally, the tooth-bearing dentary bone makes up only about the front half of the lower jaw. The rest of the jaw is formed by a series of bones such as the splenial, angular, surangular and coronoid, and the most posterior of these, the articular, articulates with the quadrate of the skull to form the jaw joint. This was the state of affairs in primitive mammal-like reptiles, such as the pelycosaurs (Fig. 11A). In the later therapsids, however, there was a progressive increase in size of the

---

Fig. 11

A–D, inner view of lower jaw of A, the pelycosaur *Dimetrodon*; B, cynodont; C, the ictidosaur *Diarthrognathus* (missing parts in broken lines); D, late embryo of hedgehog (*Erinaceus*). The figures show progressive enlargement of the dentary (stippled) and reduction or transformation of the other jaw bones. The precise extent of the dentary in C and E is uncertain.

E, skull of *Diarthrognathus*.

F, palate of cynodont.

A and B after Romer (1966). C and E after Crompton (1963), and in Joysey and Kemp (1972). D, after Parker (1885). F, after Parrington and Westoll (1940).

ang, angular. *ar*, articular. *co*, coronoid. *cp*, coronoid process of dentary, *d. ec*, ectopterygoid. *i*, incus (= quadrate). *in*, internal nostril. *m*, malleus (= articular). *Mc*, Meckel's cartilage. *mx*, maxilla. *pa*, palatine. *pm*, premaxilla. *p, pra*, prearticular (= goniale in D; becomes anterior process of malleus). *ps*, parasphenoid. *pt*, pterygoid. *san*, surangular. *sp*, splenial. *st*, stapes. *t*, trough for vestigial jaw bones. *ty*, tympanic (= angular), surrounding eardrum in D. *v*, vomer. 1, 2, joint regions of dentary and articular of *Diarthrognathus*.

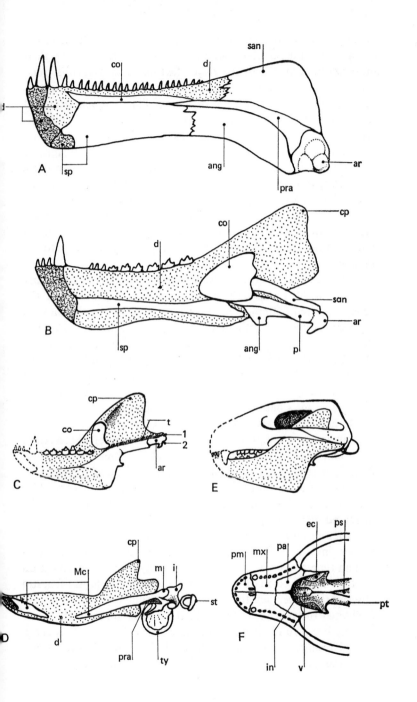

dentary (Fig. 11B) coupled with a progressive reduction in the extent of the post-dentary bones. Skeletons are moulded by their musculature and one of the major factors underlying this trend was an increase in the mass of the jaw musculature in therapsids accompanied by a separation of mammalian type masseter and temporal components, and the shifting forwards of their insertions on to the dentary bone. In the cynodonts alone (Fig. 11B) this was carried to an advanced state; the dentary formed practically the entire lower jaw, although the reptilian joint between quadrate and articular functioned behind, and it developed a large upstanding coronoid process for the new insertions of the jaw muscles. These trends reached their culmination in the first mammals with the development of the squamosal–dentary joint and the incorporation of the old reptilian jaw joint into the middle ear.

Logic demands that, in order to preserve functional continuity throughout this process, there must have been stages in which the newly acquired mammalian joint was present in association with the near redundant reptilian jaw joint. Such a stage is realized in the small (3.7cm) and very mammal-like skull of the ictidosaur *Diarthrognathus* (Fig. 11C, E). Here the articulation between the squamosal and the very large dentary lay on the outer side of that between the quadrate and articular, and most of the remaining lower jaw bones had become greatly reduced.

All these changes were concerned with the improvement of the jaw apparatus which, together with the evolution of a heterodont dentition, enabled the earliest mammals to break down their food by mastication in a manner uncharacteristic of reptiles. The reduction of a series of lower jaw bones and their replacement by the single tooth-bearing dentary (the mammalian mandible) increased the strength of the jaw. As the post-dentary bones dwindled in importance, of necessity there was a shift of the jaw muscle insertions on to the dentary. The separation of mammalian-type masseter and temporalis muscles and the provision for their increased mass by enlargement of the synapsid fenestra allowed the lower jaw to be moved in a rotary fashion and also facilitated the precise occlusion of the cusped cheek teeth. There is therefore a fundamental difference in jaw function between a typical reptile and mammal and an isolated fossil cheek tooth from the Triassic, by virtue of its wear facets, will yield considerable information about the status of its owner. The evolution of early mammals and of the mammalian jaw apparatus is thoroughly reviewed in articles by Hopson (1969), and by Crompton (in Joysey and Kemp, 1972).

There is an economy in nature and, as we have seen, the development of the mammalian jaw apparatus freed the quadrate and articular for a new function, and they were incorporated into the middle ear of the mammal to serve with the stapes as ear ossicles. The angular bone of the therapsid lower jaw was modified for support of the ear drum (Fig. 11D). Likewise one slip of the old reptilian jaw musculature did not move on to the expanded dentary but became the thread-like tympanic tensor muscle of mammals.

It would seem that with the mammalian triple system of ear ossicles the amplitude of sound vibrations is diminished while the pressure exerted on the oval window into the inner ear is increased during transmission, by virtue of the ossicle lever system and, especially, if the area of the eardrum is greater than that of the oval window. Hence sound of less intensity can be heard.

In the earliest of the mammal-like reptiles the eardrum had moved from the typically high position on the skull, seen in other reptiles, to a position close to the jaw joint. In this respect it was 'pre-adapted' to the mammalian condition. It is now generally agreed that the ear remained in a functional condition throughout the mammal-like reptiles despite the great changes that were under way in this region of the head.

Further changes in skull and tooth structure were occurring in the later mammal-like reptiles. As the temporal fossa enlarged the original contact between the postorbital and squamosal bones was lost so that the parietal formed its upper border; finally, in some forms, the postorbital bar disappeared so that the orbit and temporal fossa ran together as in primitive mammals. Other reptilian bones such as the pre- and post-frontals, ectopterygoids and parasphenoid also dwindled.

To keep pace with the increase in brain size during the transition, the epipterygoids were brought into the side wall of the braincase to form the mammalian alisphenoids, walling in the great ganglion of the trigeminal nerve. The single occipital condyle was replaced by paired structures, the atlas–axis complex was perfected, and the number of neck vertebrae became fixed at the mammalian figure of seven.

Even in some of the pelycosaurs the teeth in the canine region were enlarged to form killing weapons, and in the later therapsids the dental series was differentiated into incisors, canines and cheek teeth with ridges and cusps much like those of mammals. At some, probably post-cynodont, stage the dentition became diphyodont with but two generations of teeth as in mammals. The continual replacement of teeth in reptiles is perhaps associated with the fact that reptiles, unlike mammals, grow throughout much of their life. The presence of a secondary palate, already well formed in the cynodonts, separating the mouth from the nasal passages to allow chewing without impairing respiration, would also be necessary before the habit of suckling could develop.

The story is not so complete when we consider the evolution of the post-cranial skeleton in the mammal-like reptiles. So often in the past collectors prized the skull but shunned the skeleton in the field. We know that the therapsids had abandoned the primitive belly-crawling method of walking and had raised their bodies off the ground, turning their limbs in under their bodies and rotating their hands and feet so that they pointed forwards instead of outwards. Such changes, all tending in the direction of greater activity, were accompanied by the development of a more efficient respiratory mechanism. In forms such as the cynodonts the lumbar ribs had shortened, leaving the flanks unprotected, and suggesting the presence of a muscular diaphragm and a new mode of abdominal respiration to supplement the reptilian type of costal breathing.

The full exploitation of such improvements calls for a more effective type of temperature control than the reptilian ecto-thermic methods, and some means of insulating the body from extremes of cold, and possibly of heat. It is very possible that the advanced therapsids had actually become more or less endothermic, though the evidence for this is not as good as one might wish. Thus, the finding of a number of forwardly directed foramina in the bones of the front of the snout has been thought to suggest the presence of a muzzle covered with moist sensitive skin flanked by whiskers, as in many mammals. Yet rather similar foramina are present near the front of the maxillae of some snakes (hardly good mammalian ancestors!), and transmit nerves and blood vessels to the lip scales and adjacent structures). Again, remains of scroll-like conchae or turbinal bones within the nose of some therapsids have been regarded as an indication of warm-bloodedness, since in mammals one of their functions is that of temperature regulation. But nasal conchae, though unossified and admittedly less extensive than in most mammals, are present in the majority of living reptiles.

One interesting change which apparently occurred in the immediate ancestors of mammals was reduction in size. Advanced cynodonts were mostly at least as big as a domestic cat, while the early mammals all seem to have been tiny shrew-sized creatures (Hopson, 1973). Hopson envisages the latter as being both nocturnal and endothermic; because of their high surface to volume ratio they would have been very susceptible to heat loss. He postulates that they must have possessed both a high metabolic rate (like modern shrews) and an insulating coat of hair. This is, of course, speculative, since unfortunately no fossilized impressions of the skin of mammal-like reptiles or early mammals have been discovered.

Likewise, the fossil record cannot tell us at what stage viviparity and milk glands, the most characteristic of all mammalian features, were acquired. Since the platypus and echidna, in many ways the most primitive of living mammals, lay eggs it may seem unlikely that the therapsids had abandoned the practice. Fossils of juvenile cynodonts possess a functional dentition and so would have been able to obtain their own food. Hopson (1973) suggests that the evolution of viviparity was associated with the very small size of the first mammals. He believes that these probably laid tiny eggs from which the young emerged in a very immature state (like a new-born marsupial), requiring shelter in a nest, or perhaps, in a maternal pouch and nourishment from maternal glandular secretions. This is indeed possible, but there are dangers in over-elaborating such speculations. Viviparity occurs in many lizards and snakes, but except in a few forms with a relatively efficient placenta, the eggs are large and yolky; the young of a very few species receive the rudiments of parental care (p. 213) but even these may be potentially capable of fending for themselves.

6 | Ichthyosaurs, plesiosaurs and others

Subclass ICHTHYOPTERYGIA
Order Ichthyosauria (M. Trias.–U. Cret., W.w.): *Mixosaurus* (M. Trias., Eur., As., N.Am.), *Omphalosaurus* (M. Trias., Eur., N.Am.), *Merriamia* (U. Trias., N.Am.), *Eurhinosaurus* (L. Jur., Eur.), *Ichthyosaurus* (L. Jur.–?L. Cret.), *Ophthalmosaurus* (M. Jur.–U. Cret., Eur., N.Am.)

Subclass EURYAPSIDA
Order Protorosauria (L. Perm.–U. Trias, apart from one questionable form in U. Cret., N.Am. Mainly Eur. and N. Am.): *Araeoscelis* (L. Perm., N.Am.), *Protorosaurus* (U. Prrm., Eur.), *Tanystropheus* (M. Trias., Eur., As.), ? *Pleurosaurus* (U. Jur., Eur.)
Order Sauropterygia (L. Trias.–U. Cret., W.w.)
    Suborder Nothosauria (U. Perm.–U. Trias.), wide distribution in O.W.): *Ceresiosaurus* (M. Trias., Eur.)
    Suborder Plesiosauria (? Trias.–U. Cret., W.w.): *Plesiosaurus* (U. Trias.– M.Jur., Eur., ?As., Af., Sn.Am.), *Pliosaurus* (L.–U. Jur.–? Cret.) Eur., As., Sn.Am.), *Kronosaurus* (L. Cret., Aus.), *Elasmosaurus* (U. Cret., N.Am.)
Order Placodontia (L.–U. Trias., mainly Eur.): *Henodus* (U. Trias., Eur.)

?Subclass ANAPSIDA
Order Mesosauria to include the single genus *Mesosaurus* (L. Perm., S.Af., Sn.Am.)

The ichthyosaurs and plesiosaurs were two groups of marine reptiles in the Mesozoic which had become highly modified for aquatic life in quite different and contrasting ways. Their remains are very common in marine Jurassic deposits, and are well represented in museums in this country.

The first complete skeletons of both an ichthyosaur and a plesiosaur were discovered at Lyme Regis by Mary Anning

(1799–1847), a famous collector of fossils who made a living by selling her finds to naturalists and wealthy aristocrats who wished to set up private museums. The ichthyosaurs and plesiosaurs enjoyed quite a vogue among the geologically minded Victorians and often figured in the natural history books of the day, such as the *Bridgewater Treatise* by Dean William Buckland (1st ed. 1836), which did much to popularize extinct reptiles. Visitors to Cambridge may notice the charming 'ichthyosaur' weather-vane on the roof of the Sedgwick Museum of Geology which was opened in 1903, and today palaeontologists will note with regret the high prices that fossil marine reptiles command in the London auction houses.

The dangers inherent in the use of a single character in taxonomy are well illustrated by the confusion in the literature concerning the classification of ichthyosaurs and plesiosaurs. In the past ichthyosaurs and plesiosaurs were often placed together in the 'subclass Parapsida' on the presence of a single temporal opening situated high on the cheek on each side of the skull. A second classification has separated ichthyosaurs and plesiosaurs into the subclasses Ichthyopterygia and Euryapsida respectively on the basis of the bones which border the temporal opening; in plesiosaurs the bones forming the lower border of the opening were clearly the postorbital and squamosal, while in ichthyosaurs the two bones were believed to be the prefrontal and supratemporal, the squamosal being situated lower down on the cheek. It is now thought that the much figured lateral 'squamosal' is nonexistent and that the 'supratemporal' is the true squamosal (Fig. 12A) (Romer, 1968; McGowan, 1973). Consequently the temporal opening of the ichthyosaur is now seen to be essentially similar to the euryapsid condition.

When, however, all characters are considered it is clear that ichthyosaurs and plesiosaurs have little in common save that they were reptiles which swam in the same Mesozoic seas, and often occupy adjacent cases in museums.

The modern practice is to recognize these differences and separate the ichthyosaurs and plesiosaurs into two subclasses, retaining the names Ichthyopterygia and Euryapsida (Synaptosauria) respectively; the latter also includes the protorosaurs, nothosaurs and the placodonts.

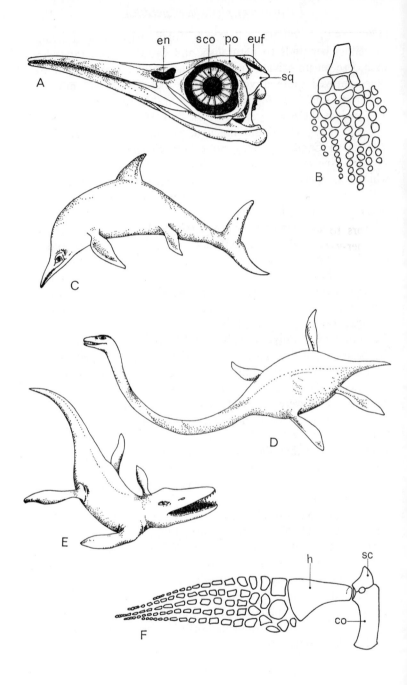

Ichthyosaurs

The ichthyosaurs ('fish-lizards') were fish-like in shape and their bodies had become so highly modified for swimming that they must have been helpless on land. They were in fact first described as fishes by a Welsh naturalist called Lluyd at the end of the seventeenth century. It was not until the earlier part of the nineteenth century that their anatomy was worked out by Cuvier and Owen, and their reptilian character was established.

In the Triassic forms, such as *Mixosaurus,* the jaws were moderately elongate but most ichthyosaurs had very long slender jaws, armed with many teeth; a few, such as *Ophthalmosaurus,* were toothless and *Omphalosaurus* had rather short blunt jaws set with button-like teeth, ideal for a mollusc diet. In *Eurhinosaurus* the upper jaw projected in front of the lower, like the bill of a swordfish, and both jaws bore teeth.

The orbits were very large and each contained a conspicuous ring of scleral plates; eyes were clearly important in ichthyosaurs. As in many other aquatic reptiles the nostrils were far back, near the eyes, but in ichthyosaurs rather low on the face. The stapes bone in the ear was massive, a condition possibly associated with its function of conducting waterborne rather than air-borne sound vibrations.

The impression of a single dorsal fin, devoid of skeleton, is shown in some fossils. There was also a large vertical tail fin of reversed heterocercal type with the lower lobe longer than the upper. The tail end of the spine was bent sharply downwards to support the lower lobe of the tail, giving an appearance which was once mistaken for post-mortem dislocation. Advanced ichthyosaurs, such as *Ichthyosaurus* (Fig. 12C), had the two lobes of the tail nearly equal in size; they were much better streamlined than earlier forms, and presumably faster swimmers.

Fig. 12

A, skull of ichthyosaur. B, paddle of ichthyosaur. C, *Ichthyosaurus* (L.-M. Jur.), after Špinar and Burian (1972). D, *Plesiosaurus* (L.-M. Jur.). E, *Kronosaurus* (L. Cret.), a giant pliosaur with a short neck; after Cox (1969). F, paddle of plesiosaur.

co, coracoid. *euf*, euryapsid fenestra. *en*, external nostril. *h*, humerus. *po*, postorbital. *sc*, scapula. *sco*, scleral ossicles. *sq*, squamosal.

The limbs were paddle-like, the front pair being the larger of the two. The pelvic girdle had lost contact with the spine, so that there was no sacrum. The bones of the hands and feet were converted into small plates and the number of digits was sometimes reduced (only three in *Merriamia*) but more commonly increased in number to seven or eight by bifurcation of the finger row (hyperdactyly). All the digits show an increase in the number of phalanges (hyperphalangy), up to nearly a dozen in some species (Fig. 12B). It is likely that the relatively large paddles of early forms, such as the Triassic *Mixosaurus*, were important organs in propulsion whereas in later forms the somewhat reduced paddles, like the paired fins of sharks, served mainly as hydrofoils for altering the inclination of the swimming plane. The skin seems to have been devoid of scaly armour although there is a suggestion that the snouts of some ichthyosaurs were encased in horny beaks.

The ichthyosaurs show a type of structural modification which has been independently acquired by a process of convergent evolution by other groups of aquatic vertebrates and, in particular, the dolphins among the mammals. Its hallmarks are streamlining of the body, elongation of the jaws into a slender beak suitable for catching cephalopods and fishes, and the development of dorsal and caudal fins. The conversion of the limbs into paddles supported by a mass of reduplicated hand and foot bones has occurred in a number of thorough-going secondarily aquatic vertebrates of quite different types.

Many ichthyosaurs were of large size, 9m (30ft) or more in length. We know that there was a general trend towards increase in size among many Mesozoic reptiles, land forms as well as water-living. Nevertheless, increase in size is another feature seen in animals which have returned to aquatic, especially marine, life and may have some value in terms of natural selection. A small creature, taking to the water, is exposed to hazards in the shape of buffeting waves and hungry fish to which a larger animal may be immune; moreover, once it has completely renounced terrestrial habits, its size is no longer so restricted by the exigencies of weight-bearing, so that circumstances all favour a tendency to gigantism.

We may suppose that the ichthyosaurs played a similar part in the Mesozoic seas to the whales and dolphins of today. They were probably inhabitants of the open waters, living near the surface and feeding on small fishes and squid; such a diet is confirmed by the fossilized excreta (coprolites) sometimes found with their skeletons. A few ichthyosaurs, such as *Omphalosaurus*, seem to have fed on shellfish for their jaws, unlike those of their relatives, were short and massive with blunt teeth.

It may be inferred from their structure that the ichthyosaurs could not have come ashore to lay eggs; in fact there is evidence that they were viviparous, for intact skeletons of small ichthyosaurs have been found within the ribs and cloacal region of adult specimens.

Ichthyosaurs first appear in the Triassic and reach their peak in the Jurassic, declining in the Cretaceous when other marine reptiles were still abundant. Not all the early forms were small for a large number of giant skeletons have been found in Triassic deposits in Nevada. The origin of the ichthyosaurs is obscure, and as in the case of their mammalian counterparts, the whales, the earliest known types were nearly as specialized as those existing 50 million years later. A relationship between ichthyosaurs and chelonians, has been suggested, but such similarities in structure that may exist are surely outweighed by the numerous fundamental differences that are apparent. Romer (1966) maintains his belief in the possibility of some sort of relationship between the ichthyosaurs and primitive mammal-like reptiles, the pelycosaurs, suggesting that both groups had a common ancestor among the cotylosaurs; this would of necessity have involved some shifting in the position of the temporal opening which was quite different in the two groups (p. 25).

Mesosaurs

Mesosaurs were a small group of freshwater reptiles which lived for quite a short time at the beginning of the Permian. The supposed presence of a single lateral temporal opening has led workers at various times to relate mesosaurs to either the synapsids or to the euryapsids, or to the ancestors of ichthyosaurs. Until the doubts concerning the presence or absence of a temporal opening are resolved, Romer advocates the placing of the Mesosauria within the subclass Anapsida.

Mesosaurs (Fig. 13A) were long-jawed little creatures, up to 1m (3ft) long, with bristle-like teeth, curiously thickened ribs and flattened swimming tails.

Mesosaurs provide a fascinating example of discontinuous distribution. The order comprises but a single genus, *Mesosaurus*, and this has only been found in a rather restricted geological horizon of Lower Permian age in South Africa and southern Brazil. As the habitat of *Mesosaurus* was apparently freshwater, it was for a long time the only piece of fossil evidence which could be used in support of the theory of 'Continental Drift' which implies, among other things, a connection between Africa and South America in the Palaeozoic (Colbert, 1973).

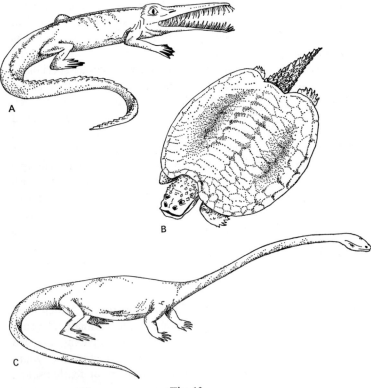

Fig. 13

A, *Mesosaurus* (L. Perm). B, *Henodus* (U. Trias); after Špinar and Burian (1972). C, *Tanystropheus* (M. Trias.).

Protorosaurs

The order Protorosauria contains a number of reptiles, in the main of Permian and Triassic age, of rather enigmatic relationships with a single temporal vacuity seemingly in the upper, or euryapsid, position. Some, like *Protorosaurus,* were lizard-like creatures, but *Tanystropheus* (Fig. 13C) from the Triassic of Switzerland was a bizzare animal with a tiny head and an extremely long neck. *Pleurosaurus,* a Jurassic form, sometimes included in the Rhynchocephalia, seems to represent a snake-like trend, having small limbs and a long slender body. *Araeoscelis* was another small lizard-like reptile, under a metre in length, with a rather long neck.

It is possible that the order includes the ancestors of the plesiosaurs and their allies, but it is unlikely that they gave rise to lizards as was formerly believed. Future work may well show the order to be a taxonomic 'rag-bag'. As it stands, it seems to have been among the less successful of reptilian experiments and mostly disappeared in the Triassic when the diapsid radiation got under way.

Nothosaurs and placodonts

The nothosaurs and placodonts were aquatic, and probably secondarily aquatic, reptiles of the Triassic which preceded the plesiosaurs in time, and though not actually ancestral to them were possibly collateral descendants of the same protorosaurian stock. Both groups are known mainly from deposits in Switzerland.

Nothosaurs were small creatures with long necks and tails In some the feet were webbed and in *Ceresiosaurus* there was a moderate degree of hyperphalangy although nothosaur feet were never truly paddle-like. The placodonts were larger and more specialized euryapsids with rather stout bodies, short necks and a tendency towards tail reduction. Like some ichthyosaurs, they appear to have fed on molluscs; their jaws were short and powerful and the teeth to the back of the mouth and on the palate were typically modified into large crushing plates. Some of the placodonts were heavily armoured and in the very turtle-like *Henodus* (Fig. 13B) the flattened body was completely encased in an armour of small bony plates; it is likely that the essentially toothless jaws in this form were covered, as in chelonians, with horny plates.

Plesiosaurs

The plesiosaurs of the Jurassic and Cretaceous were long-necked reptiles with broad flattened bodies which must have propelled themselves through the water, turtle-fashion, by sweeps of the four strong paddles. The structure of the neck skeleton suggests that this region was fairly stiff except in its most anterior part; it is unlikely that it could have been twisted in snake-like fashion, as is shown in some older reconstructions.

The ventral bones of the limb-girdles, the scapulo-coracoid and pubo-ischium were expanded into great flat plates for the attachment of the powerful muscles which worked the paddles. As in ichthyosaurs, the number of finger joints was increased, but the number of digits was never greater or less than five. The paddles (Fig. 12F) as a whole were long, sometimes with a span of more than half the length of the whole beast, and the front and hind pairs were nearly equal in size. They seem to have been fairly rigid and were probably feathered by rotation through 90° in the backstroke as the plesiosaur rowed itself along. The belly was strengthened by a series of abdominal ribs or gastralia which ran from the shoulder to the pelvic girdle. The tail was fairly short and probably finless.

It is clear that we are dealing with a very different type of aquatic adaptation to that shown by the ichthyosaurs. The latter must have swum by means of fish-like movements of the tail and body, using their paddles as hydrofoils for steering and braking; the neck was short and the head relatively im-mobile. In plesiosaurs the limbs were the main organs of pro-pulsion; the tail probably only served as a rudder, while the head had a fair range of movement on the long neck.

This account of plesiosaurs requires some qualification for there were at least two distinct types of these animals living side by side, which were clearly following different lines of adaptive evolution. This dichotomy is apparent even in the early plesiosaur faunas so abundant in the Lower Jurassic of Europe. In one of these lines the head remained of moderate size but there was a progressive tendency to elongate the neck which, together with certain changes in limb structure, became more marked as time went on. *Plesosaurus* (Fig. 12D) was an early member of this line which culminated in forms such as *Elasmosaurus* from the Upper Cretaceous, a creature with a fantastically long neck containing some 76 vertebrae.

The elasmosaurs were obviously not adapted for rapid swimming. Study of the regions of the limb girdles to which the paddle musculature was attached indicates, however, that they had the power of turning quickly by back-paddling on one side and were able to catch their prey by sweeps of the head and neck. These long-necked forms probably fed on small fish and squids.

The other type of plesiosaur, constituting the pliosaur line, was more streamlined and better fitted for rapid movement as a whole. The neck was relatively short, the jaws were large and long, and the bony areas to which the forward swimming muscles were attached were extensive. The pliosaurs had little power of turning quickly and they seem to have caught their prey by running it down by speed. These short-necked forms show a marked tendency for increase in size, some reaching about 12m (40ft); the Cretaceous *Kronosaurus* (Fig. 12E) from Australia was a massive form with a skull nearly 3m (9ft) long. All pliosaurs had long teeth and no doubt fed on the larger fishes and cephalopods.

Masses of smooth pebbles are sometimes associated with plesiosaur remains and it is certain that they were gastroliths, swallowed deliberately and retained in the stomach. They may have provided a gastric mill as an aid to digestion as in the case of some dinosaurs and birds or, alternatively, plesiosaurs like the crocodiles swallowed stones to adjust their specific gravity.

Plesiosaurs seem to have inhabited both inshore waters and the open seas; bones from both estuarine and deep-water deposits are known. Possibly, unlike ichthyosaurs, they were even capable of clumsy locomotion on land and went ashore at times like turtles, and laid their eggs on land; the well developed abdominal ribs might have protected the belly as they clambered over the beach.

Although changes in the fish and invertebrate fauna at the

end of the Cretaceous may have contributed to their extinction, the disappearance of the plesiosaurs and other marine reptiles at the close of the Mesozoic is less easy to explain than that of the terrestrial forms, since the sea has always been a more stable environment than the land.

7 | Primitive archosaurs and crocodiles

Subclass ARCHOSAURIA
Order Thecodontia (L.-U. Trias., W.w.)
  Suborder Pseudosuchia: *Euparkeria* (L. Trias., S.Af.)
  Suborder Aetosauria: *Desmatosuchus* (U. Trias., N.Am.)
  Suborder Phytosauria: *Phytosaurus* (U. Trias., Eur.)
Order Crocodilia [= Loricata] (since U. Trias., W.w.) (*some extinct suborders omitted*)
  Suborder Protosuchia: *Protosuchus* (U. Trias., N.Am.)
  Suborder Mesosuchia: *Metriorhynchus* (Jur., Eur., Sn.Am.), *Teleosaurus* (Jur., As., Eur.), *Theriosuchus* (U. Jur., Eur.)
  Suborder Eusuchia (*some extinct families omitted*)
    Family Crocodylidae
      Subfamily Crocodylinae: *Phobosuchus* (U. Cret., N.Am.), *Crocodylus* (Af., As. Aus. Pac., N.Am., S.Am.), *Osteolaemus* (Af.), *Tomistoma* (As.)
      Subfamily Alligatorinae: *Alligator* (N.Am., E.As.), *Caiman* (Sn.Am.)
      Subfamily Gavialinae: *Rhamphosuchus* (Tert., As.), *Gavialis* (As.)

The archosaurs ('ruling reptiles') have been perhaps the most varied and sensational of all the reptilian groups and include the thecodonts, crocodiles, dinosaurs, pterosaurs and the ancestors of birds. They reached their zenith in the later Mesozoic, and established themselves in all the main types of environment; only in the sea were they relatively unsuccessful.

Archosaurs are diapsids with two temporal openings in the skull. This character they have in common with members of another great subclass, the Lepidosauria, but the two lines may go back independently to remote stem-reptile ancestors. The archosaur skull has a few other distinctive features. The pterygoids tend to meet in the midline separating two wide palatal vacuities, and are often expanded into broad, downwardly directed flanges, as in crocodiles, There is usually a vacuity in front of each orbit and often a small one at the back of each side of the lower jaw. The teeth are set in sockets (Fig. 15E) and are generally absent on the palate.

The skin armour is usually well developed and osteoderms, probably covered in life by horny scutes, are often present on the back and sometimes on the belly.

There is a tendency towards bipedalism in some members of the group, culminating in certain dinosaurs and in birds. In the more advanced types the pelvic girdle becomes more firmly attached to the backbone.

The limbs are modified in accordance with this bipedal trend. The legs are longer than the arms, very much so in some forms. The pelvic girdle, which has to bear most of the weight of the body, is firmly attached to the backbone. Its constituent bones are lengthened and fan out from the acetabulum: the ilium pointing up and back, the ischium back and down, and the pubis down and forwards (Fig. 16A, p. 132). This 'triradiate' type of pelvis allows the muscles running from the various parts of the pelvis to the thigh and leg to elongate and acquire an extended range of movement. The upper end of the femur becomes bent to form a neck, so that the thighs run vertically downwards from the pelvis instead of outwards; the legs are turned forwards beneath the body in truly bipedal forms so that they move mainly in a fore and aft plane. These changes are to some extent comparable with those which have occurred in the mammal-like reptiles (p. 102) and mammals which also walk, though quadrupedally, with the belly off the ground.

Thecodonts

The most primitive archosaurs were the thecodonts, mainly a Triassic group which included the ancestors of all other types of ruling reptiles, and perhaps also of the birds (p. 151). Until recently it was widely believed that the most primitive thecodonts were bipedal and that the various later quadrupedal archosaurs, such as the crocodiles, had secondarily slumped down on to all fours. It now seems unlikely that this was so, although it is true that some of the more advanced thecodonts became bipedal.

Thecodonts such as the small agile pseudosuchian *Euparkeria* (Fig. 1) may have been 'facultative bipeds', like certain modern lizards, only rising on to their hind-legs when they wished to run at speed (p. 202).

The thecodonts enjoyed a considerable adaptive radiation. Some were slender lightly built creatures while others were big powerful carnivores; others again, such as *Desmatosuchus* (Fig. 14B), were heavily armoured with bony plates on the back and formidable spines on the shoulder region. One group, the

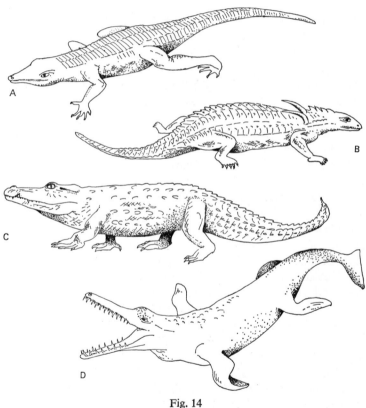

Fig. 14

A, *Protosuchus* (U. Trias. or L. Jur.), one of the earliest crocodilians. B, the armoured thecodont *Desmatosuchus*. C, modern crocodile walking with belly off the ground. D, the marine crocodile *Metriorhynchus* (M. Jur.); after Špinar and Burian (1972).

phytosaurs, resembled typical crocodiles in many ways. They differed from the latter mainly in the lack of the specialized palate (p. 121) and in that their nostrils, instead of being at the tip of the elongated snout, lay just in front of the orbits, sometimes elevated at the top of a dome-like formation of the skull. Some genera reached a length of over 9m (30ft). The phytosaurs must have followed a way of life almost identical with that of crocodiles, but for some reason were less successful and became extinct before the Jurassic.

Crocodiles

The Crocodilia appear in the Upper Triassic. Early forms, such as the small and lizard-like *Protosuchus* (Fig. 14A) with a short snout, seem to have been running terrestrial animals rather than amphibious ones. Walker (1972) has emphasized that the early crocodiles were quite closely related to the ancestors of birds, and suggests that the two groups had a common ancestry among the thecodonts.

In the Jurassic crocodiles became varied and numerous. There were long-snouted types rather like modern gharials, such as *Teleosaurus*, and tiny (under 90cm) broad-snouted ones, as such *Theriosuchus* (Joffe, 1967). One family, the Metriorhynchidae, became highly adapted to marine life and shows points of resemblance to the early ichthyosaurs. In *Metriorhynchus* (Fig. 14D), for example, the jaws were long and slender, the limbs paddle-like, the skin armour was lost and the tail bore a vertical fin. These sea crocodiles were a short-lived group and barely survived into the Cretaceous. Other more aberrant forms with toothless lower jaws and others again with deep compressed skulls appeared near the end of the Mesozoic (see Neill, 1971).

Crocodiles of modern type (suborder Eusuchia) appear in the Cretaceous and were essentially similar to those of the present day. *Phobosuchus*, a broad-snouted form which may have preyed on dinosaurs, had a skull about 1.5m (5ft) long in the dorsal midline and an estimated body length of 12m (40 ft) or more. *Rhamphosuchus*, a giant gharial from the Pliocene of North India, was of comparable size.

Living in tropical fresh waters well stocked with fish, the crocodilians were able to avoid the fate of the other archosaurians at the beginning of the Tertiary. Today about 9 genera and 23 species are known; they fall broadly into three groups: the alligators and caimans; the crocodiles; and the gharials or gavials. These animals are all basically very similar and differ from one another only in such characters as the relative length and width of the snout, the arrangement of the scutes and minor dental and osteological features.

Various aspects of the natural history of recent crocodilians are described in the books by Wettstein and Lüdicke (1931–64), Wermuth and Mertens (1961; systematics), Neill (1971) and Guggisberg (1972).

Alligators and caimans have broad rounded snouts and can be distinguished from crocodiles by usually having the fourth tooth of the lower jaw on each side fitting into a pit in the upper jaw instead of projecting outside it as in crocodiles. This traditional distinction may not be obvious in some individuals.

The snout in crocodiles varies in shape; it is very short and broad in *Osteolaemus tetraspis*, the West African broad-fronted crocodile, and short in the Indian marsh crocodile or mugger (*Crocodylus palustris*). In *C. niloticus* and *C. porosus,* the estuarine crocodile, the snout is long, but fairly wide; in *C. cataphractus*, the West African narrow-snouted crocodile, and *C. johnstoni,* from Australia, it is long and narrow. The gharial, *Gavialis gangeticus,* and the false gharial, *Tomistoma schlegeli,* can be distinguished from all other living crocodilians by the extreme length and slenderness of their snouts. Mature individuals of *Gavialis* usually have a prominent swelling at the tip of the snout; it is not a part of the bony skull and its function is unknown (Fig. 15D).

Alligator mississippiensis is the common crocodilian of the southern USA; a rare species, *A. sinensis,* is found in the Yangtse-Kiang river in China. *Caiman* is restricted to tropical Southern America. *Crocodylus* is found throughout the Old World tropics and in parts of the West Indies and Central America; one species, *C. americanus,* reaches the coast of Florida. The gharial and false gharial occur in India, and Malaya and Borneo respectively. The American alligator is the most tolerant of cold of all crocodilians, as one would expect from its comparatively northern distribution. In the Mesozoic and early Tertiary, crocodilians enjoyed a much wider range and inhabited England and other countries which now have a temperate climate; this explains the scattered distribution of some of the present-day genera.

Alligators and caimans are essentially dwellers in fresh water. Some crocodiles, however, have a partiality for brackish water and the estuarine crocodile often makes long sea journeys. In this way it has become very widely distributed, from Ceylon and the east coast of India to Malaya and the north of Australia.

The skin of crocodilians is heavily armoured. The scutes on the back and tail are reinforced by underlying osteoderms; those of the belly have little or no ossification, except in caimans, some of which have a well developed ventral bony armour. The thinner scales on the flanks, sides of the head and particularly the lower jaw are studded with darkly pigmented tubercles which are supplied by nerve fibres and seem to be organs of touch. Paired skin glands are found on the throat and lower jaw; the secretion of these has a musky odour.

The most obvious peculiarity of the skull is the elongation of the jaws, a common character of aquatic reptiles. There is no opening in the skull in front of the eyes, but the fenestrae in the palate are large; in life they are covered by the lining of the mouth. The front part of the braincase side-wall is better ossified than in most modern reptiles, for there are well developed laterosphenoids (p. 23), often miscalled alisphenoids. The epipterygoid is not ossified in the adult skull.

There is a curious belief that the upper and not the lower jaw of crocodiles is hinged to the rest of the skull. This probably originates from the fact that when the lower jaw is in contact with the ground, the upper jaw and the rest of the skull have to be tilted upwards when the mouth is opened.

The teeth are conical and sharp, especially in young specimens, and interlock, with the lower row biting slightly inside the upper. They serve only to hold the prey, being quite unfitted for chewing or cutting. A few of the teeth in the 'canine' region at the front of the maxilla are often somewhat larger than the rest. In some species of *Crocodylus* the front pair of lower teeth is very long and may perforate the tip of the snout, their points being visible when the jaws are closed; the fourth lower teeth of alligators sometimes produce a similar perforation. Tooth succession slows down in old age, but a Nile crocodile of 4m (13ft) may have replaced each of its teeth 45 times. The successional teeth grow up almost directly beneath the functional ones which fit like caps over them until they are pushed out (Fig. 15E).

As in primitive archosaurs, there are only two sacral vertebrae; in the caudal region the chevron bones are well developed, deepening the tail. There is a well developed system of abdominal ribs which are often lost in prepared specimens since they lie superficial to the abdominal muscles. The hind-legs are considerably longer than the forelegs. The carpus and tarsus show distinctive specializations (see Romer, 1956) and the fifth toe on the foot is vestigial. Both the fingers and toes are partly webbed.

The front part of the respiratory tract shows a remarkable series of modifications related to the amphibious life, which do not, however, seem to have been evolved by other groups of aquatic reptiles and are incompletely developed in the primitive Jurassic forms.

The nostrils are a pair of crescentic openings raised up on a small eminence on the tip of the snout. They are pulled open by a longitudinal dilator muscle and closed when the animal dives by a constrictor muscle which encircles the dilator and squeezes it against the back of the nostril, obliterating the aperture (Fig. 15D).

The nasal cavities lead into the extremely elongated passages of the internal nares which open near the back of the skull and are separated from the mouth by a very complete secondary palate formed from the maxillae, palatines and pterygoids (Figs. 15A, C). Projecting downwards from the palate at the back of the throat just in front of the internal nares is a muscular flap which can be pulled forwards to fit behind another flap-like extension from the back of the tongue supported by a process of the hyoid bone and known as the basihyal valve. These two flaps form a very complete valve which can close off the mouth from the windpipe and gullet. The crocodile is therefore able to submerge its head without flooding either the nose or the windpipe and lungs, even when the jaws are open under water as it is dragging down its prey.

The ear is hidden by two scaly flaps of tissue (Fig. 15A) which can be opened and closed by means of special muscles. When the head is above water the lower ear flap behind the eye is usually drawn forward a little so that there is a narrow slit between it

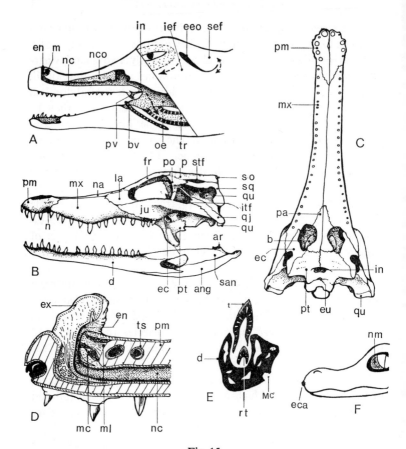

Fig. 15

A. Head of crocodile partly sectioned to show respiratory passages. Arrows show direction of airway, and movements of ear-flaps.
B. Skull of young *Crocodylus*.
C. Palate of gharial (*Gavialis*).
D. Front of snout of 3.3m (11ft) gharial, sectioned longitudinally to show narial excrescence and muscles (B. Martin and A. d'A. Bellairs, L. Bayes unpubl.). The excrescence is of immature type.
E. Cross-section through lower jaw of crocodilian showing socketed tooth with replacement. The outer surface of the jaw is on the left.
F. Late embryo of crocodile showing egg-caruncle.

ang, angular. *ar*, articular. *b*, bulla (swelling of pterygoid bones). *bv*, basihyal valve. *d*, dentary. *ec*, ectopterygoid. *eca*, egg-caruncle. *eeo*, external ear opening. *en*, external nostril. *eu*, opening of Eustachian tube. *ex*, narial excrescence. *fr*, frontal. *ief*, inferior ear-flap. *in*, internal nostril. *itf*, inferior temporal fenestra. *ju*, jugal. *la*, lachrymal. *m*, and the front of the more conspicuous upper flap. At times, however, the latter is flickered up and down, opening the external ear more widely and exposing the eardrum which lies beneath it. Both flaps are closed when the creature dives; they protect the eardrum from mechanical injury and possibly from the effects of water pressure.

The eustachian tubes of crocodiles are extraordinarily complicated. In addition to the usual lateral pair there is a third tube in the midline which leaves the skull through a large opening behind the internal nares. It joins the lateral tubes as they issue from tiny holes on either side of the median aperture to form a common passage into the throat. The two tympanic cavities are also connected by a transverse passage across the head. The functional significance of these features is not clear but they probably have some effect on sound conduction. The lagena, the organ of hearing in the inner ear, is large in crocodiles and sounds seem to play an important part in their lives. Their hearing is excellent by comparison with many birds and mammals and is most sensitive in the range 300–3000 Hz (cycles per second) (Wever, 1971).

The eyesight is keen and the eyes are advantageously placed on the top of the head as in many amphibious beasts. Seen at night by torchlight they shine brightly owing to the presence of a reflecting layer, the tapetum lucidum, at the back of the retina (see Walls, 1942). The pupil closes to a vertical slit.

The heart has been described on p. 43. Crocodiles are unusual among reptiles in possessing a complete partition between the thoracic and abdominal cavities something like the mammalian diaphragm, although its arrangement is rather different; like the coelomic partitions of reptiles in general, it deserves further study. Apparently this partition is associated with a large 'dia-

---

muscles of nostril: *mc*, circular; *ml*, longitudinal. *Mc*, groove for Meckel's cartilage. *n*, notch in upper jaw for 4th mandibular tooth. *mx*, maxilla. *nc*, nasal cavity. *nco*, nasal concha. *nm*, nictitating membrane. *oe*, oesophagus. *p*, parietal. *pa*, palatine. *pm*, premaxilla. *po*, postorbital. *pt*, pterygoid. *pv*, palatal valve. *qj*, quadratojugal. *qu*, quadrate. *rt*, replacing tooth. *san*, surangular. *sef*, superior ear-flap. *so*, supraoccipital. *sq*, squamosal. *stf*, superior temporal fenestra. *t*, tooth. *tr*, trachea. *ts*, tooth socket. *na*, nasal.

phragmaticus' muscle which runs back from the liver to the pelvis and assists the costal breathing mechanism by retracting the liver and expanding the pleural cavity in inspiration. Abdominal muscles assist expiration by pulling the liver forwards against the lungs, thus decreasing the pleural volume (Gans, 1970).

The oesophagus is fairly distensible and may be used for storing food which cannot immediately be accommodated in the comparatively small stomach. The latter consists of two compartments, a thick-walled muscular gizzard, in which gastroliths (stones) are often found, and a smaller and more glandular pyloric region which leads into the small intestine. The gastroliths may have a hydrostatic as well as a digestive function, acting as ballast.

The cloaca is a longitudinal slit leading into an extensive cloacal chamber. In the male the ventral wall of this chamber, just in front of the opening, is modified to form a single penis which is grooved on its upper surface for the transmission of sperm; the vasa efferentia open into the cloaca near the base of this groove. There is a small clitoris in the female. The more anterior part of the cloaca functions as a urinary bladder. A canal leads from the peritoneal cavity into the cloaca on either side of the base of the penis or clitoris; these canals probably correspond with the abdominal pores of some lower vertebrates. Anal glands producing a musky secretion also discharge into the cloaca and probably have some function in sex attraction.

Much remains to be learnt about the life of crocodilians and there may be significant differences between the behaviour of the Nile crocodile and the American alligator, the two best known species. Many writers have emphasized the quarrelsome nature of male crocodiles which often inflict severe injuries on each other. Such fights probably occur in defence of territory and seem to be more frequent during the breeding season. At this time the males roar frequently, perhaps to attract the females which are less vocal (Cott, 1961). Alligators are even more renowned for their ability to roar, the sound being uttered by both sexes. The roaring of one alligator may be taken up by others in chorus and captive animals may be induced to vocalize if loud sounds are made in their vicinity.

Copulation takes place in the water and may be preceded by some display or courtship. The male alligator swims alongside the female and strokes her with his head or fore-limbs. He then apparently grips her by the neck with his fore-limbs and bends the posterior part of his body to one side and under hers; the cloacae of the two animals can be brought together and the penis inserted (Guggisberg, 1972).

Most, if not all crocodilians make a nest of some kind for their eggs and exhibit some degree of maternal care which is reminiscent of birds, their closest living relatives. The Nile crocodile makes a hole in a sandbank a little distance from the water and about 60cm (2ft) deep, and covers over the eggs with soil. The eggs are hard-shelled and measure about 9×6cm (4×2in). 50 is an average number in a clutch. The female remains near the nest, covering it with her body or lying in a shady spot nearby throughout the incubation period of around three months; she does not feed during this period. It is uncertain whether the female actively defends her eggs at this time, but her mere presence probably acts as a deterrent to intruders.

The young crocodilian is provided with a horny egg-caruncle on the tip of the snout which assists it to break out of the egg-shell (Fig. 15F). Escape from the sun-baked nest is often impossible, however, without the assistance of the mother who scrapes away the sand, probably in response to the croaking of the hatchlings. She will even remove heavy obstacles placed on top of the nest. The impressive observations of Cott (still partly unpublished) reveal even further evidence of maternal care. At hatching time the mother crocodile certainly becomes aggressive in defence of her young. It is thought that she escorts them down to the water like a duck with her brood, and she may even remain with them for some days, protecting them against predators. Subsequently the young hide away among reedy shallows and backwaters. For some years they live in seclusion, avoiding places frequented by larger potentially cannabalistic members of their own species, and do not appear on basking grounds until they are about 1m (3ft) long.

Other crocodilians such as the estuarine crocodile and the American alligator make large nest mounds from decayed vegetation in which the eggs are able to develop at a suitable and relatively constant temperature. According to Neill, the nest material is piled up by the alligator's body and tail, the cavity being scooped out with a hind-foot; contrary to previous statements, the jaws are not used in nest-building. Like the Nile crocodile, the female alligator guards the nest until the young hatch.

Crocodilians grow quite rapidly at first, especially if food is plentiful. From data given by Oliver (1955) it would seem that alligators may grow about 30cm (1ft) a year for their first four years of life, and reach sexual maturity at about six years when the males are 1·8m (6ft) or more in length and the females are somewhat less. After maturity, growth slows down, but seems to continue gradually throughout life; male alligators occasionally reach a length of 3.7–4.6m (12–15ft) but females seldom exceed 2.3m (7.5ft).

The adult maximum size range of living crocodilians is from about 1.2m (4ft) to 6m (20ft), or perhaps a little more. The estuarine, Nilotic and American crocodiles and the Indian gharial are among the largest species. Giants of over 6m (20ft) have become very rare, however, since the advent of modern firearms. In many species of crocodilian (e.g. *C. niloticus*) the total length of the animal is about 7–8 times that of the head (or skull), measured in the dorsal midline from the tip of the snout to the back of the occiput. It may be noted that this is less than the overall head or skull length which would include the lower jaw; this projects backwards behind the cranium.

The two sexes look alike externally, though the males tend to grow to a larger size. The young of some species are more brightly coloured than their parents and may be marked with yellowish or greenish bands which fade with age. Alligators and crocodiles are known to have lived for about fifty-five years and may perhaps attain ages of over a century.

Alligators are believed to hibernate in holes under banks during the winter months and crocodiles may aestivate during the hot season if their pools dry up. It is well known that crocodilians of many species are in the habit of taking refuge in caves and tunnels which open beneath the surface of the waters in which they dwell.

Crocodiles spend much time basking, or lying in the water with only the eyes and nostrils exposed. They can, however, move very fast on occasion and have an alarming power of hurling the front parts of their bodies out of the water to snatch food. They can run quickly for short distances on land. Cott

(1961) has described three different types of gait adopted by the Nile crocodile; the walk with the body raised and the front and back legs working in diagonal pairs, the gallop with the two front and back legs moving together in pairs, and the run with the limbs sprawled out and the belly touching the ground, lizard-fashion. This last type of gait is often assumed when the crocodile is rushing downhill into the water. Young crocodiles are quite good climbers and may be seen on branches near the water. The tail is the main instrument for swimming, the limbs being pressed against the sides of the body. Large crocodiles can probably remain under water for longer than small ones and may withstand submergence for periods of an hour, or even considerably more.

The association between crocodiles and certain kinds of birds is well known. In Uganda the spur-winged plover, *Hoplopterus spinosus*, feeds on insects around basking crocodiles and is said to remove leeches and parasites from the gaping mouth, although this has not been firmly authenticated. The water dikkop, *Burhinus vermiculatus,* nests in the vicinity of nesting crocodiles which confer on its eggs a measure of protection. The cries of these birds are thought to warn the crocodiles of approaching danger.

Crocodiles take a wide variety of prey, especially fish. Surveys of the stomach contents of the Nile crocodile in Uganda show that young animals feed mainly on insects, snails and crabs; older individuals turn to fish; and large crocodiles over 4m (13ft) long often eat other reptiles, including young crocodiles, and mammals. Water birds are also captured. Many instances of crocodiles successfully attacking man and large mammals such as cattle on the banks of rivers or in the water have been reported; the huge estuarine crocodile seems to be a particularly dangerous species. Long-snouted crocodiles such as *C. cataphractus,* like the gharials, feed mainly on fishes.

Large prey is killed by drowning or by being torn to pieces by the simultaneous attacks of several crocodiles which will seize it by different parts and twist violently. When bolting fragments of food they throw their heads above the water, a procedure which is probably necessary because swallowing involves opening the palatal flaps. It is said that crocodiles sometimes store the carcasses of their prey in holes under the river bank before eating them, but Cott found little evidence that this was done by the Nile crocodile.

In captivity crocodiles can usually be reared without diffi-culty on a diet of worms, insects, raw meat and fish; young specimens seem to benefit from cod-liver oil. They often show signs of great interest when food is being prepared and learn to approach the person who is about to feed them. Different species vary in temperament; alligators generally become tame, but crocodiles and gharials are notoriously vicious. Even when young they can inflict painful bites, but they will seldom hang on to a limb as many lizards will. The tail of large specimens is also a powerful weapon.

The breeding of crocodiles is dependent upon the availability of suitable nesting sites and their numbers are diminished by any agency which reduces these. The newly hatched young have many enemies, being eaten by fish, storks and other birds, mongooses, larger crocodiles and particularly by monitor lizards. The latter will dig up the nest for the eggs if the mother is killed or dis-turbed and attack the emerging young.

Once they have reached a certain size, however, crocodiles have little to fear except from man. Their flesh is eaten in some parts of the world, but is barely acceptable to the European palate. Relentless persecution for their hides has led to a great diminution of their numbers, and some species are seriously threatened. Conservation is essential and this can be assisted by properly controlled tourism and farming. Fortunately, the IUCN (p. 86) has taken the crocodilians under its wing and has established a special group, like that which is concerned with turtles, to advise on protective legislation and other suitable measures. Perhaps the main problem is to deal with poachers, especially in newly emergent and underdeveloped countries where crocodiles (and other endangered animals) are mainly to be found. It would be a tragedy if the crocodilians, the last reptilian survivors of the great archosaurian dynasty, were to be exterminated just for the sake of producing a few more shoes and handbags.

8 | Dinosaurs

Abbreviations on p. 11. For some groups W.w. implies northern hemisphere only.

Subclass ARCHOSAURIA
Order Saurischia (Trias.–Cret., W.w.)
  Suborder Theropoda (Trias.–Cret., W.w.)
    Infraorder Coelurosauria (Trias.–Cret., W.w.): *Syntarsus* (U. Trias., Af.), *Compsognathus* (U. Jur., Eur.), *Coelurus* (U. Jur.– L. Cret., N.Am.), *Ornithomimus* (U. Cret., N.Am., As.). *Oviraptor* (U. Cret., As.)
    Infraorder Carnosauria (Trias.–Cret., W.w.): *Allosaurus* (U. Jur.– L. Cret., N.Am., ?E.Af.), *Megalosaurus* (L. Jur.–Cret., Eur., Af., N.Am.), *Deinocheirus* (U. Cret., As.), *Gorgosaurus* (U. Cret., N.Am., As.), *Tarbosaurus* (U. Cret., As.), *Tyrannosaurus* (N.Am., As.)
  Suborder Sauropodomorpha (Trias.–Cret., W.w.).
    Infraorder Prosauropoda (Trias.–L. Jur., W.w.): *Euskelosaurus* (U. Trias., S.Af.), *Vulcanodon* (U. Trias., Af.), *Plateosaurus,* U. Trias., Eur.)
    Infraorder Sauropoda (Jur.–Cret., W.w.): *Brachiosaurus* U.Jur.– L. Cret., N.Am., Eur., E.Af., As.), *Diplodocus* (U. Jur., N.Am.), *Brontosaurus* (U. Jur., N.Am., Eur.), *Titanosaurus* (L.–U. Cret., Eur., Af., As., Sn.Am.)
Order Ornithischia (Trias.–Cret., W.w.)
  Suborder Ornithopoda (Trias.–Cret., W.w.): *Heterodontosaurus* U. Trias., S.Af.), *Iguanodon* (U. Jur.–L. Cret., Eur., N.Af., As.), *Hypsilophodon* (L. Cret., Eur.), *Corythosaurus* (U. Cret., N.Am.), *Lambeosaurus* (U. Cret., N.Am.), *Parasaurolophus* (U. Cret., N.Am.), *Stegoceras* (U. Cret., N.Am.), *Trachodon,* U. Cret., N. Am.)
  Suborder Stegosauria (L. Jur.–L. Cret., W.w.): *Scelidosaurus* (L. Jur., Eur)., *Stegosaurus* (U. Jur., N.Am., ?Eur.)
  Suborder Ankylosauria (L.–U. Cret., W.w.): *Polacanthus* (L. Cret., Eur.), *Ankylosaurus* (U. Cret., N.Am.)
  Suborder Ceratopsia (U. Cret., W.w.): *Protoceratops* (U. Cret., As.), *Triceratops* (U. Cret., N.Am.)

E

Throughout the greater part of the Mesozoic era the land faunas of the world were dominated by two great orders of archosaurian reptiles, the Saurischia and the Ornithischia. These together comprise the dinosaurs (Greek *deinos*, terrible; *sauros*, lizard) which in their diversity approached the mammals of today. While many were fully terrestrial and adapted for fast running, others were ponderous lowland dwellers. Although the dinosaurs included the largest land animals of all time among their number, some were lightly built and hardly bigger than a pheasant. Excellent general accounts of these creatures are given by Colbert (1962, 1965, 1968) and Cox (1969) and Swinton (1970), while splendid reconstructions are figured by Špinar and Burian (1972). There are also useful guide books on fossil reptiles and birds available at the British Museum (Natural History).

Evidence favours an independent derivation of the two orders of dinosaurs from the pseudosuchian thecodonts of the early Triassic—though Bakker and Galton (1974) suggest that the two groups had a common origin. Many factors seem to have promoted the spectacular rise and success of these reptiles. Unlike their contemporaries, apart from the more advanced therapsids (p. 102), the dinosaurs had abandoned a sprawling gait and evolved fast locomotion with the limbs held in a nearly vertical position (see Charig in Joysey and Kemp, 1972). Again, in their feeding adaptations they had a marked superiority over their competitors.

Various workers such as Bakker (1972) have suggested that the dinosaurs also achieved the advantages of endothermy associated with their ability for sustained rapid movement. Bakker's reasoning has been criticized (see *Evolution*, 1973, v.27; 1974, v.31) but the sheer bulk of many dinosaurs would seem to predispose towards endothermy. The larger an animal becomes the greater is its volume in relation to its surface area. Other things being equal, this ratio would tend to minimize both heat loss and heat absorption and to stabilize the deep body temperature; this has been demonstrated to some extent in living giant tortoises. It is possible that the tendency towards gigantism, particularly exemplified in the sauropods like *Brontosaurus*, had definite selection value in terms of temperature regulation, at least in the warm climate of the age.

The anatomical distinction between the Saurischia ('lizard-hipped') and Ornithischia ('bird-hipped') is primarily based on pelvic structure. In saurischians (Fig. 16A) the pubis of each side was situated in front of the acetabulum, a condition typical for reptiles. In ornithischians the pubis was posteriorly rotated to lie parallel to the ischium; in the primitive Triassic forms, in the lower Jurassic *Scelidosaurus* (Fig. 16B), and in the Cretaceous ankylosaurs the pubis formed a simple posterior ramus, but in all other ornithischians (Fig. 16C) an anterior ramus was developed on the pubis which passed in front of the acetabulum. There has been much confusion in the literature concerning the terms 'triradiate' and 'tetraradiate' for the saurischian and ornithischian pelves; the terms are best abandoned and replaced by 'propubic' for the saurischian girdle and 'opisthopubic' for the ornithischian girdle (See Charig in Joysey and Kemp, 1972).

A feature unique to the ornithischians was the presence of a median toothless bone, the predentary, at the front of the lower jaw (Fig. 16H).

In habit, the Saurischia includes bipedal carnivores (e.g. *Tyrannosaurus*) and quadrupedal herbivores (e.g. *Brontosaurus*). The Ornithischia also includes both bipeds (e.g. *Iguanodon*) and quadrupeds (e.g. *Triceratops*) but all ornithischians were herbivores. Both orders are represented in the Triassic and both continued to evolve and diversify throughout the remainder of the Mesozoic.

Saurischian dinosaurs

We shall first review the Saurischia, the more conservative of the two orders, its members retaining a number of anatomical characters found in the pseudosuchian ancestors.

The saurischian classification as set out at the beginning of the chapter is that of Charig *et al.* (1965).

Two quite separate and divergent line of saurischian evolution can be followed throughout the Mesozoic, the theropod line and the sauropodomorph line. The theropods were strikingly different in their adaptations to sauropodomorphs for all were bipedal and these were the dominant predators of the Mesozoic. The suborder Theropoda comprises two groups, the Coelurosauria and Carnosauria. The sauropodomorphs, on the other hand, were without exception herbivores, or at the most took the occasional

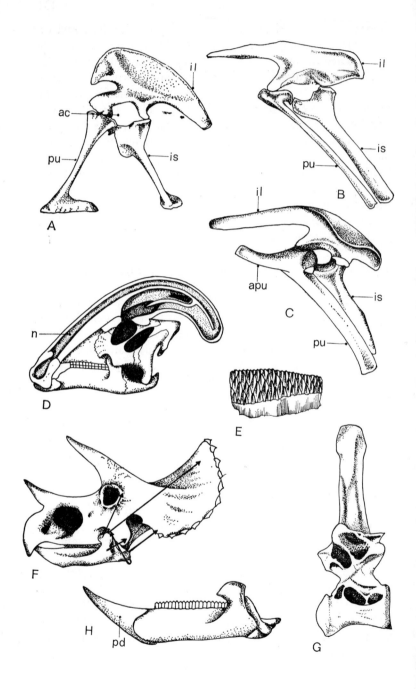

freshwater mollusc, and all post-Triassic forms were quadrupedal; the suborder comprises two groups, the Prosauropoda and Sauropoda.

Coelurosaurs had a worldwide distribution throughout the Mesozoic but, for reasons not yet clear, their fossils are more abundant in rocks of northern latitudes. They were small for dinosaurs; *Compsognathus* (Fig. 17G) from the German Jurassic was turkey-sized, while the largest genera, such as *Ornithomimus* from the Cretaceous of North America, were some 4.3m (14ft) in length. Typical coelurosaurs were lightly built reptiles with slender legs and long tails. They were clearly adapted for bipedal locomotion. Indeed there is good evidence that the upper Triassic form *Syntarsus* could move in kangaroo-like leaps, but this was probably exceptional among the group.

In the coelurosaurs the metatarsals were elongated and held close together while the fifth and often the first toes were reduced; the foot as a whole had a very bird-like appearance. Trackways indicate a fairly stiff tail which was held clear of the ground when the animal was running at speed. The fore-limbs were small with a three-fingered hand which was probably used for grasping prey. These small dinosaurs with their sharp conical teeth seem to have been active carnivores, preying on the smaller members of the Mesozoic fauna; they were probably for the most part forest dwellers. However, in the recently discovered skeleton of *Composgnathus corallestris* from the south of France the fore-limb and accompanying skin impression indicate a flipper-like development for swimming.

Coelurosaurs of a more specialized type were the 'bird

Fig. 16

A, saurischian pelvis (*Allosaurus*). B, primitive ornithischian pelvis (*Scelidosaurus*). C, advanced ornithischian pelvis (*Stegosaurus*). D, skull of *Parasaurolophus* with nasal passages extending into crest. E, tooth battery of the duck-billed dinosaur *Trachodon*. F, skull and lower jaw of *Triceratops*: arrows show directions of pull of jaw muscles. G, sauropod vertebra seen from right side. H, lower jaw of ornithischian (*Triceratops*) to show predentary bone. B, after Charig in Joysey and Kemp (1972). D, F, after Ostrom.

ac, acetabulum. *apu*, anterior pubis. *il*, ilium. *is*, ischium. *n*, nasal passage. *pd*, predentary. *pu*, pubis.

mimicking' ornithomimids which appeared towards the end of the Cretaceous. They provide an excellent example of 'convergent evolution' for as their name suggests, they were very similar in many structures to the large ratite birds of today. In *Ornithomimus* of the Upper Cretaceous the head was small and the toothless jaws were probably furnished with a beak. The neck and tail were long and, as with other coelurosaurs, the limb bones were thin-walled to reduce body weight. Although the ornithomimids were clearly fast-running bipeds their fore-limbs, unlike those of other theropods, were rather powerful and the three-fingered hand was probably used for grasping and tearing small prey. It seems likely that *Ornithomimus* and its allies were omnivores eating small vertebrates, insects and fruit. Eggs have also been suggested as a diet since the remains of one of these dinosaurs, *Oviraptor*, have been found in Mongolia beside a nest of fossil eggs belonging to the ornithischian, *Protoceratops*.

The Carnosauria, the other theropod group, includes the largest terrestrial predators known, forms such as *Tyrannosaurus*, and the almost identical *Tarbosaurus* (Fig. 17B), with a body length of over 12m (40ft) and an estimated live weight of 8130kg (8 tons). Among predatory reptiles such dimensions are matched only by giant crocodilians such as *Phobosuchus* and by some of the marine forms.

The carnosaurs show a number of interesting trends, some of which were associated with increase in size, while others would seem to be related to their methods of predation. In these bipeds, as in the coelurosaurs, the hind-limbs were highly effective for fast locomotion; the femur was held nearly upright and the lower leg bones were lengthened to increase the stride.

To support the great body weight the hind-limb bones were of massive construction and extra vertebrae were incorporated from the trunk region into the sacrum; this acted as the fulcrum for the body, with the powerful tail constituting a counterbalance for the head and thorax. The fore-limbs of carnosaurs show progressive reduction in size during the course of time; in *Tyrannosaurus* they were diminutive, too short to manipulate food at the mouth and too weak to be effective grasping organs or weapons. It is possible, however, that they assisted the animal to rise from a recumbent to a bipedal position.

Fig. 17

A, *Stegosaurus* (U. Jur.). B, *Tarbosaurus*, an Asiatic carnosaur very like the American *Tyrannosaurus* (U. Cret.). C, *Iguanodon* (U. Jur.–L. Cret.). D, *Protoceratops* (U. Cret.). E, *Brachiosaurus* (U. Jur.– L. Cret.). F, *Ankylosaurus* (U. Cret.). G, *Compsognathus* (U. Jur.), a tiny dinosaur, the size of a fowl. B–E, G, after Špinar and Burian (1972); F, after Cox (1969). (Not to scale).

The tools for predation were concentrated in the head. This became huge, over 1.2m (4ft) long in *Tyrannosaurus*, and in all carnosaurs the jaws were armed with scimitar-like teeth. To reduce the weight of the head the antorbital and other vacuities were enlarged and for its carriage the neck was shortened; in advanced carnosaurs, such as *Tyrannosaurus*, cervical vertebrae were fused. The gape of the jaw was very great and was increased in some carnosaurs by the development of a form of kinesis which allowed the upper jaw to move on the cranium; in many, such as *Gorgosaurus*, the two rami of the lower jaw were not fused in bone and must have had a snake-like horizontal gape for engulfing large portions of their prey. Carnosaurs undoubtedly predated the large sauropods. An exception to the rule that in carnosaurs the fore-limb was much reduced has been found recently in Mongolia by Polish workers. The fore-limbs of the Upper Cretaceous genus, *Deinocheirus*, were some 2.4m (8ft) long and terminated in enormous claw-like phalanges.

Little is known of the carnosaurs of the Triassic and their origin is obscure. In the Upper Jurassic the fragmentary remains of the European *Megalosaurus* and its allies are found, and in North America complete skeletons of *Allosaurus* have been excavated. The giant tyrannosaurs are all Upper Cretaceous in age, noted genera being *Tyrannosaurus* in the United States, *Gorgosaurus* in Canada and *Tarbosaurus* in Asia.

All members of the remaining suborder Sauropodomorpha were herbivorous and with the exception of some Triassic forms all were quadrupedal and attained very great size. *Brontosaurus* was some 20m (65ft) in length with an estimated weight of 30 480kg (30 tons). *Brachiosaurus,* the bulkiest dinosaur known, was some 24m (80ft) in length, despite its short tail, and may have weighed in excess of 51 000kg (50 tons); unlike other sauropods the fore-limbs were longer than the hind-limbs (Fig. 17E), a reversal of the usual archosaurian pattern.

The prosauropods of the Upper Triassic had a worldwide distribution and great diversity in form. Some such as *Euskelosaurus* and *Vulcanodon* of southern Africa were of great size and had columnar limbs for quadrupedal locomotion while others such as the European *Plateosaurus* were smaller facultative bipeds. The cheek teeth of prosauropods were leaf-like in form although some genera retained long recurved teeth at the front of the jaw, a heritage no doubt from their carnivorous pseudo-suchian ancestors. In addition to skeletal remains quadrupedal and bipedal trackways, attributed to prosauropods, are known from the Upper Triassic of Lesotho. Prosauropods disappear from the scene at the time of the Triassic–Jurassic boundary, but from them or their close relatives the Sauropoda took origin.

It is important to stress at this point that the widely held view that the sauropods proper were a secondarily quadrupedal group derived from bipedal pseudosuchian ancestors via semi-bipedal prosauropods will not stand close analysis. As we have seen in Chapter 7 the popular image of a pseudosuchian as a delicate biped is far from true, and the presence of completely quadrupedal prosauropods at the very beginning of the Upper Triassic argues against secondary quadrupedalism in the sauropod line. It is often said that the shortness of the fore-limb compared with the hind-limb and the prescence of a powerful tail in sauro-pods indicate a bipedal ancestor, but these characters are basic to all archosaurs.

Let us now consider some of the structural features in sauro-pods. The sauropod head was disproportionately small and they could therefore afford the luxury of a very long neck; the sauro-pods could crop vegetation over a large area while stationary with the minimum expenditure of energy. Sauropod teeth were simple and peg-like in form. The vertebral column was massively constructed for the support of the body but, to reduce the dead weight, the sides of each vertebra (Fig. 16G) were hollowed out without loss in structural strength. The sacrum was strengthened by incorporation of vertebrae from the caudal series. Large cable-like ligaments ran along the top of the column to winch up the neck and head. The massive pillar-like limbs were held in vertical position and terminated in elephantine pads with the digits for the most part embedded in connective tissue. The sauropod brain, as of dinosaurs generally, was absurdly small. There seems however to have been an enlargement of the spinal cord in the sacral region and perhaps another in the brachial region between the shoulders. It is possible that these areas however were for the storage of glycogen tissue; Ewer (1965) has suggested this for the thecodont *Euparkeria* by analogy to similar features in birds.

Despite their gigantic size there is no evidence that sauropods overstepped the limits of structural strength and were therefore completely dependent on the buoyancy of water for support of their weight. Yet so often they are figured as living in lagoons with only the head and neck above the surface. This seems improbable on a number of counts. It has been argued that if submerged to the level of the upper neck the pressure of water on the trachea and rib cage would prevent adequate lung ventilation. Moreover, Bakker (1971) finds considerable evidence in the structure of the vertebral column and limbs in support of a terrestrial habit for brontosaurs. It is difficult to see how sauropod trackways, which are sometimes of great clarity, could have been preserved if 30 480kg (30 ton) sauropods were moving through lake mud. The teeth of sauropods often show a high degree of wear which would indicate an abrasive plant diet rather than the soft lake and riverine plant diet so often prescribed for them. Certainly the Jurassic Morrison Formation, in which sauropods are common has a flora of open upland type. It must however be admitted that sauropod nostrils were situated high on the skull in front of the eyes; this position closely resembles that of the truly aquatic phytosaurs. In summary it seems likely that sauropods could move freely on dry land but no doubt could take to water at times.

The sauropods reached their zenith in terms of numbers and variety in the Upper Jurassic. In northern latitudes in the Cretaceous sauropod fossils are rare, but in the south *Titanosaurus* and its allies flourished in Upper Cretaceous times.

Ornithischian dinosaurs

Apart from the diagnostic pelvic pattern and the presence of a predentary bone, many other characters set apart ornithischians from saurischians. All were herbivores and the teeth tended to be set on the back half of the jaws and were often crowded together to form file-like grinding surfaces (Fig. 16E); the fronts of the jaws, typically toothless, were probably covered in horny beaks. In the bipedal forms the fore-limbs were never reduced to the extent seen in theropods and at rest forms such as *Iguanodon* could drop down on to all fours. In many respects the ornithischians were less conservative than the saurischians and show many exotic features of skull and armour. Although many were large, ornithischians never reached the gigantic dimensions of the saurischians. Towards the end of the Mesozoic ornithischians made up the bulk of the dinosaur fauna moving in great herds as do the herbivorous mammals of Africa today.

Four groups of ornithischians, representing suborders, can be recognized: the bipedal ornithopods; the quadrupedal and armoured stegosaurs; the quadrupedal and heavily armoured ankylosaurs; and the quadrupedal and horned ceratopsians.

The earliest known ornithischians are included in the Ornithopoda, for here belong the recently discovered Triassic forms from southern Africa such as *Heterodontosaurus* (Crompton and Charig, 1962), and others from China and South America. In *Heterodontosaurus* cheek teeth were still present on the premaxilla and the posteriorly orientated pubis had yet to develop an anterior ramus.

A later member of the Ornithopoda was the famous *Iguanodon* which roamed the Sussex Weald in early Cretaceous times. It was one of the first dinosaurs to be scientifically described; its remains were first found in Sussex in 1822 by Gideon Mantell (or more correctly by his wife), one of the pioneers of English palaeontology. In 1878 the remains of some thirty skeletons of *Iguanodon* were recovered from a coalmine in Belgium. The footprints of *Iguanodon* have been found in Spitzbergen.

Iguanodon (Fig. 17C) was a stoutly built dinosaur about 8m (25ft) long and 4.5m (15ft) high when standing upright. Its thumb formed a conical bony spur which may have been a defensive weapon. Its teeth were oval in shape with serrated margins; they are not unlike the teeth of some iguana lizards, a resemblance responsible for the name *Iguanodon*.

Hypsilophodon from the lower Cretaceous of the Isle of Wight has for long been described as a small and primitive ornithopod with a semi-arboreal habit. A recent study by Galton (1971) rejects this interpretation in favour of a cursorial habit; it is primitive in that teeth were present on the premaxilla.

The hadrosaurs and troödonts were two groups of more specialized ornithopods. The hadrosaurs, or 'duck-billed' dinosaurs, are first found in the lower Cretaceous of Asia and are common in the Upper Cretaceous of the Northern Hemisphere. The rare and exotic troödonts are all of Upper Cretaceous age and have been found in North America and China.

The hadrosaurs have often been regarded as amphibious. Ostrom (1964) however, thinks they lived and fed mainly on the land although the tail was flattened for swimming, and as specimens mummified in drying mud show, the front feet were webbed. The skin was covered with small irregular bony plates.

The jaws of hadrosaurs (Fig. 16D) were often flattened, forming a broad bill like that of a duck. This was toothless in front, but at the back there were remarkable batteries of teeth, sometimes about 600 on each side of each jaw. Each individual tooth was flattened from side to side and serrated on the crown. Several transverse rows of these teeth, tightly pressed together, are found in each jaw, the whole forming a kind of mill suitable for grinding up tough plants.

Trachodon was a hadrosaur with a skull of normal shape. Other duck-billed dinosaurs developed grotesque cranial excrescences. In *Corythosaurus* there was a rounded crest on the roof of the skull similar in shape to that of a cassowary bird. In *Lambeosaurus* the crest was hatchet-shaped and in *Parasaurolophus* (Fig. 16D) it was drawn out into a tubular structure which curved back behind the head. These crests were formed from the premaxillary and nasal bones and enclosed an extensive nasal passage forming in *Parasaurolophus* (Fig. 16D) an inverted U-tube. There have been many ingenious suggestions for the function of this unique nasal pattern; an air storage function or alternatively a trap to prevent water inflow during diving are common explanations. Ostrom (1962) suggests that elaboration of the nasal passage can only be explained in terms of increase in area for the nasal mucosa and that the sense of smell was important to a vulnerable herbivore. David Attenborough (personal communication) has made the interesting suggestion that the great variety in crest form, and consequent nasal development, might have been associated with vocalization.

In the troödonts (pachycephalosaurids) such as *Stegoceras*, the cranial roof was greatly thickened to form a massive dome; around the base of this and over the front of the face was a number of short spikes and knobs.

In general build, the post-cranial skeleton of hadrosaurs and troödonts was rather similar to the iguanodonts.

The three remaining suborders are the Stegosauria, Ankylosauria and Ceratopsia.

The main diagnostic feature of the Stegosauria was the armour on the back. The fore-limbs were disproportionately short indicating descent from a bipedal ancestor. Although fragmentary remains of related genera have been found in England, the famous genus *Stegosaurus* (Fig. 17A) is only known from the Upper Jurassic of North America. *Stegosaurus* was some 6m (20ft) long and furnished with an overlapping series of large upstanding and triangular bony plates along the back and some formidable bony spikes on the tail, all presumably for defence.

The Ankylosauria was another armoured group; its members had squat bodies, short legs and a 'carapace' made up of separate bony plates. These dinosaurs illustrate one of several variations on a tank-like lumbering pattern which crops up among different reptile groups; other examples are the armoured pareiasaurs, thecodonts such as *Desmatosuchus* (Fig. 14B, p. 117) and, of course, the tortoises. The ankylosaurs were restricted to the Upper Cretaceous, well known forms being *Polacanthus* from the Lower Cretaceous of the Isle of Wight and *Ankylosaurus* (Fig. 17F) from the Upper Cretaceous of North America.

The Ceratopsia, or horned dinosaurs, were the last group of dinosaurs to make their appearance for no form has been found prior to the Upper Cretaceous. Ceratopsians possessed a sharp curved beak and ran to horns on the snout and forehead and a frill-like expansion of bone from the skull which passed back over the upper surface of the neck. The horns were carried on bony horn-cores like those of ungulate mammals.

Protoceratops (Fig. 17D) from Asia was a small primitive form, almost hornless but having the characteristic neck frill. Both nests of eggs and young in various stages of growth, attributed to this genus, have been discovered in Mongolia (see Kurtén, 1968).

Triceratops (Figs. 1, 16F) was a much larger and more specialized ceratopsian which roamed the plains of North America in great herds in the Upper Cretaceous. In size it reached 6m (20ft) the huge head accounting for nearly a third of its length. Its formidable armour no doubt sometimes protected the animal from the attacks of contemporary predators such as *Tyrannosaurus*.

Ostrom (1966) has interpreted the variety of neck frill pattern in the Ceratopsia in terms of the jaw musculature; in addition to its protective function the frill provided a major area on the skull for the origin of the jaw adductor muscles (Fig. 16F) and the varieties of pattern reflect the requirements of the differing jaw mechanisms.

Dinosaur extinction

Seen through human eyes, at a distance of nearly 70 million years, the dinosaurs seem to be nature's crowning experiment in the production of the gigantic and bizarre, one that has remained quite unsurpassed by any of the mammalian extravagances of the Tertiary. The span of the dinosaurs from the later part of the Triassic to the end of the Cretaceous, a period of about 130 million years, was longer by far than the whole Tertiary period. No dinosaurs are known from even the earliest Tertiary deposits, and yet in the Upper Cretaceous new groups such as the hadrosaurs and ceratopsians were appearing, diversifying and flourishing. Why did so varied an assemblage suddenly become extinct? The reasons are far from clear.

The demise of so dramatic a group has in the minds of many overshadowed the fact that for an immense span of time dinosaurs were highly successful. The popular impression that they were a tribe of cumbersome monsters with a low state of mental organization, trapped in an ever increasing spiral of gigantism, is far from the truth. Likewise, factors such as 'racial senescence' and 'overspecialization' which have been invoked to account for their extinction savour of the mystical. Nor can their demise be attributed to mammalian competition; the mammals present throughout the Mesozoic were insignificant in size, if not in numbers. They did not become a really flourishing group until the Paleocene, by which time the dinosaurs had long since departed.

During the Jurassic and perhaps the first half of the Cretaceous, climatic and geological conditions remained comparatively stable and the character of the vegetation underwent little change. The expansion of the archosaurian group and the deployment of its various orders along different lines of adaptive radiation proceeded steadily against a partly tropical background, among coniferous uplands, cycad forests and fern-bordered lagoons. In the later part of the Cretaceous, plant evolution acquired a sudden impetus: higher flowering plants and deciduous trees became numerous and by the end of the period most of the vegetation was essentially of modern type. Some dinosaurs may have been unable to adapt their dietary habits to the floral revolution, while the carnivores would naturally have perished with their prey.

The importance of climatic factors has been emphasized by several recent workers. Towards the end of the Cretaceous there occurred widespread geological changes in which large areas of land were uplifted; these were later to form the basis of our modern mountain chains (Colbert, 1965). Besides favouring the emergence of new types of plants, these alterations in the earth's crust probably resulted in marked climatic fluctuations. Axelrod and Bailey (1968) have produced much evidence that this was a period of temperature instability, replacing the equable conditions which had prevailed for so long and to which the dinosaurs and other large reptiles had become so well adapted. It is conceivable that in some regions of 'dinosaur country' temperatures would have dropped occasionally to well below freezing. Excessively high temperatures may also have been lethal; the very bulk of the dinosaurs may have made it difficult for them to lose enough heat, especially if their swampy or shady habitats were vanishing. Even if they survived as individuals, their sensitive germ cells might have succumbed to heat stress, making them sterile.

Bakker's explanation for extinction (1972) is on similar lines, though he presupposes only a fall in temperature at the end of the Cretaceous. He regards the dinosaurs as being essentially endothermic, but his argument implies that their endothermy, unlike that of birds and typical mammals, was of a type effective only under warm stable conditions. Unlike modern ectothermic reptiles they could not survive the cold by hibernating; they were too big to shelter in burrows, and lacking the insulation of fur or feathers they were rapidly eliminated.

It should be remembered that about the same time the pterosaurs, plesiosaurs, ichthyosaurs and mosasaurs (p. 171) also became extinct. The marine reptiles may have been affected by a gradual lowering of sea temperatures which apparently occurred a across the middle and higher latitudes (Axelrod and Bailey, 1968); also perhaps by the contemporary extinction of ammonites and the replacement of many archaic bony fishes by teleosts of modern type.

In summary it is probable that the extinction of the dinosaurs and other important reptilian groups was not due to any single factor but to a combination of geological, climatic and ecological changes which cannot be satisfactorily analysed from the data available. The career of the dinosaurs was an epic one, and R. S. Lull (1947) has written them an epitaph worthy of Gibbon:

They do not represent a futile attempt on the part of nature to people the world with creatures of insignificant moment, but are comparable in majestic rise, slow culmination, and dramatic fall to the greatest nations of antiquity.

9 | Flying reptiles and the origin of birds

Subclass ARCHOSAURIA
  Order Pterosauria (Jur.–Cret., W.w.)
    Suborder Rhamphorynchoidea: *Rhamphorhynchus* (U. Jur., Eur., E.Af.)
    Suborder Pterodactyloidea: *Pterodactylus* (U. Jur.–L. Cret., Eur., E.Af.), *Pteranodon* (U. Cret., Eur., As., N.Am.)
  Class AVES
  Subclass ARCHAEORNITHES: *Archaeopteryx* (U. Jur., Eur.)
  Subclass NEORNITHES: all other birds, including *Ichthyornis* and *Hesperornis* (U. Cret., N.Am.)

The evolutionary potentialities of the archosaurs expressed themselves not only in a variety of adaptations to terrestrial and amphibious life, but also in two experiments in flight, represented by the pterosaurs and the ancestors of birds.

Pterosaurs

The precise ancestry of the pterosaurs of the Jurassic and Cretaceous is unknown, for there are no Triassic fossils, but certainly they were derived from some group of Triassic thecodontians. It is probable that the ancestors were arboreal and that the pterosaur wing membrane was evolved initially for parachuting. The later development of sustained gliding flight in advanced forms, such as *Pteranodon*, marked the culmination of two closely related trends in pterosaur evolution: the progressive increase in wing membrane area coupled with the evolution of a complex of characters serving to reduce as far as possible the body weight. Recent anatomical and computer based studies by Bramwell have led to a completely new understanding of pterosaur evolution and aerodynamics (Bramwell and Whitfield, 1974).

In the pterosaurs the wings were membranous organs supported in the main by the four greatly elongated phalanges of the fourth finger. The first three fingers were short and ended in claws; the fifth was absent (Fig. 18A). The back edge of the pata-gial membrane, impressions of which are preserved in some fossils, continued on to the thigh, leaving only the extremities of the hind-limbs free. In some species there was a narrow inter-femoral membrane connecting the thighs and typically in ptero-saurs a bony element, the pteroid, at the front of the carpal region supported a membrane which extended on to the neck. The sternum, to which the flight muscles were attached, was strongly developed and keeled in primitive forms but in the Cretaceous *Pteranodon*, which had evolved the passive gliding capacity to perfection, the sternum was reduced. Primitive genera, such as *Rhamphorhynchus* (Fig. 18C), had a long tail with a rudder-like flap at the end. In *Pteranodon* (Fig. 18D) the tail was vestigial; a long crest on the back of the head may have served as a rudder. However, Bramwell and Whitfield (1974) believe that its main function was to act as an aerodynamic counterpoise to the beak, reducing the strain on the neck muscles (and hence their size) when the beak was turned.

Pterosaur bones were extremely light and hollow; those of the fore-limb were tubes of bone of pasteboard thickness, and were strengthened by a criss-cross of struts which ran across their cavities as in birds (Fig. 18B). Tooth reduction and loss was another feature associated with reduction of weight; it is probable that the toothless forms had light horny beaks.

Casts of the braincase suggest that the brain had a similar shape to that in birds with reduced olfactory regions but enlarged cerebral hemispheres and cerebellum; the latter is particularly important in flying vertebrates in the control of balance and flight posture. The eyes of pterosaurs, judging from the size of the orbits, were large and important organs.

Bramwell (1970) suggests that the pterosaurs were endothermic and cites as contributory evidence the recent discovery in Poland of pterosaurs, preserved in fine grained sediments, which clearly demonstrate a furry insulating layer on the skin of the hind-limbs.

The earliest pterosaurs, *Rhamphorhynchus* and allied genera, appeared in the Lower Jurassic. *Rhamphorhynchus* had a wing-

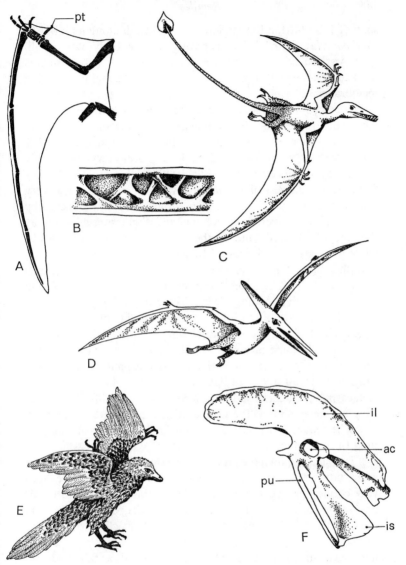

Fig. 18

A, fore-limb and skeleton of *Pteranodon*. B, metacarpal of vulture, sectioned to show internal struts, after d'Arcy Thompson (1968). C, *Rhamphorhynchus* (U. Jur.), after Špinar and Burian (1972). D, *Pteranodon* (U. Cret.). E, *Archaeopteryx* (U. Jur.). F, pelvis of kiwi (*Apteryx*), seen from left side.

ac, acetabulum. *il*, ilium. *is*, ischium. *pt*, pteroid. *pu*, pubis.

span of 1.2m (4ft), a long tail and conical teeth along its jaws. In *Pterodactylus* from the Upper Jurassic the body was small, sparrow-sized in some forms, and tail and tooth reduction was marked. These early forms probably flew by flapping the wing membranes.

Pteranodon from the Upper Cretaceous, with a wingspan of 8m (27ft) represents the culmination of pterosaur evolution in terms of thermal gliding, an experiment unsurpassed by other vertebrates or man-made gliders. It has been very thoroughly studied by Bramwell and Whitfield (1974). Apparently the key factor in the success of *Pteranodon* was the combination of very low body weight and large wing area; the former was achieved by reduction of the vertebral column and flight musculature, by the loss of all teeth and further thinning of the bone walls, while wing area was increased by elongation of the metacarpals and phalanges. The calculated live body weight for a full grown animal is only 17kg (36lb) and yet the wing area was 6sq.m (63sq.ft); the wing loading, a vital factor in gliding performance, was only a quarter of that of the albatross and man-made gliders. *Pteranodon* had only to spread its wings in winds above 24km/h (15mph) to become airborne and it could remain aloft without stalling at only 15mph. It is likely that the pteroid membranes acted both as an anti-stall flap and air brake. The very flexible metacarpal–phalangeal joint in *Pteranodon* allowed for a variable wing geometry so that the normal high aspect ratio of the wing could be reduced at speed on a straight flight path, or during a tight turn in a thermal.

It is difficult to imagine how the pterosaurs were able to manage when not airborne. The long trailing wings would have been very clumsy on the ground and clearly the limb structure was unsuitable for any form of bipedal or quadrupedal locomotion. Possibly the smaller kinds at least were able to cling to branches or rocks with their hands or to hang upside down by the feet, like bats. In *Pteranodon* the hind-limbs had a rather dorsal articulation with the pelvis and the foot formed an admirable grapple for suspension; it is likely that this and other large forms restricted their landing sites (and presumably nesting places) to cliff tops and faces.

The causes of the extinction of the pterosaurs at the close of the Cretaceous remain a mystery although the vulnerability of the wing membrane and avian competition seem likely factors.

Birds

The birds are far more reptilian in their organization than the mammals and to the comparative anatomist they seem little more than highly specialized archosaurian reptiles, although of course they have elaborated courtship, nesting and migratory behaviour to a degree unknown in any reptiles. It is thought that feathers could quite easily have been derived from scales of reptilian type. These appendages were as efficient as mammalian hair for the purposes of heat conservation; it is quite likely that they were evolved in the first place for thermal insulation and that their flight function, though essential in birds, was a secondary development. The total separation of the arterial and venous blood streams due to the completion of the ventricular septum and the loss of the left systemic arch were improvements which, for all we know, may have been effected in pterosaurs and dinosaurs. It would seem, however, that the special mode of lung ventilation, together with development of air sacs and their extension into the bone, was restricted to the avian line.

The structure of a bird's wing seems more robust and certainly more adaptable than that of a pterosaur. It is mainly supported by the fairly stout bones of the arm and forearm instead of by the long fragile bones of a single finger, while the nature of the joints at its articulation with the shoulder girdle, and between its different segments, allows it to be folded back over the body in a manner which seems to have been impossible for pterosaurs. The greater part of the wing area is made up of feathers instead of a vulnerable membrane; a few of these can be lost with impunity, and they can in any case be replaced, though not very rapidly. The fact that a bird's legs are not involved in its wings is a further advantage, since bipedal locomotion remains unimpaired.

Both birds and pterosaurs share the features of aerodynamic instability, essential for great manoeuvrability (J. M. Smith, 1962), but it should be emphasized that in contrast to the pterosaurs, which specialized in passive gliding flight, the adaptive radiation of birds, has in the main been concerned with active flapping flight.

The earliest known birds appear rather later on the scene than the pterosaurs, towards the end of the Jurassic. Until recently *Archaeopteryx*, the only Jurassic bird, was known, apart from a solitary feather impression, from only two specimens, the fine skeletons with feathers in the British and East Berlin Museums (de Beer, 1954). A third fragmentary skeleton was found in 1956 and Ostrom has described a fourth but incomplete specimen which he re-discovered in the Teyler Museum in Holland, where it had been since 1855 mislabelled as a pterosaur. Eichstadt Museum possesses a fifth specimen, recently described by Wellnhofer (see p. 232). All these specimens have come from the Upper Jurassic lithographic stone of Bavaria; these deposits are marine in nature and most probably the birds were blown out to sea and became fossilized in the silty mud on which they finally came to rest.

Archaeopteryx (Fig. 18E) was about the size of a jackdaw. Yalden (1971) estimates its wingspan as 58cm (22in) and its weight as about 200g (7oz). The majority of its features were frankly reptilian, while others were completely avian in character. It had a long tail, abdominal ribs and teeth in both jaws. The sternum, long believed to be absent, was small and lacked a keel. The wings carried three clawed fingers and the metacarpals were unfused, though the second and third seem to have been closely applied to each other. The fibula was the same length as the tibia instead of being reduced as in modern birds, and the metatarsals were incompletely fused, the first toe (hallux) being opposable and well adapted for perching on branches; the sacral region of the spine was comparatively unspecialized. The bones of *Archaeopteryx* do not appear to have been pneumatized, and the endocranial cast suggests a brain of reptilian proportions. The clavicles, however, were fused to form a 'wishbone' or furcula as in almost all modern birds except the ratites (ostrich, etc.), while both the structure of the feathers and their arrangement on the wings was very similar to that of birds today.

This ancient bird was probably a forest dweller. Yalden suggests that it was able to manage flapping flight, despite the absence of a sternal keel, but does not think that such flight could have been sustained for very long. He envisages the creature fluttering somewhat uncertainly among the leafy canopy. Its claws would have been useful for climbing and also for 'effecting sprawled crash landings on the foliage, beyond the reach of predators dependent on substantial branches for their progress'.

The origin of birds

There can be no doubt that the birds were descended from archosaurian reptiles of some kind, but in the absence of earlier known birds than *Archaeopteryx*, the precise identity of the ancestors presents an intriguing problem—still unresolved despite a recent flurry of papers on the subject. A long-standing, traditional view, expressed by Swinton (in Marshall, 1960), by Romer (1966) and in Fig. 1 of this book, is that the birds were directly descended from primitive thecodonts of the suborder Pseudosuchia (p. 117). According to this theory the dinosaurs, though also of thecodont origin, arose independently from birds; the many undoubted similarities between the two groups can largely be explained away on grounds of parallel evolution. This view would not conflict with Walker's suggestion that the birds came from the same thecodont stock as the crocodiles.

An alternative idea is that the birds originated 'higher up' on the archosaurian tree, not directly from thecodonts but from their primitive dinosaurian descendants. This was a popular theory over 50 years ago but was rejected by Heilmann in his classical book *The origin of birds* (1926) on the grounds that clavicles are present in most birds but absent in dinosaurs. However, this difficulty has now been removed by the discovery of clavicles in some dinosaurs.

Ostrom (1973) believes that the skeleton of *Archaeopteryx*, particularly of the limbs, both fore and hind, shows many close resemblances to that of a coelurosaurian dinosaur (suborder Theropoda, order Saurischia). He suggests that these common features are too numerous and complex to be merely attributable to parallel evolution, and that the immediate ancestors of birds were most probably small coelurosaurs. His ideas are now followed by Bakker and Galton (1974), although previously Galton (1970) regarded the ornithischian dinosaurs as being more closely associated with the birds than the saurischians. Certainly the ornithischian and modern avian pelves are both opisthopubic

(Figs. 16C, 18F), whereas the pelvis of coelurosaurs was propubic (Fig. 16A). Ostrom suggests, however, that the pelvis of *Archaeopteryx* may have differed from that of later birds and that its structure can be interpreted along coelurosaurian lines. It is hoped that studies of the new *Archaeopteryx* material will resolve this and other problems.

It is attractive to envisage the birds as feathered dinosaurs— a concept which implies that the dinosaurs did not become extinct without issue at the close of the Cretaceous. Indeed, Bakker and Galton in their stimulating paper propose that the two orders of dinosaurs should be united with the birds in a single 'Class Dinosauria', comprising all sauropsid vertebrates which (supposedly in the case of extinct forms) exhibited 'endothermy and a high aerobic exercise metabolism'. In view of Bramwell's work one wonders why they did not include the pterosaurs as well!

The way in which avian flight was evolved is another fascinating field for speculation which has been reviewed by Ostrom (1974). Some workers have believed that the ancestral bird ('pro-avis') was arboreal and used its fore-limbs as a kind of parachute when leaping from a higher to a lower branch. Others notably the brilliant but ill-fated palaeontologist Baron Francis Nopcsa, regarded the 'pro-avis' as a cursorial biped (in this context either a thecodont or a primitive dinosaur would do)— which ran fast over the ground flapping its fore-legs to increase its speed and eventually becoming airborne (see Lull, 1947, and Colbert, 1968, for an account of Nopcsa's remarkable life). Galton (1970) has the best of both worlds for he suggests that the birds evolved in two stages, through a cursorial 'pro-proavis' to an arboreal 'pro-avis' before achieving true flight.

The history of land birds in the later Mesozoic is virtually unknown but a number of marine forms, of which *Hesperoronis* and *Ichthyornis* are by far the best known, occurred in the Upper Cretaceous. *Hesperornis* was a large diving and swimming bird without a keel on its sternum, and with wings which had already become vestigial and quite useless for flight. *Ichthyornis* was a much smaller, strongly flying bird, perhaps rather gull-like in appearance. It has been suggested that the toothed jaws associated with the *Ichthyornis* remains really belonged to a small mosasaur (p. 171), but Gingerich (1973) has confirmed the presence of socketed (or thecodont) teeth in both this genus and in *Hesperornis*, as Marsh had maintained in his original account.

Gingerich has also given a valuable re-description of the skull of *Hesperornis* with new information concerning the palate. The palate proves to be remarkably similar to that found in the flightless ratites such as the ostrich, and quite unlike that in carinate birds. Some workers have argued that the ratite palate is not primitive but has been derived from the neognathous condition of carinates by a process of neoteny (see Bellairs and Jenkin, in Marshall, 1960); it has even been suggested that *Archaeopteryx* had a carinate type of palate. Gingerich has not only underlined the genuinely primitive nature of the ratite condition but has also shown that the supposed pattern in *Archaeopteryx* is purely hypothetical, in view of the poor preservation of this part of the skull. It now seems likely that Lowe (1928) was right in supposing that the ratites do indeed represent a natural and primitive group and are not a taxonomic rag-bag resulting from wholesale convergent evolution.

Toothed birds are not confined to the Mesozoic for a variety of forms has been found in the Eocene of England (C. Walker, personal communication). By early Tertiary times most of the modern avian orders had appeared on the scene.

Addendum

The remains of a flying reptile with an estimated wing span of 51 feet has been discovered in Texas (*The Times*, 13 March 1975). Unlike *Pteranodon*, it seems to have lived away from the sea and possibly fed on carrion rather than fish.

10 | The tuatara and the ancestors of lizards

Subclass LEPIDOSAURIA
Order Eosuchia (U. Perm.–early Tert., W.w.)
  Suborder Younginiformes: *Youngina* (U. Perm., S.Af.)
  Suborder Choristodera: *Champsosaurus* (U. Cret.–Eocene, Eur., N.Am.)
  Suborder Prolacertiformes: *Prolacerta* (L. Trias., S.Af.)
Order Rhynchocephalia (since L. Trias., W.w.): *Scaphonyx* (M. Trias., S.Am.), *Rhynchosaurus* (M.–U. Trias., Eur.), *Sphenodon* [= *Hatteria*] (New Zealand).
Order Squamata: lizards and snakes, *etc.* (since U. Trias., W.w.)

One is inclined to picture the Mesozoic landscape as a scene dominated by enormous reptiles such as the giant dinosaurs. It is likely, however, that then as now small animals outnumbered large ones and, although their fragile remains are less abundant in the fossil record, they doubtless played a very important part in the life of the time. Among the smaller reptiles of the past were many members of the subclass Lepidosauria.

The lepidosaurs were presumably derived from cotylosaurs, perhaps from a group of small Permian forms called millerettids (e.g. *Milleretta*). Some of these possessed a single temporal opening, which technically would make them synapsids. Their true position, however, is believed to lie between the more primitive stem-reptiles on the one hand and the lepidosaurs on the other; they are provisionally classified with the stem-reptiles (p. 66). (See C. E. Gow, *J.Zool.*, 1972, **167**, 219).

The earliest and most primitive lepidosaurs, such as *Youngina* from the Upper Permian, are placed in an order known as the Eosuchia. These were mostly lightly built animals with slender limb bones and delicate rather loosely constructed skulls in which there were two temporal openings, each bounded by complete arcades of bone. From such forms the Rhynchocephalia, and the Squamata, have probably been derived. Most of the eosuchians disappeared in the early Mesozoic, possibly because they could not compete with the much more enterprising and adaptable lizards.

The Rhynchocephalia have been an extremely conservative group, retaining many primitive features such as the completely two-arched condition of the skull. Although they have developed a few minor specializations, for instance, a small beak at the tip of the upper jaw, they differ comparatively little from eosuchians. During the Triassic certain herbivores called rhynchosaurs were briefly abundant, but all save *Sphenodon* became extinct during the Mesozoic. Creatures almost identical with *Sphenodon* were alive in the late Triassic about 200 million years ago, so that this line has had one of the slowest rates of evolution known among amniote vertebrates.

The tuatara, *Sphenodon punctatus* (Fig. 1) from New Zealand, resembles a rather clumsy lizard, two feet or more in length when adult, with a big head and a low crest down its back and tail. When first discovered in the early nineteenth century it was described as a lizard, and it was not until later that it was placed in a separate order, the Rhynchocephalia ('beak-headed'). It is not surprising that such a unique animal should have been extensively studied by zoologists. Dawbin (1962) and Sharell (1966) have described its natural history, while Gabe and Saint Girons (1964) have produced a valuable atlas of its microscopic structure.

Anatomically, *Sphenodon* has many features of interest. It has perhaps the best developed parietal eye of all living reptiles. Its vertebrae, unlike those of most modern forms, are amphicoelous (p. 27). Its ribs have hook-like uncinate processes about half-way along their length which give attachment to muscles; these are also found in birds and certain other reptiles. As in many lizards the tail has fracture planes for autotomy (p. 198) and is able to regenerate when broken off.

The dentition shows some remarkable features. Teeth are present on the palatines as well as along the jaw margins and all of them are attached to the bone in the acrodont fashion (p. 189). The appearance of the teeth changes during the life of the animal. There is virtually no tooth replacement and the bone of the jaw margins grows down to cover the bases of the teeth as their points become worn away; thus in very old animals the biting edges are formed almost entirely by bone. In such specimens the originally separate teeth at the front of the premaxilla have more or less disappeared but the downgrowth of bone on either side looks like a pair of large wedge-shaped teeth. To these the animal owes its name, *Sphenodon* meaning 'wedge-toothed'. Cooper and Poole (1973) have described rather similar changes in the agamid lizard *Uromastyx*, but here the premaxillary downgrowths fuse across the midline to produce a single median chisel-like surface which functionally replaces the worn-down front teeth.

The characters in which *Sphenodon* differs from lizards deserve special note. Perhaps the most striking of these are the presence of a complete lower temporal arcade formed by the jugal and quadratojugal bones (Fig. 23G), and the absence of copulatory organs in the male. There are true abdominal ribs or gastralia (as opposed to the parasternal apparatus of some lizards), and the young have a horny egg-caruncle like crocodiles and chelonians, instead of a true egg-tooth (p. 189).

Today the tuatara is confined to a few rocky islands off the coast of New Zealand, although the distribution of its remains shows that up to a few thousand years ago it was common on the mainland. It is good to know that the New Zealand government's policy of strict protection has now resulted in the tuatara becoming very abundant on Stephen Island, which is only about a mile in length, and some other even smaller islands near the Cook Strait.

The islands where *Sphenodon* lives are also inhabited by very large numbers of petrels and other sea birds, which have burrowed extensively into the soil and modified its chemical composition through the agency of their excreta. As far as is known, the tuatara does not now occur on islands where the birds are not found.

It has often been stated that the reptile lives peaceably alongside the birds in burrows made by the latter, but this has not been confirmed by recent work. On the contrary, the tuatara normally excavates its own burrow, although when disturbed it will take cover in the nearest retreat, which often happens to be a burrow made by a bird; it also preys on the nestling petrels, and possibly on the adults and eggs when it gets the chance. Its main food, however, consists of large crickets, and just why its present-day distribution should correspond so closely with that of the birds is not known.

The tuatara spends much of the day in its burrow, coming out at night to hunt when the weather is not too severe. It is often active at quite low temperatures; some individuals have been found foraging with body temperatures of around 8°C (46°F), a degree of cold which would reduce most reptiles to a state of immobility. It is not known how *Sphenodon* managed to reach its isolated habitat in the first instance, but it may well be that its low thermal requirements were important in allowing it to colonize a region where the climate, not unlike that of Britain, is inhospitable to most reptile life. Its survival in New Zealand may be due to the absence of mammalian predators, which were only introduced by man at a comparatively recent date.

The tuatara is normally rather sluggish, although it can run quickly for a short distance. Its rate of metabolism is apparently lower than that of turtles, lizards and even frogs at comparable temperatures. When active it only breathes about once in seven seconds, and it may go for at least an hour without breathing at all. It occasionally makes a croaking sound, something like that of a frog.

Sphenodon lays about a dozen oval parchment-shelled eggs. each about 2.5cm long. They are deposited in a shallow nest and covered with debris. The incubation period is about fourteen months, much longer than is usual in reptiles. Development of the embryos is at first rapid, but becomes almost completely arrested during the winter months before hatching. The subsequent growth rate of the animal also seems to be very slow and the life span is long, possibly over fifty years.

The ancestors of lizards

We have seen that *Sphenodon* differs from lizards in several important respects, but it also has many features in common with them, especially with those of the agamid group with which it was originally confounded. These similarities suggest that the lizards, despite their diverse adaptations to various modes of life, still retain many of the characters of the earliest two-arched reptiles, the eosuchians, which *Sphenodon* so much resembles.

Lizards, typically, have only a single complete temporal arcade, the upper one, and their relationship to eosuchians and rhynchocephalians was not at first apparent to all workers. The discovery, however, of a small fossil reptile known as *Prolacerta* in the Lower Triassic provides strong evidence that the lizards are really of eosuchian descent, and that they are modified diapsids which have lost the lower temporal arcade. In *Prolacerta* there is a gap between the tiny quadrato-jugal and the jugal so that the lower temporal bar is incomplete; the animal has all the appearances of an eosuchian becoming a lizard and may actually have been a lizard ancestor.

The main skeletal differences between lizards and eosuchians or rhynchocephs lie in the construction of the cheek region of the skull but it can be appreciated that the interpretation of these delicate bones in small fossil reptiles is often difficult. Quite numerous remains of such creatures have been recovered from widespread Upper Triassic deposits in Europe and it is likely that some of these will turn out to be lizards rather than members of the other groups mentioned above. It has been suggested. for example, that the thalattosaurs, a small group of paddle-limbed long-snouted marine reptiles, are aberrant lizards and not eosuchians, as has generally been thought. Other fossils of more obviously saurian character are known from pre-Jurassic deposits.

Colbert (1970) and Robinson (1973, etc.) have described remains of remarkable lizards from the Upper Triassic which seem to have glided on rib-supported 'wings' like the modern *Draco*. One of these is aptly named *Icarosaurus*, after Icarus of Greek mythology who flew too close to the sun so that his wax wings melted. These and other late Triassic lizards of more 'normal' appearance can provisionally be grouped in an infraorder of their own, the Eolacertilia.

Lizards are not plentiful as fossils until the later Cretaceous, when many forms allied to those of today become recognizable. It now seems certain, however, that the origin of the lizards occurred far back, at some time in the Triassic. Even by the end of this period some highly specialized forms were in existence, and these nimble little reptiles had begun to develop the versatile qualities for which they are renowned today.

11 Lizards, amphisbaenians and snakes

Abbreviations, p. 11.

Subclass LEPIDOSAURIA
Order Squamata
  Suborder Sauria [= Lacertilia] (since U. Trias., W.w.) (some extinct families omitted)
    Infraorder Eolacertilia (p. 158): *Icarosaurus* (U. Trias., N.Am.), *Kuehneosaurus* (U. Trias., Eur.)
    Infraorder Gekkota
      Family Gekkonidae (W.w.): *Gekko* (Aus., E.As.), E.Ind.), *Hemidactylus* (Af., As., Eu., E.Ind., Pac., ? introduced Sn.Am., W. Ind.), *Palmatogecko* (S.Af.) *Ptychozoon* (S.As., E. Ind.), *Sphaerodactylus* (Sn.Am., W. Ind.), *Tarentola* (Eu., N.Af.)
      Family Pygopodidae (Aus.): *Lialis, Pygopus*
      ? Family Dibamidae (Aus., E.As., E. Ind.)
      ? Family Anelytropsidae (N.Am.)
    Infraorder Iguania
      Family Iguanidae (N.W., Mad.): *Amblyrhynchus* (Gal.), *Anolis* (N.Am., Sn.Am., W. Ind.), *Basiliscus* (Sn.Am.), *Conolophus* (Gal.), *Crotaphytus* (N.Am.), *Iguana* (Sn.Am.), *Liolaemus* (Sn.Am.), *Phrynosoma* (N.Am., Sn.Am.), *Sauromalus* (N.Am.) *Sceloporus* (N.Am., Sn.Am.) *Tropidurus* (Sn.Am., Gal.)
      Family Agamidae (O.W., Aus.): *Agama* (Af., As., Eur.) *Amphibolurus* (Aus.), *Calotes* (E. Ind., S.As.), *Chlamydosaurus* (Aus.) *Draco* (E. Ind., S.As.), *Lophura* (E. Ind.), *Moloch* (Aus.), *Physignathus* (Aus., E. Ind.), *Uromastyx* (N.Af., W.As.)
      Family Chamaeleontidae (Af., Eu., Mad., S.As.): *Chamaeleo* (Af., Eur., As.), *Microsaura* (S.Af.)
    Infraorder Scincomorpha
      Family Scincidae (including Feyliniidae) (W.w.): *Chalcides* (As., Eur., N.Af.), *Eumeces* (As., N.Af., N.Am., Sn.Am.), *Lygosoma* (Af., Aus., As., E. Ind.), Af., As., *Mabuya* (E. Ind., Af., As., Sn.Am., W. Ind.), *Riopa* (Af., S.As., E. Ind., Aus.), *Trachysaurus* (Aus.)

Family Xantusiidae (N.Am., Sn.Am., W. Ind.): *Xantusia* (N.Am.)

Family Lacertidae (Af., As., Eur.): *Lacerta* (Af., As., Eur.)

Family Teiidae (N.Am., Sn.Am., W. Ind.): *Ameiva* (Sn.Am., W. Ind.), *Cnemidophorus* (N.Am., Sn.Am.), *Tupinambis* (Sn.Am., W. Ind.)

Family Cordylidae (including Cordylidae and Gerrhosauridae) (Mad., S.Af.): *Chamaesaura* (S.Af.), *Cordylus* (Af.), *Gerrhosaurus* (Af.)

Infraorder Anguimorpha

Family Anguidae (including Anniellidae) (As., Eur., N.Af., N.Am., Sn.Am., W. Ind.): *Anguis* (Eu., N.Af., W.As.), *Anniella* (N.Am.), *Celestus* (Sn.Am., W. Ind.), *Gerrhonotus* (N.Am., Sn.Am.), *Ophisaurus* (As., Eur., N.Af., N.Am., Sn.Am.)

Family Xenosauridae: *Shinisaurus* (E.As.), *Xenosaurus* (Sn.Am.)

Infraorder Platynota (often given status of superfamily of Anguimorpha only)

Family Aigialosauridae (L. Cret., Eur.)

Family Dolichosauridae (Cret., Eur.)

Family Mosasauridae (U. Cret.): *Globidens* (E. Ind., Eur., N.Af., N.Am.), *Tylosaurus* (U. Cret., Af., As., Eur., N.Am.)

Family Varanidae (all recent forms O.W. & Aus.): *Megalania* (Tert., Aus.), *Varanus* (Af., As., Aus., E. Ind.)

Family Lanthanotidae: *Lanthanotus* (Borneo)

Family Helodermatidae: *Heloderma* (N.Am.)

Suborder Amphisbaenia

Family Amphisbaenidae (Af., Eu., N.Am., Sn.Am., W.As., W. Ind.): *Amphisbaena* (Sn.Am.), *Bipes* (N.Am.), *Rhineura* (N.Am.)

Family Trogonophidae (N.Af., W.As.): *Trogonophis* (N.Af.)

Suborder Serpentes [= Ophidia] (since L. Cret.)

Infraorder Scolecophidia

Family Typhlopidae: *Typhlops* (W.w.)

Family Leptotyphlopidae: *Leptotyphlops* (Af., As., N.Am., Sn.Am., W. Ind.)

Infraorder Henophidia [= Booidea]

Family Simoliophidae (Cret.): *Lapparentophis* L. Cret., N.Af.)

Family Palaeophidae: *Palaeophis* (Eocene, N.Af.)

Family Dinilysiidae: *Dinilysia* (U. Cret., Sn.Am.)

Family Anilidae: *Anilius* [= *Ilysia*] (Sn.Am.), *Cylindrophis* (E. Ind., S.As.)

Family Uropeltidae: *Uropeltis* (S.As.)

Family Xenopeltidae: *Xenopeltis* (E. Ind., S.As.)

Family Boidae (W.w.): *Madtsoia* (U. Cret.–Eocene, Mad., S.Am.), *Chondropython* (Aus.), *Constrictor* (Sn.Am., W. Ind.), *Eryx* (As., Eur., N.Af.), *Eunectes* (Sn.Am., W. Ind.), *Liasis* (Aus.), *Python* (Af., As., E. Ind.)

Family Acrochordidae: *Acrochordus* (Aus., E. Ind., S.As.)

Infraorder Caenophidia

Family Colubridae (W.w.): *Ahaetulla* [= *Dryophis*] (S.As.), *Chrysopelea* (E. Ind., S.As.), *Coluber* (As., Eur., N.Af., N.Am.), *Coronella*, Eur., N.Af.), *Dasypeltis* (Af.), *Dispholidus*, (Af.), *Elachistodon* (S.As.), *Elaphe* (As., E. Ind., Eur., N.Am., Sn.Am.), *Erpeton* (S.As.), *Heterodon* (N.Am.), *Langaha* (Mad.), *Lampropeltis* (N.Am., Sn.Am.), *Natrix* (Af., As., Aus., E. Ind., Eur., N.Am.), *Ptyas* (As.), *Storeria* (N.Am.), *Thamnophis* (N.Am., Sn.Am.), *Thelotornis* (Af.)

Family Elapidae (nearly W.w. except Eur.): *Acanthophis* (Aus.), *Bungarus* (E. Ind., S.As.), *Dendroaspis* (Af.), *Hemachatus* (Af.), *Maticora* (E. Ind., S.As.), *Micrurus* (N.Am., Sn.Am.), *Naja* (Af., E. Ind., S. & E.As.), *Notechis* (Aus)., *Ophiophagus* [= *Hamadryas*] (E. Ind., S.As.), *Oxyuranus* (Aus.)

Family Hydrophiidae (mainly Aus., E. Ind., S.As.): *Pelamis* (nearly W.w. exc. Atlantic)

Family Viperidae (nearly W.w. except Aus.): *Agkistrodon* (As., Eur., N.Am., Sn.Am.), *Atractaspis;* true systematic position uncertain (Af.), *Bitis* (Af.), *Cerastes* (N.Af.), *Crotalus* (N.Am., Sn.Am.), *Echis* (N.Af., As.), *Lachesis* (Sn.Am.), *Sistrurus* (N.Am.), *Trimeresurus* [in part = *Bothrops*] (As., E. Ind., N.Am., Sn.Am.), *Vipera* (Eus., As.).

The lizards and snakes are the most abundant of modern reptiles both in the number of kinds, and no doubt also in the number of living individuals, which must make up by far the greatest part of the world's reptile population. About 300 living genera and 3000 species of lizards and amphisbaenians, and 300 genera and 2700 species of snakes are known.

Anatomically the Squamata are distinguished from other living reptiles by a number of anatomical features, such as the modified diapsid condition of the skull, which usually shows kinesis (p. 186), the tendency to reduce the limbs in various groups, the specialization of the tongue and of Jacobson's organ (p. 207), the transverse position of the cloaca (also found in *Sphenodon*) and the presence in the male of paired copulatory organs.

F

There are obvious differences between 'typical' lizards and 'typical' snakes; the former have four limbs, movable eyelids, a visible eardrum and numerous small scales on the belly, whereas in the latter the limbs and eardrum are absent, the eyes are covered by a transparent spectacle (p. 205) and there is a single row of wide scales along the belly. There are, however, many snake-like lizards and some rather lizard-like snakes, and it may be difficult to distinguish between the two, except by resort to somewhat recondite characters. To avoid repetition in describing the many features which lizards and snakes have in common they are dealt with here under one chapter heading.

Of all the existing types of reptiles the lizards show the widest range of adaptive modification for various ways of life. Adaptations of a similar type seem to have arisen independently in different groups as a result of parallel evolution; the assumption of a snake-like form, for example, has occurred in members of about 7 out of the 20 or so families, generally in association with burrowing or secretive habits.

The classification of lizards presents a difficult problem and many different systems have been used. It seems likely that the lizards, after their origin from *Prolacerta*-like ancestors in the early Mesozoic, split up into several groups of more or less equal distinctiveness. These groups are here given the rank of infraorders, each containing one or more families.

It is difficult to decide just how these infraorders are related to one another, and the allotment of the various families among them depends on an assessment of detailed anatomical characters, ranging from chromosomes to skull structure, such as are beyond the scope of this book to discuss. The families of lizards, however unlike the infraorders, are fairly homogeneous well defined units, and there is not much difference of opinion about their nomenclature and composition. For this reason the different kinds of lizards are described mainly under their familial groupings in the following account.

The different kinds of lizards

The Gekkonidae are very distinctive little creatures which are common in warm countries all over the world and have been among the few kinds of reptiles to reach New Zealand. Kluge

(1967) has discussed the taxonomy and evolution of this very large family. As fossils they are poorly known, but a related and possibly ancestral form, *Ardeosaurus*, occurs in the Jurassic.

Geckos (Fig. 19I) have flattened bodies covered with small granular scales, their skins are thin and some forms appear almost translucent in strong light. In most species the eyes are protected by a spectacle instead of eyelids.

Many of the numerous species of geckos live on rocks or trees, and some, like *Hemidactylus*, the common house lizards of the east, have a predilection for buildings. Such species have specialized digital pads which help them to climb (p. 199). There are also some ground and desert-living types; in some forms the tail is swollen and serves as a fat reservoir. The great majority of geckos lay eggs which are often deposited in pairs; as a rule these eggs have hard shells, instead of being parchment-shelled like the eggs of other oviparous Squamata.

Most geckos are partly nocturnal, appearing in the evenings when they can be seen stalking insects on walls, especially where these congregate round a light. At such times the lizards are often extremely vocal, making cheeping or clucking sounds from which their name is onomatopoetically derived. Their calls are familiar to all who have lived in the tropics and seem to play a part in the social behaviour of the more gregarious species. Geckos have excellent hearing and their main auditory receptor (papilla basilaris) in the inner ear is relatively larger than in other lizards (I. L. Baird in Gans *et al,*. 1970, v. 2.).

The oriental 'tokay' (*Gekko gecko*) is a massive, pugnacious lizard up to 30cm (1ft) long, but many geckos are less than half this size. Indeed, this family probably contains the smallest lizards known; some species of the New World genus *Sphaerodactylus* are under 5cm (2in) long.

The Pygopodidae (snake-lizards) is a small group of virtually limbless forms with a spectacle eye-covering, found in Australasia. *Pygopus* and *Lialis* (Fig. 19D) are the biggest, 30–60cm (1–2ft) and have scaly flap-like vestiges of the hind-limbs. They live under stones, logs, etc., and feed on smaller reptiles and invertebrates. Other members of the family are burrowers; Bustard (1970) gives a good account of these interesting and little-known reptiles. Despite their dissimilar appearance, the pygopodids have certain anatomical resemblances to the geckos (such as the

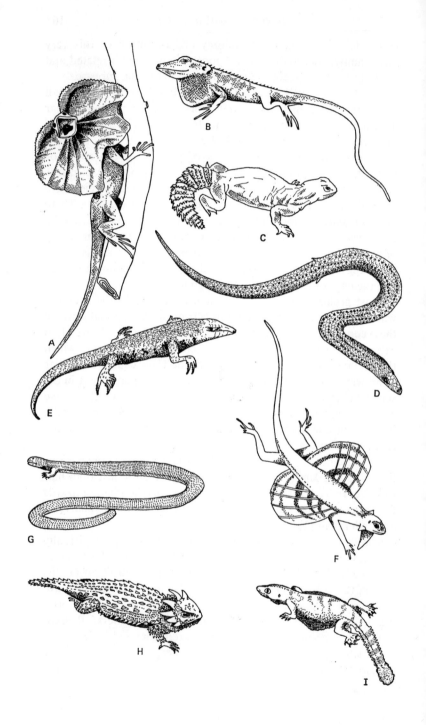

structure of the inner ear) and are probably allied to them. The small families Dibamidae and Anelytropsidae contain a few small limbless burrowers and may be related to the Pygopodidae (see Underwood, 1957).

The very large family Iguanidae consists of lizards of varied type, mostly found in the New World. The iguanas of the American tropics (e.g. the green *Iguana iguana*) are large animals, some reaching a length of nearly 2m (6ft) with a crest down the back and often a prominent dewlap beneath the throat. The green iguana is partly arboreal but also takes to water; some other forms are ground dwellers.

Amblyrhynchus of the Galapagos Islands is the only modern lizard with truly marine habits, living among the lava rocks along the coast, swimming in the surf and feeding on seaweed. Most marine iguanas are sooty in colour, like the lava, but on one island (Hood or Española) some members of the population at least, probably the breeding males, have green crests and are red on the flanks (cover); these are magnificent animals. A large herbivorous ground iguana (*Conolophus*) is also found on the Galapagos, together with small lava lizards (*Tropidurus*) belonging to the same family. Their display patterns have been studied by C. C. Carpenter (see Milstead, 1967) and are reviewed by Thornton (1971). The mainland of tropical America is the home of the basilisks (*Basiliscus*, Fig. 20F, also p. 202); these are large iguana-like tree lizards furnished with a helmet-shaped eminence on the head and a high crest along the tail. Like many of the iguanas they feed partly on plants.

The anoles (*Anolis*) or 'American chameleons' are smaller lizards that lead an active life among foliage, climbing with the aid of digital pads which are furnished with tiny bristles like those of geckos (p. 199). The males have a large distensible fan-like structure beneath the throat (Fig. 19B). Anoles are often

---

Fig. 19

A, frilled lizard, *Chlamydosaurus* (Agamidae). B, *Anolis*. with throat-fan extended (Iguanidae). C, *Uromastyx* (Agamidae). D, *Lialis* (Pygopodidae), after Bustard (1970). E, sand skink, *Scincus* (Scincidae). F, flying lizard, *Draco* (Agamidae). G, *Bipes* (Amphisbaenidae). H, horned lizard, *Phrynosoma* (Iguanidae). I, 'flying' gecko, *Ptychozoon*.

brightly coloured and rival and true chameleons in their powers of colour change.

The chuckwallas (*Sauromalus*) are fairly big herbivorous desert-dwellers with stout flattened bodies, while the collared lizards (*Crotaphytus*) and swifts (*Sceloporus*) are smaller agile lizards found in the arid parts of North America. The horned toads (*Phrynosoma*, Fig. 19H) are peculiar desert lizards which spend much of their time buried beneath the sand. They have flattened toad-like bodies covered with spiny scales, short tails and prominent spines projecting backwards from the head. One iguanid genus, *Liolaemus*, can withstand very severe climates, being found in the inhospitable region of Tierra del Fuego, and also occurring at altitudes of 5000m (over 15 000ft) in the Andes of Peru.

The Agamidae are the Old World counterparts of the Iguanidae. It has been suggested that the agamids were descended from the iguanids and replaced them throughout the Old World, except in one or two isolated regions, such as Madagascar and Fiji, where iguanids are still found (Darlington, 1948). Like the majority of iguanids, they are oviparous.

Calotes is a genus of insectivorous tree agamids of medium size with crested backs and long tails. The males of some species possess a throat-fan. *C. versicolor,* a common oriental form, has received the vernacular name of 'bloodsucker' on account of the scarlet hue which the head and throat assume when the creature is agitated.

Agama is an allied genus which includes both desert-living and partly arboreal types, among the latter being the rainbow lizard, *Agama agama* (Fig. 20E) so well described by Harris (1963, 1964). *Uromastyx* (Fig. 19C), another inhabitant of the North African deserts, is a heavily built lizard resembling the iguanid *Sauromalus* except that the tail is armed with spines. The flying dragons (*Draco*, Fig. 19F) of Malaya are described on p. 202.

Some of the most striking of the agamid lizards are found in Australia. The frilled lizard (*Chlamydosaurus,* Fig. 19A), a creature nearly 1m (3ft) long, is distinguished by the large frill-like expansion of skin around the neck, which, like the throat fans of *Anolis* and *Calotes*, is operated by the hyoid skeleton and muscles. It is erected like a ruff when the lizard is angry and gives it a frightening aspect. *Amphibolurus barbatus*, the bearded lizard, is a slightly smaller form also with a frill-like appendage which in this case is restricted to the underside of the throat. Allied to these lizards are the Australian water dragon (*Physignathus*) and the sailed lizard (*Lophura*), rather large animals resembling the iguanas and basilisks. Another agamid type is the Australian *Moloch*, a small desert lizard which shows a close parallel with the American *Phrynosoma*. *Moloch* is said to be extremely selective in its food habits and feeds exclusively on ants.

The chameleons are probably specialized descendants of the agamid stock; they are placed together with the agamids and iguanids in the infraorder Iguania. They are restricted to the Old World, the majority of species occurring in Africa and Madagascar. The grotesque appearance of these tree lizards is too well known to necessitate general description, but certain of their characters, such as their feet, tongues and powers of colour change are described elsewhere under the appropriate headings. Most chameleons lay eggs which they bury in the soil beneath their bushes, but a few species bear their young alive.

The Scincidae is a large and cosmopolitan family of lizards mostly with smooth shiny scales, elongated bodies and rather short tails and legs. *Chalcides* from Europe and Africa, and *Mabuya*, are typical genera; some forms such as the 'sand-fish' (*Scincus*; Fig. 19E) from north Africa are adapted for desert life. *Trachysaurus rugosus* from Australia is a large and rather unusual skink with a thick stumpy tail and very rough scales.

Skinks are characteristically ground lizards, but have made themselves at home in environments as different as deserts and the leaf-strewn floors of tropical forests. As a group they show a widespread tendency to limb reduction, the snake-like forms mostly dwelling under stones or earth, or among the roots of vegetation. Many skinks are viviparous.

The Xantusiidae or night lizards contains a few genera of small nocturnal forms, rather like geckos in appearance, occurring in North America. They inhabit crevices among rocks and one species, *Xantusia vigilis,* lives in association with the Joshua tree (*Yucca brevifolia*), being constantly found beneath its fallen limbs. They are viviparous.

The Lacertidae, found in the Old World, are lizards of small or moderate size, which show little tendency to develop specialized adaptations. The green lizard, *Lacerta viridis,* and the wall lizard, *L. muralis,* are common in Europe and are often sold in pet-shops in this country. Although many individuals of both species must at various times have been liberated in England, neither has succeeded in becoming truly native, although the wall lizard has bred in recent years in certain restricted habitats (M. Smith, 1973). Both lizards occur in the Channel Islands. The sand lizard, *L. agilis,* is found in Dorset and adjoining counties in England, and also in parts of Lancashire, but needs urgent conservation; the bright green colour of the males may lead to its confusion with the green lizard. The common lizard, *L. vivipara,* is widespread throughout the British Isles including Ireland, and in Europe ranges a few degrees inside the Arctic Circle, probably being the most northerly distributed reptile. It is unusual within its family for being viviparous.

The Teiidae of America is a rather similar group to the Lacertidae, although it contains snake-like forms. Teiids such as some *Ameiva* and *Cnemidophorus* are small active lizards resembling the smaller lacertids in appearance and habits. The tegus (*Tupinambis*) are much larger creatures, growing up to about 1m (3ft) in length, and able to prey on small birds and mammals.

The Cordylidae is a family of African lizards now regarded as including two groups (subfamilies) which were previously given separate familial status; the cordylines, zonures or girdle-tailed lizards, and the gerrhosaurs or plated lizards. Most cordylines are four-legged rock-dwellers, with bands of spiny scales around the tail, and in some species, around the neck and body also. The gerrhosaurs are rather skink-like in shape with long bodies and short legs; their bodies are covered by flattened closely fitting plates, reinforced by an underlying bony sheath of osteoderms. Both groups also include some snake-like forms such as *Chamaesaura* (subfamily Cordylinae).

The Anguidae, as the name of the family suggests, contains a number of snake-like forms, although many of its members, such as the West Indian *Celestus,* have well developed limbs. The slow worm, *Anguis fragilis,* is a familiar member of the family. It is common in many parts of England where it may be found under stones or along banks; it can burrow quite well in soft ground. The slow worm is viviparous, producing up to a dozen nimble silvery or golden-brown young in August or September. It will live for many years in captivity and feeds readily on slugs and small earthworms. The glass 'snakes' (*Ophisaurus*), of North America, Europe and Asia, are similar forms, though some species reach a larger size and lay eggs. *Anniella*, placed by other writers in a family of its own, is much like the slow worm in appearance but more highly adapted for burrowing life. It is found in sandy regions in California. The Xenosauridae is a small family related to the Anguidae, and contains *Xenosaurus* from Mexico and *Shinisaurus* from China, both with well developed limbs.

The remaining families of lizards make up the infraorder Platynota, a group which is perhaps more homogeneous than some of the other infraorders, though it has affinities with the Anguidae. It is very ancient and has a special interest in relation to the problem of the origin of snakes (p. 174).

Many of the Varanidae or monitor lizards are creatures of large size and striking appearance, popular exhibits in zoological gardens and widely distributed throughout the hotter parts of the Old World; the greatest number of species is found in Australasia. They are often called iguanas, or, in Australia, 'goannas', but they are quite different from the large members of the family Iguanidae to which the name iguana is properly applied.

The appearance of a monitor lizard (Fig. 20C) is unmistakable, and so similar are all the existing species that they are usually classified in the single genus *Varanus*. A typical monitor gives a curious impression of slinkiness due to the elongation of every part of the body and the absence of projecting crests or spines such as are so characteristic of the iguanas. A few species, however, such as the Cape monitor, *V. albigularis,* are more thickset and resemble the tegus (p. 168) in proportions. The neck of a monitor is long, so that the shoulders seem to be set back, and very mobile. The eyes are conspicuous, giving the creature an alert expression which is enhanced by the habit of rearing up the head and neck on the fore-limbs and looking deliberately about. The forked tongue is long, snake-like and retractile. The tail is very powerful, and unlike that of most other lizards, cannot easily be broken off. The feet are armed with heavy claws. Many monitors have a rather uniform brown, grey or blackish colouring, although when young they tend to be more brightly marked.

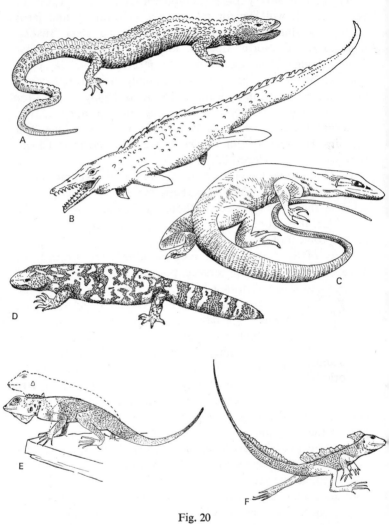

Fig. 20

A, *Lanthanotus*. B, mosasaur, a giant sea lizard from the Upper Cretaceous. C, *Varanus*. D, Gila monster, *Heloderma suspectum*. A–D all belong to the platynotid group. E, Territorial challenge display of male *Agama agama* towards rival male; the head and part of the tail are orange, the body blue and the tail tip black in the breeding colour phase. Broken lines show position of body at upthrust. After Harris (1964). F, *Basiliscus* running bipedally (after Snyder, 1949).

The largest of existing lizards belong to this family. The Komodo dragon, *V. komodoensis*, from the East Indies, grows about 3m (10ft) long, and some Australian Pleistocene forms (*Megalania*) may have been about twice that size. The water monitor, *V. salvator*, from Malaya reaches a length of over 2m (7ft) and some other species are nearly as big. There are, however, a few dwarf Australian species only 30cm (12in) or so long.

Some monitors live in arid, rocky country; *V. griseus*, from North Africa, is predominantly a desert form. Others, such as *V. salvator* and *V. niloticus*, are partly aquatic and have laterally compressed tails for swimming. Most species can climb readily.

Monitor lizards are highly predacious, feeding on vertebrates and carrion, as well as invertebrates. They sometimes raid poultry runs, killing the chickens and stealing the eggs. Some species are important predators on the eggs and young of crocodiles. Monitor lizards are usually fierce creatures and defend themselves with tooth and claw and by blows of the tail. The natural history of the Komodo dragon, which can sever the Achilles tendon of a buffalo and kill it when it has fallen on the ground, has been described by Auffenberg (1972). This formidable scavenger and predator has occasionally been tamed in captivity.

Probably the Varanidae are among the most ancient of existing lizard families with a history going far back into the Mesozoic, though the earliest known fossils date only from the Cretaceous. At the beginning of this period other platynotid types, however, were embarking on a course of aquatic adaptation which was to bring the lizards among the front ranks of the legion of water reptiles.

The least highly modified of these aquatic Platynota were the Aigialosauridae of the Lower Cretaceous, which seem to have been intermediate between monitor-like forms and the more highly aquatic dolichosaurs and mosasaurs. The Dolichosauridae had slender, almost snake-like bodies, small heads and rather short limbs.

The Mosasauridae, mainly a late Cretaceous group, were much more successful. They were essentially huge sea-going monitor lizards, differing from the varanids mainly in those features which are the hallmarks of aquatic adaptation: gigantism, lengthening of the jaws, flattening of the tail which may have been furnished with a low fin and conversion of the limbs into paddles in which the number of phalanges, though not of digits, was increased.

Some types of mosasaurs, such as *Tylosaurus* (Fig. 20B), reached a length of over 9m (30ft) and probably preyed on large fishes and other aquatic reptiles. Another type, represented by *Globidens*, probably ate molluscs, and like the placodonts and certain ichthyosaurs it had massive rounded teeth in place of the sharp recurved ones of its relatives. In many mosasaurs the bones of the lower jaw were so constructed as to permit movement between the front and back halves on each side. This intramandibular hinge is developed to a variable extent in other platynotids and in snakes. As in snakes also, the two halves of the lower jaw were only loosely connected in front. Presumably such features were adaptations for feeding on large prey.

The mosasaurs seem to have lived mainly in coastal waters and it is possible that even the most advanced types were able to slide out on to a sandbank to bask. Indeed they must have retained some ability to move on land if, like the monitor lizards, they laid eggs.

McDowell and Bogert (1954) have clearly shown that two more families, the Lanthanotidae and the Helodermatidae, should also be referred to the platynotid group. The former is represented by a single genus and species, *Lanthanotus borneensis,* a rare and nocturnal lizard from Sarawak. McDowell and Bogert believe that this creature has many anatomical resemblances with the extinct aigialosaurs and dolichosaurs and might almost be regarded as a living member of that group. It is a long-bodied lizard, somewhat over 30cm (12in) long, with a large head, no external ear, short limbs and a rather incongruously slender tail (Fig. 20A). Recent observations on its habits show that it burrows and swims well, eating pieces of fish in captivity.

The heloderms or beaded lizards (Fig. 20D) from the arid regions of the USA and Mexico are notorious as the only poisonous lizards. They are stoutly built with stumpy tails and have a rather striking coloration. *Heloderma suspectum,* the Gila monster, up to 60cm (24in) long, has salmon-pink and black markings, while the larger *H. horridum* is black and white or orange. Heloderms are normally sluggish creatures and appear to feed mainly on eggs, although small vertebrates are included in their diet. The Gila monster is nocturnal, and takes shelter in a burrow from extremes of heat. In captivity it often soaks in a dish of water.

Bogert and del Campo (1956) have produced a superb monograph on the Gila monster and its allies in which the habits, heat requirements and venom of these lizards are fully discussed. They suggest that the coloration is primarily for concealment in their natural semi-desert surroundings, though it may also serve an ancillary warning function. The heloderms are oviparous.

Amphisbaenians

The amphisbaenians, or 'worm-lizards' are a most interesting group of small reptiles which have become specialized for burrow-life. It is probable that the group separated off from other Squamata at a very early time and the modern trend is to classify them in a suborder of their own called the Amphisbaenia, distinct from, and of equal rank to, the lizards and the snakes. Two families, the Trogonophidae and the Amphisbaenidae, may be recognized. Gans (1960, 1969, etc.) has made notable contributions to our knowledge of the group (see p. 232).

The eyes of these reptiles are greatly reduced and the head is hard and compact; the bones of the skull roof articulate very firmly by means of interlocking sutures (Fig. 21E). In one genus, *Bipes* (Fig. 19G), there is a single pair of well developed limbs, the front ones, but in the other genera neither pair is externally visible.

Amphisbaenians are distinguished from both lizards and snakes by certain anatomical features, such as the high degree of ossification of the anterior sphenoid region of the skull (which in other reptiles is mostly cartilaginous, p. 23), the elongation of the extra-stapes (Fig. 21E), which is applied to the outer side of the lower jaw, the reduction of the right instead of the left lung (p. 204) and the arrangement of the body scales into rings which encircle the girth of the animal. The tail is usually short and stumpy and resembles the seemingly eyeless head; travesties of the animal are shown with two heads in medieval bestiaries. This, together with the fact that some species are able to crawl backwards, is responsible for the name amphisbaena, meaning 'going both ways'.

Amphisbaenians are found in tropical and subtropical parts of America, Africa and Western Asia; there is one species in the south of Spain and Portugal. *Trogonophis*, a green and yellowish form, is common in Algeria where it is frequently found in coastal regions quite close to the sea. The worm-lizards pursue a secretive existence beneath stones and underground, sometimes appearing on the surface at night or after heavy rain. They feed mainly on insects and their larvae, some species subsisting on ants and termites and living in their nests. The ears of these subterranean creatures are probably important for picking up sounds made by the movement of their tiny prey (Wever and Gans, 1973). Little is known of their embryology or mode of reproduction, but the females of some species are thought to breed only once in two or three years. The north American *Rhineura* is said to be oviparous, while certain other forms are thought to bear their young alive.

The origin of snakes

In structure the different types of snakes seem to resemble each other much more closely than do the different kinds of lizards, not only in gross anatomy, but also in the character of their chromosomes. The range of differences between, say, a sea snake on the one hand and a boa constrictor on the other, is probably much less than that between lizards such as a gecko and a monitor. In habits, however, the snakes have become almost as diverse as the lizards. Indeed one of the most striking features of the Serpentes is the fact that the different species have become adapted for such various ways of life without departing very greatly from a single, and in some respects rather simple, body-pattern, one characterized above all by elongation and flexibility of the body and loss of the limbs. It is interesting that the snakes should have had such a more successful radiation than any of the other groups of vertebrates which have adopted a similar body form: the existing snake-like lizards, for instance, the apodous amphibians or the eels. Most of these animals live out their lives within rather narrow confines, beneath stones, underground or in mud; yet the snakes as a group have invaded both the trees and the water in addition to establishing themselves in a variety of terrestrial and subterranean habitats. Indeed even as individuals some types of snakes are so highly adaptable that they can range at will throughout most of the different types of environment available in their localities, grass and trees, rocks, sand, mud and water.

The origin of snakes is a fascinating problem, though it is still largely a matter for speculation; the palaeontological data are so sketchy that one is dependent mainly on evidence derived from the study of living forms. The earliest known snakes are found in the Cretaceous, but there is much to suggest that the group originated at an earlier time, possibly during the Jurassic, and almost certainly from lizards of some kind.

Incomplete remains of snake-like creatures occur in the Lower Cretaceous, but without better preserved skulls one cannot always be certain whether they were true snakes or forms such as dolichosaurian lizards. Upper Cretaceous and early Tertiary formations have yielded remains of undoubted boid snakes (p. 178), some as large as any which exist today, and also of certain marine forms which are mostly placed in the family Palaeophidae; their remains are sometimes associated with those of primitive whales. Perhaps the most interesting fossil snake is the 1.8m (6ft) *Dinilysia* from the Upper Cretaceous of Patagonia. The well preserved skull shows a curious mosaic of primitive (lizard-like) and specialized characters, and also indicates a relationship with the modern snakes of the family Anilidae (Estes *et al.*, 1970). Probably, however, it is too late in time to throw much light on the origin of the Serpentes.

None of the existing types of snake-like lizards appear to have any specially close affinity with the snakes, though some, such as *Pygopus* (p. 163) mimic the external appearance of a snake in a remarkable fashion (Bustard, 1970). Many authorities believe, however, that the snakes are rather closely related to the platynotid lizards (*Lanthanotus*, monitors etc.) even though no known member of this group, living or extinct, shows extreme limb reduction. This view has been strongly argued by McDowell and Bogert (1954) and McDowell (1972); they conclude that *Lanthanotus* has many significantly snake-like features (such as the presence of a well developed intramandibular hinge) and is at the same time closely allied to the extinct platynotids of the aigialosaur–dolichosaur group.

Another approach to the problem is to consider the type of overall adaptive modification which the ancestors of snakes may have showed. They may, for example, have been aquatic forms resembling (and perhaps related to) the dolichosaurs of the Lower Cretaceous. On the other hand, Walls has pointed out in his brilliant book (1942) that the ophidian eye shows many peculiarities (p. 206) which are not found among lizards; the eye structure of *Lanthanotus* is still largely undescribed. He suggests that the conditions in snakes can be most readily explained on the assumption that their ancestors were burrowers which had greatly reduced their eyes. Subsequently, according to Walls, most of the snakes emerged above ground and underwent extensive radiation as surface-living types and their almost vestigial eye structures became refurbished and transformed in such a way as to build up an efficient organ of rather unique character.

Certain other considerations seem to support this interesting theory. Burrowing or semi-burrowing habits predominate among the existing types of lizards which have assumed a snake-like form, while the more primitive groups of living snakes contain a high proportion of burrowing representatives. Anatomical characters such as the loss of the upper skull arcade and of the eardrum are found in all snakes and in the great majority of lizards which are modified for burrowing life, including *Lanthanotus*. Admittedly, however, these features (though not usually all together) are also found in some other lizards which have well developed eyes and limbs and show no inclination towards life underground.

In many ways *Lanthanotus* seems to provide a satisfactory meeting ground for the prevalent theories of ophidian origin; it is both a platynotid and a burrower, though perhaps not a highly specialized one. Better still, it also spends much of its time in water, at least in captivity, and swims by graceful undulations of its elongated body. This brings it more into line with the extinct aquatic platynotid groups.

Underwood is firmly opposed, however, to the idea of special affinity between *Lanthanotus* and the snakes. He believes that the snakes originated from some unknown group of burrowing or secretive lizards which split off from the rest of the Squamata in very ancient times, and not from platynotids, or indeed from any other surviving groups of lizards. His views are based in particular on his important studies of the retina and carry much weight (see Underwood in Gans *et al.*, 1970, v.2). The problem of the origin of snakes therefore still lies open to all lines of investigation and will probably only be solved by the discovery of new fossil material. Recent work is reviewed by A. d'A. Bellairs (in Joysey and Kemp, 1972), while Senn and Northcutt (1973) have discussed some relevant neurological findings.

The different kinds of snakes

Underwood (1967) proposed a revised classification of living snakes in which several new families and subfamilies were recognized. Here we retain the traditional family groupings, but follow Underwood in dividing the suborder into three infra-orders, the first two containing the more primitive or 'lower' snakes and the third the more advanced or 'higher' forms. We feel that detailed consideration of the numerous groupings proposed by various workers in recent years is beyond the scope of this book, and refer by name only to some of the traditionally recognized subfamilies.

Of the existing families, the Typhlopidae is of particular interest. *Typhlops* and its allies are small worm-like creatures (though a few species grow to 60cm (2ft) or more) from the New and Old World and Australia. They are specialized for burrowing life and have tiny eyes. The head is blunt, the tail very short and the body is covered entirely by small closely fitting scales of equal size. The dentition is much reduced, the palate and lower jaw being quite or almost devoid of teeth, and the diet probably consists of insects and earthworms. Some species at least lay eggs of an elongated shape. Vestiges of hind-limb girdles are present.

The Leptotyphlopidae of the New and Old World tropics much resemble the Typhlopidae in habits and general appearance and together with them make up the infraorder Scolecophidia. The two families differ, however, in many anatomical features; for example, in the Leptotyphlopidae the upper jaw instead of the lower one is toothless. The hind-limb vestiges of *Leptotyphlops* are very well developed.

The Uropeltidae are small burrowing snakes found in damp wooded parts of Ceylon and South India. The body scales are smooth and in some species brightly patterned, and the short truncated tail is covered with a conspicuous shield-like scale which may possibly be of assistance in burrowing. There seem to be no vestiges of the pelvis. They are described by Gans (1973).

The Anilidae is another group of burrowing snakes, from the tropics of America and Asia. These possess pelvic rudiments, and as in the Uropeltidae, the belly scales are scarcely enlarged. The South American *Anilius scytale* is one of the types of 'coral snakes' (p. 218), the body being pink with black rings. Unlike the other burrowing snakes described, the Anilidae feed to a large extent on vertebrates. They are viviparous. The Xenopeltidae contains a single form from South East Asia which lacks limb vestiges but shows some primitive features. The last three families are sometimes reduced in status and grouped together in a single family Anilidae (Romer, 1956; Bellairs, 1969).

The presence of such characters as pelvic rudiments among the above-mentioned families of living snakes marks these groups as comparatively primitive ones. If one accepts the theory that the ancestors of snakes were specialized burrowers, many other features which they show, such as the small size of the eyes, the narrow gape and fairly rigid construction of the jaws and face which seem to be adaptations to burrowing life, may be regarded as primitive also. These snakes would then seem, broadly speaking, to be surviving representatives of a stage in evolution through which all the Serpentes have passed. If, on the other hand, one believes that the snakes have originated from surface-living ancestors, these families appear to be specialized, in some respects degenerate offshoots of the ophidian stock which still retain some primitive characters. Such forms live in the same manner as many of the limbless lizards, burrowing underground or hiding beneath stones. Their narrow non-venomous jaws and weak dentition confine them to small, often invertebrate, prey and they are mostly of small size.

The Boidae (boas and pythons), though also retaining vestiges of the pelvis, possess many of the characters of the more advanced and typical snakes: wide mobile jaws, fairly large ventral scales which assist in locomotion (p. 203), and except in the burrowing types, well developed eyes. They are not poisonous but kill their prey by constriction, an extremely rapid and effective method which causes death by stopping the action of the heart and lungs rather than by actually crushing the tissues.

The modern boids are grouped into several subfamilies including the Boinae and Pythoninae. The former are found in western Asia, Africa, Madagascar and certain islands in the Indian Ocean, but most species occur in the New World; the latter occur in the Old World, with many species also in Australasia. Both groups contain some very large types reaching at least 9m (30ft) in length, like the reticulated python of Malaya and the anaconda (*Eunectes murinus*) from South America, as well as some small burrowing forms such as the desert-living sand boas (*Eryx*) which are only about 1m (3ft) long. The large pythons and boas tend to be partly arboreal and partly aquatic; the anaconda is a particularly water-loving species. Pythons lay eggs, but most boas are viviparous.

The Acrochordidae is a small family of curious water snakes from the Far East; it is placed by Underwood (1967) in the infraorder Henophidia, with other primitive groups.

About two-thirds of the existing snakes belong to the family Colubridae, which has a virtually worldwide distribution. It seems to have appeared in the Oligocene, rather earlier than the other groups of advanced snakes. The Colubridae is divided into a considerable number of subfamily groups: the Colubrinae, Dipsadinae, Dasypeltinae, Boiginae and Homalopsinae. Older workers have used another system of classification based on the condition of the teeth. The harmless colubrids in which none of the teeth (Fig. 22O) are adapted for transmission of venom were placed in the series Aglypha, while the (generally) mildly poisonous 'back-fanged' forms are referred to the series Opisthoglypha (p. 191). This system does not always entirely conform with the subfamilial classification given previously, but by and large it may be said that the members of the first two subfamilies are aglyphs, while those of the last two are opisthoglyphs. The family contains some viviparous species.

The Colubrinae consists mainly of generalized adaptable snakes such as the grass snake, *Natrix* [= *Tropidonotus*] *natrix* found in England and many of the species styled as whip snakes and racers (*Coluber* and *Zamenis*). A number of forms, particularly those belonging to the genus *Natrix*, are, however, markedly amphibious, while others, such as *Heterodon*, are burrowers. Most of these aglyphous snakes have no special means of killing their prey, which is simply eaten alive, but some, such as the smooth snake (*Coronella austriaca*), a rare species in England, have lesser or greater powers of constriction. Most colubrines reach only a moderate size but a few, e.g. the four-lined snake (*Elaphe quatuorlineata*) from southern Europe and the Indian rat snakes (*Ptyas*), may grow to 2.4m (8ft).

The Boiginae, another considerable group, contains most of the rear-fanged snakes, many of which are tropical. A number of species, such as *Ahaetulla mycterizans*, the green whip snake of the orient, are highly arboreal. *Ahaetulla* is an extremely slender creature, about 1.2m (4ft) in length, with a body little thicker than a pencil and an elongated snout. The African boomslang (*Dispholidus typus*) deserves special mention, for unlike that of most of the back-fanged snakes, its bite may be dangerous to man. It is a greenish-coloured tree snake and grows about 1.5m (5ft) long; when alarmed it has the habit of inflating its throat with air.

In 1957 a small boomslang which had been sent to America killed a distinguished herpetologist, Dr. K. P. Schmidt, whose informative and beautifully illustrated book on reptiles (in collaboration with Inger) is cited in the bibliography. Schmidt died 24 hours after being bitten and has left an admirably dispassionate account of his symptoms; these are recorded by Pope (1958).

The Homalopsinae is a group of oriental water snakes, while the Dipsadinae contains a few small terrestrial species distinguished by their curiously large and chunky heads and their habit of eating slugs and snails. The Dasypeltinae contains a single genus (*Dasypeltis*) of egg-eating snakes (p. 198) from Africa; *Elachistodon* is a similar but rear-fanged genus, sometimes placed in a subfamily of its own.

The family Elapidae contains many highly poisonous snakes in which the deeply grooved or canalized fangs (p. 191) are fixed to the front of the upper jaw (Fig. 22Q); for this reason they are often termed proteroglyphs. To this group belong the cobras (*Naja*, *Hemachatus*) of Africa and Asia, the kraits (*Bungarus*) of Asia, the mambas (*Dendroaspis*) of Africa and the coral snakes (*Micrurus*) of America. Also placed in this family are almost all the poisonous snakes of Australia, which include such dangerous types as the tiger snake (*Notechis scutatus*) and the death adder (*Acanthophis antarcticus*). Most of these elapine snakes are swift, slender-bodied forms; *Acanthophis,* however, is thickset and viperine in appearance. Some elapids reach a considerable size, the largest, the king cobra or hamadryad (*Ophiophagus hannah*), occasionally reaches 5.5m (18ft), while the Australian taipan (*Oxyuranus scutellatus*) may be about 3m (10ft) in length.

The Hydrophiidae or sea snakes appear to be a group of elapids which has taken to marine life. Most sea snakes are viviparous and have no need to leave the water; indeed many of them are rather helpless on land and lack the broad belly scales which help typical snakes to move on the ground. The eyes and nostrils of the sea snakes are placed near the top of the head, and the tail is much flattened for swimming. They feed mainly on fish, but their bite is dangerous, sometimes fatal to man; some forms exceed 1.8m (6ft) in length. Sea snakes are found in the tropical waters of the east and one species, *Pelamis platurus*, is truly pelagic, ranging as far as south east Africa, and the west coast of South America.

The Viperidae are in many ways the most specialized of all the poisonous snakes. The fangs are large and completely canalized; unlike those of the proteroglyphous snakes they can be erected at will. From its fang structure, this group is often termed the Solenoglypha.

Two subfamilies are recognized, the Viperinae and the Crotalinae, the former being restricted to the Old World. Among the Viperinae are such well known snakes as the Russell's viper (*Vipera russelli*) of Asia, the African puff adder (*Bitis arietans*) and the adder (*Vipera berus*), the only poisonous snake found in England. The latter is the most northerly distributed of all snakes, for in Scandinavia it is found just within the Arctic Circle.

The crotalines or pit-vipers are distinguished from the viperine snakes by the presence of a deep pit, a heat-sensitive organ (p. 209), in front of each eye and nostril. To this group belong the rattlesnakes (*Crotalus* and *Sistrurus*) of America, the fer-de-lance (*Bothrops atrox*), and the bushmaster (*Lachesis muta*) of the American tropics including the West Indies. The bushmaster is the largest member of the Viperidae and grows to a length of nearly 4m (13ft). A number of pit-vipers are also found in Asia.

Most vipers are sluggish, thick-bodied snakes with large bluntly triangular heads covered with small scales instead of by a comparatively small number of large plates, as is the case in most colubrid snakes. Many species inhabit rocky or arid country, and some such as the Egyptian asp (*Cerastes cornutus*) are desert-livers; a few, as the water moccasin (*Agkistrodon piscivorus*), are amphibious, or as some of the oriental pit-vipers (*Trimeresurus*), arboreal. The African mole 'vipers' (*Atractaspis*) are burrowers. But it is doubtful if they really belong to this family at all. Most of the Viperidae are viviparous.

Books by the following authors containing information on the natural history of lizards and snakes (in some cases on other reptiles) are listed in the bibliography: Bellairs; Bustard; Klauber (a magnificent two-volume compendium on rattlesnakes); Mertens; Minton; Oliver; Parker; Pope; Schmidt and Inger; H. M. Smith; M. A. Smith; Steward.

12 | The biology of lizards and snakes

The scientific literature on the lizards and snakes is so much greater than that on any of the other groups of modern reptiles that it is necessary to discuss the biology of the Squamata in more detail, and more systematically, than has been done in the case of the other orders. Nevertheless the following account is only a brief and superficial one, and it has been possible to do little more than try to outline the main aspects of the structure, function and behaviour of these animals, and to touch on some of the more interesting trends of current research.

The skull and jaws

At first sight, the skulls of a typical lizard and a snake (Fig. 21) look very different; they are, however, both derived from a common pattern, the diapsid condition found in primitive lepidosaurs such as *Sphenodon*. In a lizard such as *Lacerta* this condition is only altered by the loss of the lower temporal arcade. In many other lizards, however, the upper as well as the lower arcade has disappeared. This reduction of the bones in the temporal region, which is widespread among specialized burrowing forms such as *Anniella* and the amphisbaenians, also occurs in some surface-living types, as the geckos, and is universal in snakes. It is probably associated with changes in the mechanism of kinesis (p. 186).

In most lizards the skeleton around the front part of the brain is composed only of a flimsy cartilage and membrane fabric, and there is a slender conspicuous epipterygoid bone. In snakes the braincase is much more rigid, the front of the cranial cavity being enclosed by downgrowths from the bones of the skull roof, the frontals and parietals, which have replaced the absent or

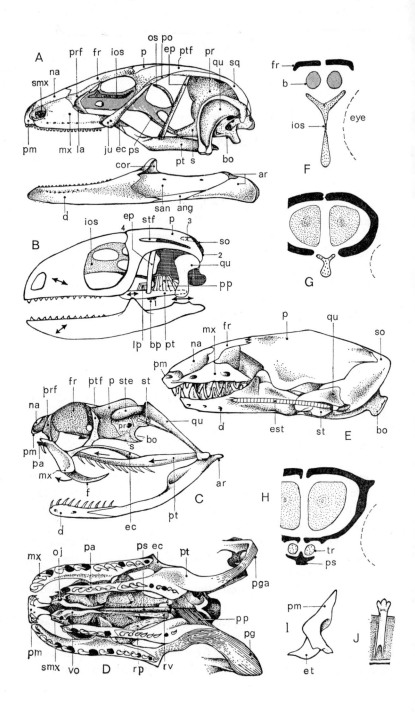

vestigial orbitosphenoid cartilages (p. 23). Here again, however, we find that some of the burrowing lizards have developed a compact cranial box and have reduced or lost the epipterygoid, much as the snakes have done.

In lizards the eyes are separated by a thin vertical inter-orbital septum (Figs. 21A, F), but in snakes this structure is absent and the width of the bony braincase is interposed between the orbits. On either side below this, however, lies one of a pair of cartilaginous rods, the trabeculae cranii (Fig. 21H). These

---

Fig. 21

A. Skull of skink, *Mabuya carinata*. Cartilaginous regions shown in machine stipple. After Rao and Ramaswami (1952).
B. Diagram showing kinesis in skull of lizard. Directions of movement of upper and lower jaws shown by arrows. The fixed occipital segment is shown in cross-hatching and the cartilaginous parts of the skull are stippled. The numbers 1–4 indicate the positions of the main kinetic joints; at 3 a cartilaginous peg from the supra-occipital projects into the back of the parietal in the midline.
C. Skull of the viper *Cerastes aegyptiacus*. Arrows show direction of movement of jaw bones during fang erection. After Phisalix (1922).
D. Ventral view of skull of *Python sebae* showing a few of the numerous jaw muscles, mainly on left. After Frazzetta (1966).
E. Skull of *Amphisbaena manni*, showing extra-stapes. After Wever and Gans (1973). Some bones unlabelled in C–E.
F, G, H. Transverse sections through skull at mid-eye level in F, lizard; G, burrowing lizard; H, snake.
I. Egg-tooth (*et*) of *Natrix natrix* attached to premaxilla, from left.
J. Pleurodont tooth of the herbivorous marine iguana (*Amblyrhynchus*) (adult) from inner side.

ang, angular. *ar*, articular. *b*, brain. *bo*, basioccipital. *bp*, basipterygoid process of basisphenoid. *cor*, coronoid. *d*, dentary. *ec*, ectopterygoid. *ep*, epipterygoid. *est*, extrastapes (= extra-columella). *f*, fang. *fr*, frontal. *ios*, interorbital septum (calcified region shown in darker stipple in A). *ju*, jugal. *la*, lacrimal. *lp*, levator pterygoidei muscle (cut). *mx*, maxilla. *na*, nasal. *o.j*, opening for duct of Jacobson's organ. *os*, orbitosphenoid. *p*, parietal. *pa*, palatine. *pg*, pterygoideus muscle. *pga*, accessory *pg*. *pm*, premaxilla. *po*, postorbital. *pp*, protractor pterygoidei muscle. *pr*, prootic. *prf*, prefrontal. *ps*, parasphenoid. *pt*, pterygoid. *ptf*, postfrontal. *qu*, quadrate. *rp*, retractor pterygoidei muscle. *rv*, retractor vomeris muscle. *s*, basisphenoid. *san*, surangular. *smx*, septomaxilla. *so*, supraoccipital. *sq*, squamosal. *st*, stapes (= columella auris). *ste*, supratemporal. *stf*, superior temporal fenestra. *tr*, trabecula. *vo*, vomer. II, foramen for optic and other nerves.

structures are present in the embryonic skulls of all vertebrates, and it is interesting that while in the embryos of other reptiles they fuse to form part of the interorbital septum, in snakes they remain separate in the eye region throughout life. In burrowing lizards with tiny eyes (Fig. 21G) the interorbital septum is very low, and the study of embryos suggests that only a small alteration of the growth pattern might be necessary to convert such a condition into that seen in snakes. However, while many of these detailed features of the skull are clear enough when sections of embryos are studied under the microscope, they are almost impossible to follow on macerated skulls of adult specimens.

One further and very striking difference between the skull of a typical lizard such as *Lacerta* and that of a typical snake like *Natrix* may be noted. In the former the front part of the upper jaw is fairly firmly attached to the rest of the skull, whereas in the snake the upper jaw is only very loosely attached to it, and most of its component bones are reduced to slender tooth-bearing rods—except for the tiny premaxilla which remains jointed to the face. In a primitive burrowing snake such as *Anilius*, however, the upper jaw is not nearly so loose, and its general appearance and contacts with other bones are more like those in lizards. Such conditions suggest that the burrowing lizards and burrowing snakes are in some ways structurally intermediate between the typical lizards and typical snakes, and seem to support the view that the snakes have been derived from burrowing ancestors.

The skulls of most lizards show an interesting phenomenon known as kinesis, in which the upper jaw is able to move in relation to the cranium. This has been previously mentioned in connection with certain other groups of reptiles (p. 136), and is developed to an even greater degree in snakes.

In most lizards kinesis (Fig. 21B) involves movement in several regions: at the back of the skull roof there there is a kind of hinge in the midline between the parietal and occipital bones; at each side between the paroccipital process and the parietal, supratemporal and neighbouring bones; and at the skull base between the pterygoids and the basipterygoid (or basitrabecular) processes which project from either side of the basisphenoid. Since the anterior part of the braincase is cartilaginous and elastic, the front of the skull, including the upper jaw, is able to move as a 'maxillary' segment on the back part ('occipital segment'), represented by the solidly ossified occipital, otic and basisphenoid bones. Raising of the snout is apparently initiated by movement of the pterygoids which are pulled upwards and forwards by the levator and protractor pterygoidei muscles; this movement is imparted via the palate to the front of the skull as a whole. The epipterygoid probably has a steadying effect during kinetic movements, running as it does like a strut between the pterygoid and the skull roof. This type of kinesis, with the hinge in the skull roof well back, between parietal and occipital, is known as metakinesis. In some lizards the bending plane lies further forwards, between the parietal and frontal (mesokinesis); in such forms, which include some specialized burrowers, the postorbital bar is lost and the upper temporal arcade often disappears as well. Lizards such as *Varanus* which have a hinge in both the mesokinetic and metakinetic situations are called amphikinetic.

Mobility of the quadrate is another characteristic feature of the Squamata. An essential difference between a lizard and a rhynchocephalian or some other primitive type of lepidosaur is that in the former the quadratojugal bone and lower temporal arcade have disappeared. This has the effect of freeing the lower end of the quadrate which thus becomes mobile (a condition known as streptostyly), pivoting on the articulation between its upper end and the skull. The lower end of the quadrate is loosely attached to the back end of the pterygoid but it would seem that in lizards, as in snakes, the quadrate does not actually push the pterygoid forwards, as is sometimes stated. Since the jaw joint lies between the lower end of the quadrate and the articular, an obvious effect of streptostyly will be to bring about protraction and retraction of the lower jaw. Streptostyly and kinetism are usually, though not invariably, associated in lizards. Thus chameleons have a movable quadrate, but little if any intracranial mobility; they also lack the epipterygoid bone.

Various types of kinesis and streptostyly are found among different vertebrates, e.g. in sharks and many birds. Their precise function in lizards is not fully understood but has been the subject of much discussion. It seems probable that they allow some increase in the gape of the jaws and also facilitate adjustments in the alignment of the upper and lower tooth rows, so that the prey can be gripped by the maximum number of teeth. Their most important function, however, is probably to help in pulling struggling prey back into the mouth by a series of successive snaps (see Bellairs, 1969).

In typical snakes the mechanism of biting and chewing is of a rather different type. The braincase is comparatively rigid and well protected underneath by the massive parasphenoid bone, so that the brain cannot be injured by violently struggling prey. The facial part of the skull is usually fairly loose (prokinesis) and both upper and lower jaws are exceedingly mobile. The quadrate is highly streptostylic, and can swing back to give the lower jaw an immense gape of well over a right angle; the absence of any firm union between the two sides of either the upper or the lower jaw enables each side to work independently. The jaw bones, armed with recurved teeth and operated by a fantastically com- plicated set of muscles (see G. Haas, in Gans *et al.*, 1973 v.4), are able to work their way over the body of the prey, drawing it back into the throat where the contraction of the pharyngeal muscles propels it on its path. The skin of the throat is extremely distensible and prey much wider than the head can be swallowed, though often by a process so slow and seemingly painful that it is suggestive of a birth, in reverse. There can be little doubt that these elaborate specializations of the jaw apparatus, which dis- tinguish typical snakes from snakelike lizards, have contributed a good deal to the success of the snakes as a group. When they are associated with special methods of killing as by poison or constriction, the snakes become formidable creatures, able to overcome quite large animals and in some cases reaching a large size themselves.

In the Viperidae, and to a lesser extent in certain other snakes, the arrangement of the jaw bones, makes it possible for the fangs to be erected. The maxilla of the vipers (Fig. 21C) is short and very deep, and is hinged above to the prefrontal, so that the whole bone can pivot when pressure is exerted on it from behind by the ectopterygoid, which is itself pushed forward by movement of the pterygoid. The final effect is to swing the fangs into the erect position, when, owing to the upward tilting of the head, they will point forwards as the snake strikes. Fang erection is not confined to the act of striking, for it may occur when the snake opens its mouth as if to yawn. The jaw mechanism of vipers has been studied by Boltt and Ewer (1964).

The teeth and salivary glands

In lizards the teeth are present along the jaw margins, and sometimes also on the palate. In amphisbaenians, there is a big tooth in the midline at the front of the premaxilla. The teeth usually have a simple shape, being conical, peg-like (Fig. 21A) or slightly recurved. In the iguanas the tooth crowns are generally serrated or three-lobed (Fig. 21J), while in a few monitors (and other forms) they are blunt and rounded, probably in association with a diet of molluscs and crabs. In the heloderms some of the mandibular teeth have a groove in front and behind for the conduction of the venom.

The way in which the teeth are attached to the jaw bones varies among lizards. In the agamids and chameleons (and also in *Sphenodon* and some amphisbaenians) the bases of the teeth are set squarely on the biting aspect of the jaw, a condition known as acrodont. In such cases ankylosis between the tooth and bone is very firm; there is hardly any tooth replacement so that in old specimens the dentition may become very worn. In other lizards the teeth are attached to the inner side of the jaw so that their bases are oblique; this is the pleurodont condition (Fig. 21J). In many agamids the front teeth are pleurodont while those behind are acrodont.

In the embryos of lizards and snakes an egg-tooth is developed on the premaxilla (Fig. 21I). It projects forwards from the snout and is used for piercing the egg-shell. It is present in most viviparous as well as oviparous forms, though in the former it can have little function and may be degenerate. The egg-tooth is shed within a day or so of hatching. In geckos there are paired egg-teeth instead of a single one in the midline.

Snakes are carnivorous, though a few instances of individuals taking fruit are on record. Their sharp recurved teeth (Fig. 22O) are adapted for seizing and holding prey, and in most snakes they are present on all the upper jaw bones except the premaxilla and ectopterygoid, as well as on the dentary below. Premaxillary teeth (apart from the egg-tooth) occur, however, as a primitive feature in some snakes such as pythons (Fig. 21D), while in

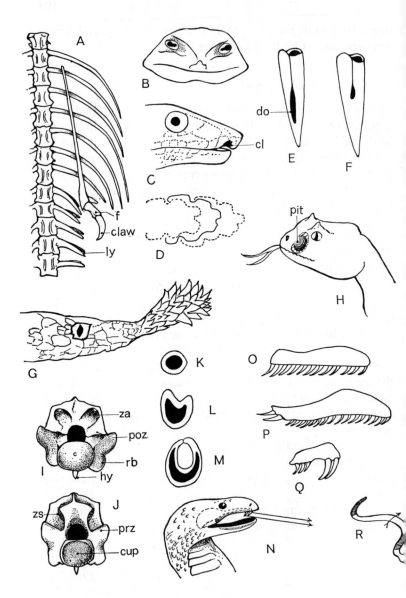

Fig. 22

A. Vestigial pelvis and hind-limb of python from below. *f*, femur.
  ly, lymphapophysis.
B. Tree-snake *Ahaetulla* [= *Dryophis*] showing binocular fields and
  grooves in front of eyes. After Walls (1942).

specialized burrowers the dentition may be reduced or absent on the palate, or even on the dentary or maxilla. The teeth are fairly lightly ankylosed to the jaw bones and are sometimes broken off when the snake bites.

In many snakes one or more of the teeth on each side of the upper jaw are enlarged and modified to form poison fangs. In the opisthoglyphs the fangs lie at the back of the maxillae and each is furrowed by a groove for the conduction of the venom (Figs. 22L, P). The situation of such fangs must make them difficult to engage and the snake may have to persevere, hanging on to and chewing its prey, in order to drive them into the wound.

In the proteroglyphs, e.g. the cobras, mambas and sea snakes, the fangs have become almost or completely tubular, hypodermic-like structures owing to the approximation of the lips of the groove (Fig. 22M). Some cobras, notably the African ringhals (*Hemachatus haemachatus*) and the black-necked cobra (*Naja*

C. Late embryo of anaconda (*Eunectes*) showing anomalous cleft lip (*cl*). The palate is also cleft.

D. Longitudinal section of three interlocking rattle segments of rattlesnake. After Klauber (1972).

E, F. Fangs of (E) non-spitting cobra (*Naja haje anchietae*), and (F) spitter (*Naja nigricollis*) seen from in front and showing discharge orifice (*do*).

G. Head of snake *Langaha nasuta*, female. The rostral appendage of the male is simpler. After Guibé (1949).

H. Head of horned rattlesnake (*Crotalus cerastes*) showing sensory pit with inner and outer chambers separated by membrane and exposed by cut (slanting lines).

I, J. Anterior trunk vertebra of the Eocene marine snake *Palaeophis* (I) from behind. (J) from in front. After Swinton (1965). *c*, condyle. *cup*, cup at front of centrum. *hy*, hypapophysis. *poz*, post-zygapophysis. *prz*, pre-zygapophysis. *rb*, rib-bearing process. *za*, zygantrum. *zs*, zygosphene.

K, L, M. Tooth of aglyph and fangs of opisthoglyph and proteroglyph respectively, in cross-section. Pulp cavity in black.

N. Cobra (*Naja nigricollis*) spitting twin jets of venom. Outline of venom duct and gland in broken lines; positions of superior and inferior labial glands stippled. E, F and N after Begert (1943).

O, P, Q. Right maxilla of (O) *Coronella* (aglyph); (P) *Langaha* (opisthoglyph); Q, *Naja* (proteroglyph). After Phisalix (1922).

R. Sidewinder. Only the shaded regions of the body are in contact with the ground. Arrow shows direction through which raised loop has been moved.

nigricollis), are able to spit a jet of venom from each fang for several feet, and when this is successfully directed into the eyes of an aggressor it can cause severe pain and temporary blindness (Fig. 22N). Bogert (1943) has shown that the fangs of these spitting cobras differ from those of allied non-spitters, the discharge orifice being smaller, presumably to increase the force of the jet, and facing directly forwards (Figs. 22E, F).

In the Viperidae the fangs are always completely canalized. They are the only teeth present on the maxillae, and instead of being more or less fixed like those of the proteroglyphs, they can be erected by the rotation of the maxillae. As they lie along the roof of the mouth when not in use they are able to grow very long, the fangs of a large Gaboon viper being about 2.5cm (1in) in length, while those of a king cobra, a much longer snake, may be less than half this length.

Armed with its long erectile fangs a viper is able to inject a lethal dose of venom deep into the tissues of its victim in a single stroke, often withdrawing its head in a flash to avoid any chance of retaliation. Although the prey may run for a short distance before succumbing to the venom it can be trailed at leisure and devoured.

The fangs are replaced like the other teeth in a more or less alternating fashion. There are usually two sockets side by side at the front of each maxilla and as the more mature one is shed, its function is taken over by its neighbour. Behind these lies a battery of replacement fangs in various stages of maturity, which move forwards into position as the front ones are shed. It is therefore often possible to find more than one fang on each maxilla, although it is probably seldom that two functional venom-conducting fangs coexist side by side for very long. Young snakes are born ready to bite, usually with functional fangs on the inner position on each maxilla (Bogert, 1943). Artificial removal of a snake's poison fangs is, unless the injury is very extensive, only a temporary method of rendering a snake harmless, since the fangs are continually being renewed.

Lizards and snakes are equipped with salivary glands, both along the edges of the jaws and on the palate (see Kochva and Gans in Minton, 1971). These are particularly well developed in snakes, for although these creatures do not cover their victims with slime before swallowing them, like the boa constrictor in

The Swiss Family Robinson, their method of feeding calls for a plentiful supply of saliva for lubricating the prey.

In harmless snakes there is a strip of glandular tissue beneath the scales of the upper and lower lips. In some forms, such as some species of *Natrix*, the back part of the upper-lip gland is enlarged to form a partly distinct 'parotid' portion, more properly known as Duvernoy's gland. This tendency is carried further in the opisthoglyphs, where the secretions of the 'parotid' are markedly toxic; they are discharged through one or more large ducts into the grooves on the fangs. In the proteroglyphs (Fig. 22N) and the Viperidae the venom gland is quite distinct from the lip glands and lies behind and below the eye. Its long duct runs forward and ends in the immediate neighbourhood of the orifice at the base of the functional fang (Fig. 22N). A slip from one of the jaw muscles is inserted into the venom gland and helps to express the venom from it when the snake bites. In a few snakes the venom gland has migrated back into the neck and may even extend down the body as far as the heart region. In the heloderm lizards the glands of the lower instead of the upper jaw have become converted into poison glands.

In many snakes, even in some aglyphous species which are for practical purposes innocuous to man, the saliva is more or less poisonous. A survey carried out some years ago suggested that perhaps 30 000 people die every year from snake bites, the great majority of these deaths occurring in India and south east Asia (see Buckley and Porges, 1956). In view of the difficulty of obtaining accurate statistics in underdeveloped countries, one suspects that this figure is much too high. It is not surprising, however, that in tropical countries much research is being done on the properties and treatment of snake venoms. The reader in search of special information on the subject is referred to the bibliography by Russell and Scharffenberg (1964) and to the books edited by Buckley and Porges (1956), Bücherl *et al.* (1968–71) and Minton (1971), and to the US Navy Manual on poisonous snakes (1968), revised by Russell and other authorities (p. 232).

It would appear that snake venoms contain complex enzymes and protein-like substances which have a rather specific action on various animal tissues; they produce no injury to the intact skin. Speaking very broadly, the venom of most vipers and rattle-snakes acts mainly on the blood system and on the tissues

G

in general, especially in the region of the bite, and produces much swelling. In most of the front-fanged snakes the venom predominantly affects the nervous and muscular systems. Circulatory or respiratory failure, internal bleeding and massive tissue destruction or gangrene are usually the causes of death in viper bites, while in the cases of bites by cobras, mambas and their allies, death is often due to respiratory paralysis caused by blocking of the neuro-muscular junctions. Venoms of the latter type are on the whole quicker acting than those of the former and death from a cobra bite has been known to occur in as short a time as a quarter of an hour, although such rapid fatality is unusual. The venom of any one species of snake contains active principles of many different types, although one may predominate and mask the effects of the others. It should be emphasized that there are many exceptions to the generalizations above; e.g. the venom of the tropical rattlesnake (*Crotalus durissus*) has a powerful effect on the nervous system, and that of some cobras causes mainly local necrosis. The poison of *Heloderma* may produce severe local pain and swelling and also seems to affect the respiratory system. It would seem that its bite is occasionally fatal in man (Bogert and Del Campo, 1956).

The severity of a bite depends upon many factors: the species of snake and toxicity of its venom, the site of the injury, the depth to which the fangs have penetrated and the amount of venom injected, which may depend on the period which has elapsed since the snake last emptied its venom glands. Snakes such as the big vipers, cobras and mambas can theoretically inject a lethal dose (or much more) at one bite, and the venom of certain sea-snakes is even more powerful. On the other hand, bites by authenticated poisonous snakes may 'misfire' and produce little if any injury at all. The bite of the adder (*Vipera berus*) is seldom dangerous to a healthy adult, although its effects may be quite unpleasant; in Britain less than ten people have been killed by this species during the twentieth century.

The most effective treatment for snake bite is the injection of antiserum into the tissues or veins of the victim. This is usually prepared from the blood of horses which have been immunized by the injection of graded samples of venom and contains substances (antibodies) which neutralize its effects. The venom is obtained in the first instance by forcing the snake to bite over the edge of a glass, the head being squeezed if necessary to milk out the venom from its glands. Polyvalent antisera, prepared against the venoms of several species of snakes, are often used.

Antiserum should normally only be administered under skilled supervision; it may be unnecessary, and its use carries the risk of evoking dangerous reactions of allergic type.

First aid measures for snake bite treatment have for long been controversial, partly perhaps because the venoms of different species of snakes vary so much in their mode of action. The classical remedies of sucking the wound and incising it so that the blood flow can wash away the venom may (at least theoretically, and if carried out almost immediately) be of value, but are not in general recommended. Incision by unskilled hands may be dangerous and it is an essential principle that the treatment should do less harm than the bite—which may quite possibly have been inflicted by a non-poisonous or only mildly poisonous species such as the adder of northern Europe. The following recommendations, slightly modified from the *Trans. Roy. Soc. Tropical Medicine* and *Hygiene,* 1962, **56**, 93, are listed below.

(1) Identify snake if possible.

(2) Reassure victim and keep him at rest.

(3) Wash the bitten surface with water without rubbing.

(4) Apply a lightly constricting ligature to occlude veins and lymphatics draining the bitten area – but not the arterial circulation. This must be released for one minute in every thirty.

(5) If bitten on a limb, immobilize it by splinting if possible, as if for a fracture.

(6) Get the victim to a doctor as soon as possible. A lone victim should exert himself as little as he can while reaching medical aid (possibly this is utopian advice!).

Animals such as king snakes (*Lampropeltis*) and mongooses which are liable to eat poisonous snakes tend to have a partial immunity to their venom, or at least to that of some of the prey species. Generally speaking, poisonous snakes are quite (though perhaps not absolutely) resistant to their own venom, somewhat less resistant to that of closely allied species and still less immune to the bites of unrelated poisonous snakes—but there is some conflicting evidence (see Minton and Minton, 1969).

The skeleton and limbs

In most lizards the limbs are well developed and possess five fingers or toes of which the fourth is usually the longest. The shoulder girdle is often poorly ossified and contains windows between the scapula and coracoid; the sternum, is more or less cartilaginous. In some forms structures rather like abdominal ribs are present but are probably not homologous with those of other reptiles, so that they have been distinguished by the term parasternum. In male geckos there is a pair of small bones behind the cloaca.

In a substantial minority of lizards the limbs are reduced, often drastically; in some, for example the Pygopodidae, only the hind pair are visible, while in others, such as the amphisbaenian *Bipes*, only the front pair can be seen. In others again, as the slow worm (*Anguis fragilis*), neither pair of limbs is externally visible. The limb girdles and their muscles are, of course, reduced also, but in few if any lizards have both girdles disappeared completely, as they have in the majority of snakes.

Of all the groups of snake-like lizards, the skinks perhaps afford the most interesting examples of limb reduction. Within this family it is possible to find all gradations in limb structure, from a pentadactyl member of normal appearance at one extreme to complete absence of the free appendage at the other. In the intermediate forms the limbs are often tiny and may bear one to four toes, the number differing in some cases on the hand and foot, and possibly showing individual variation. Genera such as *Chalcides* and *Riopa* show good examples of such limb reduction.

In most snakes all traces of the limbs and their girdles have been lost. No snake is known to possess a shoulder girdle, but in some members of the more primitive groups vestiges of the hind-limbs and pelvis are found, though often they can only be demonstrated by dissection, X-rays or histological methods. In some forms such as *Python* the girdle consists of little more than a single elongated bone (Fig. 22A); in others such as *Trachyboa* and *Leptotyphlops* it has a more complex structure and attempts to identify the ilium, ischium and pubis can be made. The girdle has a curious position, inside the ribs, which recalls that in turtles. The outer part of the limb is represented by one or more small bones and usually carries a claw which projects from the scales on either side of the cloaca. These claws show sexual variation, being larger in the males and supposedly used to stimulate the female during coitus. The limbs are operated by quite an elaborate set of muscles which are supplied by an interlacing nerve plexus from the pelvic region of the spinal cord. The vestigial limbs of both snake-like lizards and snakes have been studied by Gasc (1970, 1974), and by Raynaud (1972). The latter has shown that the early limb buds show premature regression of the apical cap, the epidermal thickening which is apparently responsible for inducing the later differentiation of the limb.

The vertebrae of most Squamata are of the ball and socket variety, the socket being on the front of each vertebra (procoelous); most geckos, however, have amphicoelous vertebrae with both ends hollowed out. In snake-like lizards and snakes the vertebrae are very numerous, ranging in snakes from less than 200 to 400 or more. The first two vertebrae may be devoid of ribs but these are present on the remainder although in the tail they are fused with the vertebrae. In the cloacal region the ribs end in forked claw-like processes known as lymphapophyses (Fig. 22A) which surround the contractile lymph hearts (p. 45) on each side of the body.

The spine of a snake is a remarkable structure, quite flexible, yet at the same time very strong, as it must be to resist the stresses imposed upon it; in the case of the large heavy constricting snakes these are doubtless very considerable. Each vertebra is closely moulded against its successor and articulates with it at five points; there is the usual joint between the centra of the vertebrae at the ball and socket, and two between the paired zygapophyses. In snakes (and some lizards including some of the extinct Platynota) a pair of extra joints is also developed. On the anterior surface of each vertebra above the zygapophysis on each side is a process known as the zygosphene which fits into a corresponding hollow, the zygantrum, on the back of the vertebra in front (Figs. 22I, J). Movement of about 25° laterally is possible between any two adjacent vertebrae, giving a total range of 50° from side to side. There is considerably less movement in the vertical plane, about 13° of ventral flexion and 15° of dorsal flexion as a rough average in many snakes. The zygosphenal joints, together with the zygapophyses, form something resembling a tenon and mortise; they prevent extreme bending of the backbone such as might injure the spinal cord.

Mention must be made here of the remarkable adaptations of the vertebrae in certain egg-eating colubrid snakes, notably in *Dasypeltis*; though less than 1m in length it can swallow eggs as large as a fowl's. The hypapophyses (ventral processes) of the 'neck' vertebrae are specialized, some being long and pointed. These penetrate the oesophagus and rip open the egg-shell, which is ejected from the mouth while the egg contents are swallowed (see Gans, 1952).

Autotomy and regeneration

In many lizards the tail can easily be broken off, and such shedding (autotomy) seems to be due more to active contraction of the tail muscles than to mechanical injury by the aggressor. The writhing of the detached fragment may distract the attention of the predator while the lizard escapes, and in some species the tail is brightly coloured as if to enhance this effect.

The fracture takes place at a predetermined plane of weakness through a vertebra and not between two vertebrae; the position of this plane may vary in different species, being near the middle of the vertebra in *Lacerta* and towards the front of it in *Anguis*. As a rule, all the caudal vertebrae are autotomous, except for those near the base of the tail and therefore in the neighbourhood of the male reproductive organs. There are also modifications of the muscles and other soft tissues. Such fracture planes are also found in *Sphenodon*, some amphisbaenians and a few extinct cotylosaurs. They are absent in monitors, agamids, chameleons and certain other lizards, and in almost all snakes (Etheridge, 1967: Sheppard and Bellairs, 1972).

Lizards with the power of autotomy are in general able to grow new tails though the power of regeneration is greater in some species than in others. The new tail may become virtually as long as the original one, or (as in the slow-worm *Anguis*), no more than a short conical stump (Bryant and Bellairs, 1967). The scales of the regenerate may differ somewhat in appearance from those of the original and the internal structure is always different; the vertebrae are not renewed but are replaced by an unsegmented tube of cartilage. The regenerated spinal cord is very thin and much of the nerve supply of the new tail is derived from fibres which grow back from the stump. The growth of the new tissue seems to be dependent on the influence of the ependymal lining of the spinal cord and abnormal regenerates can be induced by implanting pieces of ependyma. In many lizards, at least, regeneration will occur if the tail is experimentally amputated between two fracture planes (instead of being broken off through one of them as in normal autotomy), and also if a pre-existing regenerate is broken or cut off. Occasionally, perhaps after an incomplete fracture, a lizard can be seen with a bifurcated tail. The limbs of lizards may very exceptionally undergo incomplete regeneration but no new digits are formed.

Locomotion

In most lizards the limbs are the principal agents in loco-motion, and as might be expected they show various adaptations to the mode of life and habitat of their owners. In some desert-living geckos, lacertids and skinks, for example, the edges of the digits are fringed with scales which prevent the feet from sinking into the sand. The remarkable *Palamatogecko* which lives in the shifting sands of the Namib desert in south west Africa has webbed feet which act like snow-shoes. On climbing geckos the digits are usually expanded proximal to the claws, and the under surfaces of the expansions bear a number of large specialized scales known as lamellae or scansors (Fig. 23D). The arrange-ment of these lamellae differs in various groups of geckos and is of considerable taxonomic importance. Each lamella is fur-nished with large numbers of very fine branching bristles or setae which are expanded at their tips. A similar type of digital specialization is found in the highly arboreal *Anolis* lizards of the family Iguanidae (Ruibal and Ernst, 1965; Maderson, 1966).

Many theories have been put forward to account for the way in which geckos are able to climb so well up smooth vertical surfaces and even to cling upside down. Some workers believe that the necessary adhesive power is produced merely by the setae which engage in tiny irregularities in the substratum; the claws are mainly important in climbing rough surfaces. Others have supposed that there is some vacuum mechanism, and it has

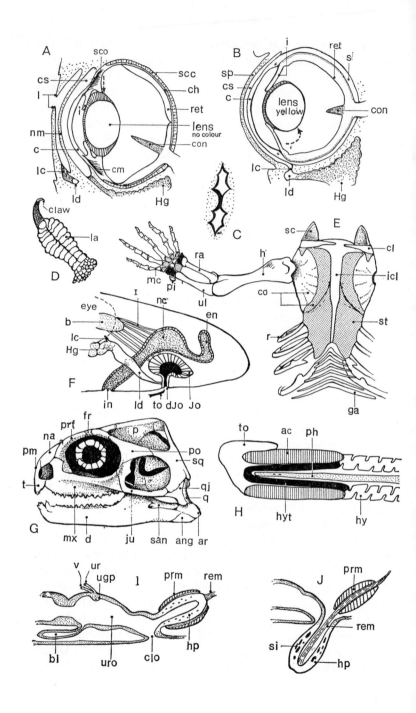

been suggested that the expansions at the tips of the setae act as minute suction cups. The mechanism is not yet fully understood, however, and it is possible that other factors, for example electrostatic phenomena, may be involved.

In the chameleons the feet are also modified, though along very

---

Fig. 23

A, B. Diagrams of eye in cross-section of A, lizard; B, snake. The lachrymal duct and nictitating membrane actually lie near the front of the eye, not the middle as shown. Arrows show direction of force applied in accommodation.

C. Serrated pupil of gecko.

D. Under surface of digit of gecko (*Hemidactylus*). The microscopic bristles are borne on the lamellae.

E. Shoulder girdle and fore-limb of *Sphenodon* from below. The radiale and ulnare are in black, the intermedium and distal carpals stippled and the centralia unshaded.

F. Diagram showing nose and organ of Jacobson in snake, as seen in partly reconstructed longitudinal section.

G. Skull of *Sphenodon*.

H. Diagram of longitudinal section through retracted tongue of chameleon. Sudden contraction of the accelerator muscle shoots the tongue tip off the hyoid process, the hyoglossus tendon becoming turned inside out.

I, J. Diagrams showing hemipenis of a squamate reptile in longitudinal section, retracted in I, everted in J. Left of figure is anterior.

A–C, after Walls (1942). E, after Miner (1925). G, after Romer (1966). H, after Gans (1967).

---

ac, accelerator muscle. *ang*, angular. *ar*, articular. *b*, brain (olfactory bulb). *bl.* bladder. *c*, cornea. *ch*, choroid. *cl*, clavicle. *clo*, cloacal opening. *cm*, ciliary muscle. *co*, coracoid. *con*, conus papillaris. *cs*, conjunctival space. *d*, dentary. *dJo*, duct of *Jo*. *en*, part of nasal cavity leading to external nostril. *fr*, frontal. *ga*, gastralia. *h*, humerus. *Hg*, Harderian gland. *hp*, hemipenis. *hy*, hyoglossus muscle. *hyt*, tendon of *hy*. *i*, iris. *icl*, interclavicle. *in*, internal nostril. *Jo*, Jacobson's organ. *ju*, jugal. *l*, eyelids. *la*, lamella. *lc*, lachrymal canaliculus. *ld*, lachrymal duct. *mc*, metacarpal. *mx*, maxilla. *na*, nasal. *nc*, nasal cavity. *nm*, nictitating membrane. *p*, parietal. *ph*, processus entoglossus of hyoid. *pi*, pisiform. *pm*, premaxilla. *po*, postorbital. *prf*, prefrontal. *prm*, propulsor muscle of hemipenis. *q*, quadrate. *qj*, quadratojugal. *r*, rib. *ra*, radius. *re*, rectum. *rem*, retractor muscle of hemipenis. *ret*, retina. *san*, surangular. *sc*, scapula. *scc*, scleral cartilage. *sco*, scleral ossicle. *si*, blood sinus. *sp*, spectacle. *sq*, squamosal. *st*, sternum. *t*, tooth-like projection of premaxilla. *to*, tongue tip. *ugp*, urogenital papilla. *ul*, ulna. *ur*, ureter. *uro*, urodaeum. *v*, vas deferens. I, olfactory nerves and vomeronasal nerves to *Jo*. II, optic nerve. *s*, sclera.

different lines. The digits on each extremity are divided into two groups by webs of skin; in the foot three of the claws are on the outside and two on the inside, and in the hand the situation is reversed. Each hand or foot is thus divided into an outer and an inner part and these can be opposed to one another as the animal grasps the twigs in its slow deliberate movements. The chameleon's tail is highly prehensile; when not in use it is coiled vertically like a watch-spring.

Certain tree lizards are able to glide or parachute through the air by means of expansions of the skin (or patagia) along the flanks and elsewhere; in this way they can descend from great heights without injury. The most adept gliders are the flying dragons (*Draco*, Fig. 19F, p. 164) where the patagia are supported by ribs. The flying geckos (*Ptychozoon*, Fig. 19I) can probably do little more than parachute at a steep angle and their narrow patagia are composed only of skin and soft tissue. Certain species of *Anolis* which have expanded digital pads are also able to parachute and can be dropped from a height of 12m without sustaining damage. David Attenborough has shown in a film that the oriental flying snake (*Chrysopelea*) is able to fall from a branch and descend obliquely to the ground with its body in horizontal undulations. During this process the body is much flattened and the belly drawn in to form a concave surface, increasing resistance to the air.

Some terrestrial lizards of the agamid and iguanid families rise up on their hind legs when they are running at speed. This type of locomotion recalls that of the bipedal dinosaurs and is seen in *Agama, Amphibolurus* and *Chlamydosaurus*, the frilled lizard, and also in the large iguanid *Basiliscus*. The basilisk is able to run in this way over water for a short distance, supported by the surface film, before it plunges into the depths. In such bipedal locomotion the tail is stretched out backwards and upwards (Fig. 20F) and acts as a counterpoise. Snyder, who has made interesting studies of lizard locomotion, (1949, 1962), found that removal of sections of the basilisk's long heavy tail prevented it from running on its hind legs.

In snake-like lizards undulatory movements of the body are of prime importance in locomotion and the ventral abdominal musculature has become highly complicated, gaining attachment to the belly scales and, in some forms at least, probably helping to hitch the body along. The snakes have perfected limbless locomotion and the mysterious ease with which they glide along has aroused the wonder of man since the days of antiquity. In recent times, however, the way of a serpent on a rock, which baffled even King Solomon, has been carefully studied and is described by Gans (1966) and Gray (1968). In the usual type of ophidian locomotion progress is essentially due to the thrust of the sides of the animal against irregularities of the ground as the body is thrown into lateral undulations by the contraction of the muscles on one side and the relaxation of those on the other. The process is rapid and continuous and as the snake glides along each part of the body follows a path, the curvature of which is continually changing. The free edges of the broad ventral scales catch against the ground and prevent the snake from sliding backwards. If the animal is placed on a flat smooth surface it is almost unable to progress.

This horizontal undulatory or 'serpentine' type of locomotion is practised by all snakes. For example, when a snake is creeping along a narrow tunnel, or sometimes when climbing it may move by alternately bunching up and straightening out parts of its body; this is known as 'concertina movement'. Desert vipers and rattlesnakes use a method called sidewinding in which loops of the body are raised and thrown sideways (Fig. 22R). This type of movement is particularly effective over shifting sand.

Some of the heavy thick-bodied snakes such as the pythons, boas and big vipers employ a method of rectilinear locomotion when they are not in a hurry. The body is stretched out almost in a straight line and waves of contraction pass along the elaborate belly musculature from head to tail so that the ventral surface of the body moves forwards in a series of steps, the enlarged ventral scales being raised, carried forwards and then anchored on the ground. By cutting windows in the side of a snake's body, Bogert has shown that the ribs do not move even in this type of locomotion although some of the muscles which control the waves in the ventral scales are attached to them.

The speed with which snakes travel has been much exaggerated. Amongst dense vegetation they appear to slip away in a flash, but in the open even the fastest-moving species seem to be limited to about 6km/hr (4mph). A record of 11km/hr (7mph) is held by a mamba, however.

The internal organs

It is perhaps surprising that an animal like a slow worm or a snake should preserve so much of the usual arrangement of the vertebrate organs tucked away in its long flexible body. We find, however, that in these creatures most of the paired viscera have become asymmetrical, being reduced on one side, for example the lungs, or else lying at rather different levels in the body; while the intestine is less coiled than it is in animals of more usual proportions. Bergman has written a series of articles on the relative lengths and positions of the viscera in different kinds of snakes (see Bergman, 1962), while Bragdon (1953) has shown that the organs in any species have a constant relationship to the belly scales. Counting these scales down the body may therefore guide one to a particular organ on which it is desired to operate for experimental purposes.

In most snakes the neck seems, so far as can be ascertained in the absence of a shoulder girdle, to be very long, for the heart may lie about one-third of the way down the body. In limbless lizards it is usually much nearer the head. Elongation of the neck is associated with asymmetry of the carotid arteries. In most snakes the right common carotid is tiny and the blood to the head is carried in the left vessel, which after arising from the right aortic arch runs up the neck alongside the trachea as far as the back of the head. Here it divides into left internal and external branches and also sends one or more branches across the midline from which the right external and internal carotids are derived. In the more primitive snakes such as the pythons and boas, however, the right common carotid may persist.

In snake-like lizards, apart from amphisbaenians (p. 173), and in snakes, the left lung is reduced. In the more primitive forms it is still a sizeable organ but in the majority it is rudimentary. The right lung, however, is very long and sometimes extends down to the cloaca, as in sea snakes where it must have a hydrostatic function. Its back part is a simple air-sac and contains no alveoli. The glottis (p. 45) of snakes can be pushed forward to the front of the mouth and the trachea of some species (e.g. vipers) has taken on the structure and function of a lung; both the protrusible glottis and the tracheal lung seem to be adaptations to the mode of feeding, and may help a snake to breathe when its mouth or gullet is blocked by prey. In some lizards the lining of the pharynx acts as an accessory organ of respiration. The oesophagus of snakes is highly distensible; it may have to accommodate a part of a large victim while the rest is being digested in the stomach. In the larger snakes a big meal may take a week or more to be digested completely. Faeces are usually passed after each meal.

The eyes

The eyes of lizards are of the usual reptilian pattern (p. 34; Fig. 23A), except in specialized burrowers such as the amphisbaenids, where they are degenerate and may lack lack scleral bones eye muscles or even a lens. Most Squamata are keen-sighted, though they perceive moving objects much more readily than static ones. Binocular vision is especially well developed in monitor lizards, and in tree snakes such as *Ahaetulla* (Fig. 22B), where the face is grooved in front of each eye to increase the overlap of the visual fields. In the chameleons the bulging eyes can be swivelled round independently, giving the animal a very wide range of monocular vision. Once the prey has been located both eyes converge upon it and it is held under binocular vision while the chameleon stalks it and gets it within striking range of his tongue. The eyelids of these beasts are of a peculiar design, forming a complete ring round the front of the eyeball with a small circular opening in the centre.

Partly nocturnal Squamata usually have slit pupils, and in geckos the edges of the slit are often serrated (Fig. 23C). When the pupil is completely closed the apposed notches form a series of pinhole apertures each of which forms a sharp image, and the images formed by all of them are superimposed on the retina (Walls, 1942).

In quite a number of lizards, for example in most geckos, the eyes are covered by a transparent spectacle and the nictitating membrane is absent; in other lizards, including certain skinks and *Lanthanotus*, the lower eyelid contains a transparent window. In snakes a spectacle is always present, and this is responsible for the lidless glassy stare for which these creatures are renowned. Embryological studies show that the ophidian spectacle is developed from the fusion of the eyelid primordia and not from the nictitating membrane which seems to have disappeared entirely.

The spectacle seems to be an adaptation to life near the ground, eliminating the necessity for blinking when the delicate cornea is threatened by abrasive sand particles or brushing vegetation. Its outer layers are shed when the skin is cast.

In most snakes there is only a single eye gland (p. 36), the Harderian, which is always quite big, and in small-eyed types relatively enormous. It usually discharges, not directly into the conjunctival space as in lizards, but into the upper end of the tear duct which has only a single opening into the eye. In all Squamata the front end of the tear duct opens into the duct of Jacobson's organ (p. 207), or into a groove on the palate nearby; probably some of the eye gland secretions which the tear duct carries enter the organ and it is possible that they are in some way concerned in its function.

The eyes of snakes (Fig. 23B) differ from those of lizards far more than might be expected. The sclera lacks cartilage and bone, and the eye muscles are simplified, the retractor bulbi being absent and the levator bulbi (p. 36) apparently being transformed into a couple of extra jaw muscles, the retractors of the pterygoid and vomer. The muscles of accommodation are of a peculiar type and adjustment for close vision is brought about by the lens being pushed forwards, instead of by being pressed from its edges into a more spherical shape. The yellow oil droplets which diurnal lizards have in their retinal cones, and which reduce chromatic aberration by filtering off light at the blue end of the spectrum, are absent, but instead the lens itself often has a yellow colour and acts as a filter. Rods and cones of various types occur in the retina, but among them a unique type of double cone, quite different from anything in lizards, is often found in diurnal snakes.

These and other less striking peculiarities render the snake's eye a compound of oddities, impossible to derive from the condition of the eye in any known surface-living lizard. Walls (1942) has argued with great skill that the typical ophidian eye has been built up from the remnants of a degenerate, or at least simplified organ, in which structures such as the scleral skeleton had been lost, while in the rebuilding process some new ones, like the unique double cones, have appeared. His views are generally supported by the more recent work of Underwood (in Gans *et al.*, 1970, v.2). The evolutionary implications of his findings have been discussed in Chapter 11.

The ear

In many lizards the eardrum is rudimentary or absent and in some the middle ear cavity has disappeared. Degeneration of the ear is common in burrowing forms, but has also taken place in some surface-living lizards which might be expected to need good hearing. In all snakes a similar process has taken place, and in these reptiles the outer end of the stapes is applied to the quadrate. It has been supposed that the snakes and 'earless' lizards are practically insensitive to airborne sounds unless these are sufficiently loud to be conducted by the skull bones; the snake-charmer's cobra probably sways to the movement of his hands, not to the music of his pipe. Snakes are certainly sensitive to ground vibrations transmitted to the quadrate and stapes through the bones of the lower jaw and in this way they may take warning at the approaching footfall. There is evidence, however, that the inner ear of snakes responds electrically to airborne sounds as well as earthborne vibrations and are quite sensitive to a limited range of sounds of low wave-length (100–500Hz) (Wever and Vernon, 1960). It is not known what part, if any, such responses play in their normal behaviour.

The organ of Jacobson and the tongue

The paired (vomeronasal) organs of Jacobson are important in the lives of most Squamata, and the fact that they are so large and elaborate may be one of the reasons for the success of these animals. Each organ is a hollow domed structure situated beneath the nose and above the palate near the front of the snout (Fig. 23F). A large mushroom-shaped body projects into its cavity from below, and the cavity continues down into a duct which opens on to the roof of the mouth on one side of the midline. The dorsal dome is lined by sensory epithelium very similar to that which covers the olfactory part of the nose, and it receives a rich nerve supply from branches of the vomeronasal nerve which run back into the well developed accessory olfactory bulb (see T. S. Parsons, in Gans *et al.*, 1970, v.2).

There is much evidence that the organ serves to 'smell' odorous particles which are picked up from the air or ground on the tongue and that these particles are wafted up into its cavity by ciliary action, or perhaps in some species with forked tongues introduced directly into it. Noble (1937) and other workers have performed various experiments in which the organ of Jacobson was put out of action by such methods as amputating the tongue tips and compared the responses of these animals with those of others which had been blindfolded or had their nostrils plugged. Their results show that the vomeronasal apparatus is involved in many different aspects of behaviour: in following trails left by prey and potential mates; in sex recognition and courtship; in joining other members of the same species prior to hibernation (p. 215); and in enabling certain lizards to return to their own nests during the brooding period (p. 213). Noble's experiments show that the ordinary sense of smell is important in many forms as well. Both the sensory areas of the nose and the organ of Jacobson tend to be reduced in arboreal lizards such as *Anolis*; however it is interesting that in monitors and in the majority of sea snakes the nasal sense areas are also small, but the organs of Jacobson are well developed (H. Saint Girons, personal communication).

In the majority of Squamata the tongue tip is forked, though the extent of the bifurcation varies greatly, being very deep in monitor lizards and all snakes, and very slight (just a notch) in geckos. Although the organ may retain the function of taste, there is little doubt that its shape and its flickering movements, so characteristic of the monitors and snakes, are related to the role of Jacobson's organ. In the snakes there is often a notch beneath the tip of the upper jaw through which the tongue can be protruded without opening the mouth. It is retracted by muscles attached to the hyoid skeleton into a kind of sheath which extends back into the neck beneath the trachea. Tongue structure in Squamata has been studied by McDowell (1972).

In the chameleons the tongue has become specialized along different lines; the organ of Jacobson is vestigial, and the tongue is used for seizing insects which adhere to its sticky knob-like tip. The mechanism by which the tongue can be shot out of the mouth has been described by Gans (1967); its basis is essentially muscular and it does not involve a penis-like engorgement of the organ with blood or lymph as is sometimes stated. The chameleon's tongue is hollow and when it is retracted a spike-like projection from the hyoid skeleton, the processus entoglossus, fits into the whole length of its cavity. Just before the act of projection the tongue is pulled forward to the front of the mouth by extrinsic muscles. Then its intrinsic muscles, a powerful sleeve-like accelerator muscle which surrounds the tip and longitudinal hyoglossus muscle which run along its sides, contract simultaneously. Since the action of these muscles is antagonistic the tongue goes into a momentary state of spasm; suddenly the hyoglossi relax and the unopposed action of the sleeve muscle shoots the tip forwards off the slippery spike of the processus entoglossus at its target (Fig. 23H). The strain of the shot is taken by elastic fibres which run from the tip of the processus to the lining of the tongue cavity. The tongue is finally retracted by the hyoglossi and its stalk bunches up in concertina fashion.

The sensory pits

Pythons and some boas have a series of pits in the labial scales along the margins of the jaws; in rattlesnakes and other pit-vipers a rather similar pit (but divided into two chambers by a thin membrane) is found between the eye and nostril on each side of the head (Fig. 22H). These pits receive a rich nerve supply from branches of the trigeminal nerve. They are exceedingly sensitive to infra-red radiations and act as heat receptors, enabling these partly nocturnal snakes to locate and attack warm-blooded prey in the dark. The boa constrictor does not possess sensory pits, but is nevertheless provided with a heat sensitive mechanism associated with the labial scales and trigeminal nerve. A response can be recorded from the boa's brain within 35 milliseconds after the animal has been exposed to a brief pulse of infra-red radiation; the mechanism is activated by as little heat energy as 0.00002 cals per sq cm (Gamow and Harris, 1973).

Social and territorial behaviour

The social behaviour of lizards has proved a particularly interesting field for study. These reptiles often have more or less

H

defined home ranges, areas which they habitually frequent, such as a particular rock or tree-stump. During the breeding season this awareness of space becomes intensified and the males of many species appropriate territories for themselves and for their females (one or more in number) from which invading males are driven off. Some fighting between the females may also sometimes occur. Such territories differ from home ranges in that they are defended whereas the latter are not. Under some circumstances, especially when space is limited, as when a number of animals are kept together in captivity, a hierarchy of dominance may be established. In some cases one male will become a 'despot', claiming the only available territory and doing most of the courting of the females (C. C. Carpenter in Milstead, 1967).

Territorial behaviour of this kind is, of course, widespread among vertebrates and may well be important in man, as Robert Ardrey and others have argued. Its main function is probably to prevent overcrowding and to assist in the dispersal of the species over a wide area; it may also have some more subtle role in strengthening the sexual bond between male and female.

Harris (1964) has given a fascinating account of the social life of the rainbow lizard, *Agama agama* in West Africa. The male threatens any rival who encroaches on his territory, expanding his dorsal crest and the fold of skin beneath his throat, changing colour and raising his head and fore-quarters in a characteristic fashion which suggests the gymnastic exercise known as 'press-ups' (Fig. 20E). Fighting, mainly by lashing with the tail, may then take place and continue until one of the contestants runs away, leaving the territory and females to the victor. Females and young are not challenged by the males, and a female will sometimes posture in front of a male with her tail raised in the air; this is generally followed by mating. Other gestures such as bobbing of the head are also employed by both sexes in various social situations. Experiments with painted models show that sex recognition in *Agama* is accomplished almost entirely by sight and depends to a large extent on colour, the males being brighter-hued and bigger than their mates.

Territorial fighting between male lizards often has a somewhat ritualistic character; the formidable teeth are seldom used and the vanquished animal is unlikely to suffer serious injury. This principle is well illustrated by the duels of the male Galapagos iguana, which have been compared with the jousts of medieval knights (see Thornton, 1971). Rival males will first challenge each other by opening their mouths, nodding their heads and strutting with elevated bodies and dorsal crests. They then lower their heavily armoured heads and clash them together, each pushing the other until one is toppled over. The vanquished lizard may then retreat at once, or alternatively adopt a posture of submission, lying limp and flat on the ground with his limbs outstretched; he is then allowed to flee unmolested. On the other hand, a male who wanders accidentally into a territory which another is patrolling and omits to give the proper formalities of challenge is attacked much more viciously by biting, and is driven away without ceremony. Females also joust in competition for the relatively scarce nesting sites—places where the ground is soft enough to dig a hole in which the only two eggs laid each season can be deposited.

Carpenter (see Milstead, 1967), who has made many studies of aggression and social behaviour among iguanids, found that baby lizards with their yolk-sacs still attached will perform 'press-up' display within minutes of hatching—long before sexual or territorial behaviour develops. His time-and-motion analyses, based partly on cinematography, have revealed that some of the finer points of adult display patterns are specific to each species. He found that each of the seven species of lava lizards (*Tropidurus*) on the Galapagos has a distinct pattern; only one species is found on any one island. It is possible that in other less isolated kinds of lizards, small differences in the display pattern may act as cues which enable different but related species to distinguish between each other in geographical areas where their ranges overlap.

Such elaborate types of social behaviour are particularly striking in agamid and iguanid lizards, and are probably also manifest in chameleons. These three families are related and comprise the infraorder Iguania; they are all characterized by visual dominance, diurnal habits, marked sexual dimorphism and powers of colour change. The geckos, a very different group, may well also prove to show interesting patterns of community life, but as yet have hardly been investigated. Social organization is less noticeable in most other lizards, although some are certainly territorial and many exhibit some form of male rivalry during the breeding season. For example, displays of threat and fights between male sand lizards (*Lacerta agilis*) have often been witnessed, the lizards shaking each other in their jaws and rolling over (Smith, 1973). A remarkable form of combat has been described in certain monitors, the two males rearing up and grappling each other with their fore-legs.

Although snakes may have home ranges they are not certainly known to stake out and defend special territories. In some species (e.g. vipers), however, the breeding males indulge in protracted combats in which the heads and front parts of the bodies are reared up, each snake trying to push his rival over (Fig. 24B). These performances were for a long time regarded as dances between male and female, but identification of the sexes has shown that this is probably never the case (see Bogert and Roth, 1966).

Mating and reproduction

The mating of lizards may be preceded by some form of courtship which may involve nodding or bobbing of the head, gestures characteristic of many agamid and iguanid species. The male ground gecko (*Coleonyx*) approaches the female with body low and tail weaving, pokes her with his snout and licks her (Pope, 1956). In other species mating may occur without preliminary formalities. The procedure for copulation appears to be essentially similar in most lizards. The male seizes the female by the flank or neck with his jaws. He then brings the rear of his body against that of the female and twists the base of his tail beneath her cloaca, when one of his hemipenes can be inserted.

In lizards (apart, no doubt, from specialized burrowers with reduced eyes) courtship seems to depend mainly on vision, whereas in snakes, where marked sexual differences in form or colour are usually less evident, smell, touch and the organ of Jacobson play the leading roles. This is a difference, incidentally, which might be expected if the snakes have arisen from burrowing ancestors.

Male snakes apparently trail the females by picking up with the nose or Jacobson's organ the scent left by secretions of the skin and perhaps those of the anal or cloacal glands. In the courtship of many species the male rubs his chin along the female's back, playing his tongue in and out. During the act of coitus, the two snakes often lie extended side by side, the tail of the male being coiled round that of the female so that the two cloacae are in apposition. The chin-rubbing procedure apparently stimulates special touch corpuscles in the skin of the lower jaw, and Noble has shown that these and other similar structures in the cloacal region have an important role in the final stages of court-ship.

Male lizards and snakes possess paired organs of intromission known as hemipenes which normally lie in the base of the tail behind the cloaca; in some species they produce a thickness of this region which betrays the sex of their owners. The organs are tubular and the inner surface of each is traversed by a deep groove for the conduction of the sperm, which begins in the cloaca near the opening of the vas deferens. The lining of the hemipenis is often pleated and in many snakes is armed with spines which help to anchor it in the oviduct. In some snakes such as the adder (Fig. 4B, p. 46) each hemipenis is forked at the tip; the appearance of the organ is important as a systematic character. In erection the organ is turned inside out and pro-truded from the cloaca, the mechanism depending in part on the action of propulsor and retractor muscles and in part on the engorgement of blood sinuses in the tissues of the hemipenis (Figs. 23G, H). Only one organ is inserted at a time, and the process of coitus may extend over several hours in snakes where the male sometimes finds it difficult to disengage and is dragged about by the female. The anatomy of the male genital organs of snakes is described by Dowling and Savage (1960).

The eggs of Squamata have shells which are usually parchment-like in consistency. They are composed of layers of thin fibres, the outermost ones being lightly calcified. Eggs are usually deposited in clutches, under stones, in holes which may be dug by the mother, or among rotting vegetation. Manure heaps are a favourite nesting place for the grass snake in England, while in the tropics some lizards such as the Nile monitor may nest in termite mounds which act as natural incubators.

In some species the eggs are brooded or guarded by the mother. Certain skinks of the genus *Eumeces*, for example, lay their eggs in nests underground and periodically come in to brood them; probably the eggs gain heat from the sun-warmed body of the parent. The female *E. obsoletus* turns her eggs daily and at hatching time pokes the eggs with her snout to stimulate the young to struggle free from the egg-coverings. She retains interest in the young for some days after hatching and even cleans them by licking with her tongue. Indian cobras may guard their eggs and it is said that the male takes his share of the duty. The female king cobra (*Ophiophagus hannah*) is the only snake known to build a nest out of vegetation, which she piles up with a loop of her body.

It is well known that female pythons brood their eggs in their coils and that in the Indian species (*Python molurus*), at least, there is a definite rise in the snake's body temperature. Spasmodic contractions of the coils are noticeable every few seconds and probably help to generate the additional heat.

A considerable number of lizards and snakes have adopted a viviparous (or as it is sometimes called, ovoviviparous) mode of reproduction. The egg-shell is greatly reduced or lost, and the membranous eggs are retained within the oviduct until the young are ready to emerge from them. Sometimes the young are born within their membranes and may remain there for a short period until they hatch. The distribution of viviparity often cuts across taxonomic boundaries, as for example in lizards of the families Scincidae and Lacertidae, and snakes of the families Boidae and Viperidae, where some species lay eggs and others are viviparous.

Viviparity may have certain advantages, for the unborn young are protected from the hazards of predator and climate by the defensive and locomotor powers of the mother; a pregnant reptile can incubate its eggs by basking and shield them from cold by retreating underground, and it is perhaps partly for this reason that species such as the adder and viviparous lizard are able to inhabit cold regions. There is little evidence that the young of lizards and snakes receive maternal care after birth; stories of adders and rattlesnakes swallowing their young to give them refuge are probably based on the appearance of viable foetuses within the ruptured body of a parent which had been killed by a blow.

Quite a number of viviparous reptiles have evolved some form of placenta, and this has been demonstrated in *Xantusia* and many skinks, and in snakes of various groups, including sea snakes. The placenta is formed by the application of the vascular chorio-allantois to the lining of the oviduct; sometimes these membranes are thrown into folds or villi which increase the area available for physiological exchange between the mother and the embryo. The thin covering of the yolk-sac may also participate in the formation of an additional or alternative placenta. Even when a placenta of some kind is present, however, the yolk generally, perhaps always, is the main source of embryonic nutrition.

The yolk sac may be broken off at hatching or birth, or retracted into the body cavity of the young, where it may provide a useful source of food during early post-natal life. In the embryo the stalk of the yolk-sac forms part of the umbilical cord which also passes to the chorio-allantois. The site of the cord attachment can often be seen in baby reptiles as a navel scar on the belly in front of the cloaca.

Hibernation and longevity

Some species of lizards and snakes are prone to hibernate gregariously if suitable shelter is available, although they do not always do so. From time to time clusters of slow worms and adders dug up in the winter are reported, and there are many accounts of rattlesnake dens in the USA. Group hibernation may have some value in terms of natural selection, for it ensures a good supply of breeding pairs in the early spring when the reptiles emerge from their retreat.

Longevity seems to vary greatly in different species. Among the lizards the record is probably held by a slow worm which lived for 54 years but some species have a life-span of a few years only. Pythons and certain other large snakes have lived for 25 years or more in captivity.

The skin and its appendages

The scales of the head are symmetrically arranged and in most forms are large; on the body they are usually small, though in the majority of snakes the ventrals are enlarged and correspond more or less with the number of the vertebrae. In snakes there is often a groove between the scales along the midline of the chin, and in some lizards there is a rather similar lateral groove or fold along the flank; presumably these in both cases allow for distension.

The form and arrangement of the scales varies considerably in the different families. The body scales may be smooth and overlapping as in many skinks, or they may form a mosaic of flat plates as in the gerrhosaurid lizards. In many snakes their surfaces are ornamented with tubercles and keels. Osteoderms (p. 20) are present beneath the head and/or body scales of many lizards (e.g. *Anguis*), where they form a complete, flexible bony sheath, but are not found in snakes. The system of naming and counting scales for identification purposes is described in the fine book the *British Amphibians and Reptiles* by Malcolm Smith (1973).

The skin is shed piecemeal by most lizards, and often in a single piece by snakes which rub away the old skin round the nose and after freeing the head creep out of it, leaving a reversed slough behind. Captive snakes must be provided with bricks or other rough objects to rub against while they are shedding their skins. Some time before shedding the colours of a snake become dull and the spectacle bluish so that vision is impaired. This clears up shortly before sloughing actually starts. At shedding time snakes seldom feed, but often enter the water, possibly to counteract excessive loss of moisture through the skin. Shedding often occurs several times each year.

The initiation of moulting is assisted by a special device for engorging the head veins, causing the head and eyes to swell with blood and stretch the epidermis. The histology of shedding is very interesting. It depends essentially on the ability of the epidermis of a lizard or snake to build up a new keratinised layer (known as the inner epidermal generation) beneath the old one (outer generation) while the latter still remains *in situ*. A cleavage zone then appears between them so that the old layer is shed, leaving the new one at the surface. The cycle is partly controlled by the thyroid gland, but is manifest in isolated pieces of epidermis in tissue culture; here, however, actual shedding does not take place. Important histological studies on the skin and skin-shedding cycle in reptiles have been made by Maderson and his collaborators (see Maderson, 1968; Maderson *et al.*, 1972).

The skin is furnished with a variety of appendages. In many snakes some of the scales bear special tubercles or pits which probably have a sensory function (see Underwood, 1967), while some lizards have sensory bristles projecting from certain scales (see Harris, 1963). In a few species of snakes poisonous skin glands have been demonstrated. Many lizards have a row of femoral pores, little blind tubes along the inner surface of the thighs, which become filled with cellular debris. They may have some sexual function, but this is uncertain (Cole, 1966).

Appendages of a very different type are the crests, horns and other excrescences with which many lizards and a few snakes are supplied. Among them are such structures as the throat fan of the male *Anolis* the beard of *Amphibolurus barbatus* and the frill of *Chlamydosaurus*, which seem to be devices for intimidating rivals or foes. Many lizards, particularly desert forms like *Moloch*, run to spines, presumably a deterrent to predators. Certain chameleons have one, two or three scaly 'horns' on the snout—incidentally the casqued appearance of the head in these lizards is mainly due to the bone structure and is not a mere thickening of the skin. In some vipers and rattlesnakes the head is also equipped with horns (Fig. 22H) above the eyes or on the snout. A few lizards and snakes have long appendages projecting from the tip of the snout. Such are present in the snakes *Ahaetulla nasuta* and *Langaha* (Fig. 22G), for instance, and in a water snake, *Erpeton tentaculatum,* there is a pair of tentacles on the front of the snout.

Perhaps the most interesting skin appendage of snakes is the crotaline rattle. This is composed of up to ten or more hollow horny segments, each consisting of three lobes with constrictions between them, which partly fit inside those of the segment behind (Fig. 22D). The terminal vertebrae of the spine in front of the rattle are fused together and form a core for the tail-tip or 'end-body' which is a region of active growth, adding a new segment to the rattle with each skin moult, perhaps three times a year. The rattle grows continuously by the addition of new segments throughout the life of the snake, but when it reaches a certain length it becomes broken short so that segment counts of ten or more are uncommon. In young snakes the rattle terminates in a button-like segment, which of course, eventually becomes broken off.

Contact between the loosely fitting, but securely articulated, segments of the rattle is responsible for the dry sinister sound

H*

produced when the tail is elevated and vibrated at a rate of 50 or more cycles per second. The rattle is only sounded voluntarily and presumably is a warning device, scaring away a potential aggressor and enabling the snake to save its venom for its prey. The structure of the rattle and the way in which new segments are added to it are described by Klauber (1972).

Colour and colour change

The colours of many reptiles lend themselves to concealment. Forest-living snakes like the boas, for instance, have a well marked disruptive pattern which breaks up the body outline and harmonizes with the leafy background. In some forms dark longitudinal bands run across the head including the iris, and disguise the otherwise conspicuous eye. The cutaneous fringes along the head and flanks of bark-living geckos are also devices for camouflage, and there are many other examples of this kind. There has been much discussion about the problem of warning coloration. This has been attributed to the venomous coral snakes (*Micrurus*) and the similar markings found in other harmless species which inhabit the same locality have been regarded as examples of mimicry. It is possible, however, that the red, black and yellow markings of these snakes, and of other reptiles such as heloderms, are really examples of disruptive coloration for concealment which have been acquired by parallel evolution in different forms. Mimicry in snakes is discussed by Gans and Latifi (1973).

Many lizards and a few snakes can change colour, the latter only to a very limited extent. The performance varies from a simple blanching and darkening seen in rattlesnakes, in the iguanid *Phyrnosoma* and in certain geckos, to the much more complicated changes shown by the anoles and chameleons.

The adaptive significance of reptilian colour change is not always obvious. Only in some circumstances may it serve the purpose of concealment, and one may see a green chameleon or anole on a brown background or vice versa. Under other conditions it appears to play some part in temperature regulation (p. 54), and under others again it comes into play when a lizard is alarmed or is threatening a rival. Generally speaking, however, colour responses seem to be mainly influenced by the intensity and wavelength of the light to which the animal is exposed, by its background and by the temperature. Changes in these conditions may impose a rhythmic dark and light phase alternation, such as that which follows the sequence of day and night.

At least four types of pigment cells are found among the lizards, but only in one of these, the melanophores, does the pigment seem to undergo active concentration and dispersal; colour change is therefore due to the optical effects of the shifting dark brown melanophore pigment seen through and against the pigment in the other chromatophore types. In general, the animal grows light when the pigment is concentrated and dark when it is dispersed.

Much work has been done on the means of control of the melanophores. Experiments involving section of the spinal cord and peripheral nerves show that in chameleons, and probably also in *Phrynosoma,* these cells are under nervous control, probably through the autonomic system. In *Phrynosoma,* hormones (p. 33), e.g. intermedine, secreted by the intermediate lobe of the pituitary gland, and adrenalin, also influence melanophore activity, the effect of intermedine being to darken the animal and that of adrenalin to blanch it. In *Anolis* the melanophores seem to be controlled entirely by intermedine and are not under the influence of the nervous system.

Although visual stimuli seem to be mainly responsible for initiating colour change, some other mechanism must sometimes operate as well. This is apparent from experiments on blinded lizards and can be demonstrated in the intact chameleon. If an area of its skin is shielded from light for a few minutes the outline of the shield will appear as a pale patch (see Carr, 1964). Such responses may be due to the reflex activity of special light receptors in the skin, or perhaps is the result of the melanophores themselves reacting directly to light. The problems of colour change in reptiles are very complicated, and the mechanisms may vary from one species to another. The subject is described in greater detail by Bellairs (1969).

Warning and defensive behaviour: 'fascination'

From time to time references have been made to various types of warning behaviour adopted by reptiles towards rivals or foes, such as the erection of throat fans and other appendages. These and other responses are discussed in a long paper by Mertens (1946) and some of them, not previously mentioned here, are of sufficient interest to deserve note.

When threatened or threatening, many reptiles inflate the body with air, an expedient which increases their apparent size and presumably gives them a more formidable appearance. Angry chameleons often behave in this manner, and it is a well known habit in puff adders and other snakes, which rid themselves of the excess air by expiring it in a powerful hiss. Sometimes only the throat is blown up, as in monitor lizards, and in certain snakes such as the boomslang. In the latter the effect is enhanced by the exposure of the skin between the stretched scales, which shows up in a vivid black and white check pattern. Such examples of 'flash colour change' occur in other Squamata, and this mechanism is responsible for the bright pink appearance of the extended throat fan of certain *Anolis* lizards. It is of course quite different from the kinds of physiological colour change previously described. Flattening of the neck is a warning gesture in many snakes and the cobra's hood, operated by elongated neck ribs, is an extreme development of this method.

Some snakes which do not normally bite will make passes at an aggressor with closed jaws. In the primitive snake *Cylindrophis* (Fig. 24A) the passes are made with the tail which is brought round and jerked menacingly while the head is hidden beneath the coils. The little horned toads (*Phrynosoma*) are able to eject a thin stream of blood from ruptured capillaries in the eyes for several feet when disturbed, the mechanism for this phenomenon being similar to that responsible for the venous engorgement of the head prior to skin-shedding.

When hard-pressed, certain lizards and snakes will sham dead, lying motionless with the belly upwards. This behaviour is common in the American hog-nosed snakes (*Heterodon*) and has been noticed in the English grass snake (*Natrix*). Another procedure followed by the monitors and some snakes such as the grass snake is to discharge the foul-smelling contents of a large pair of glands, the anal glands, which lie along the base of the tail and open into the cloaca. Although all snakes possess these glands, only a few use them in this way and their significance is rather puzzling. It has, of course, been suggested that their

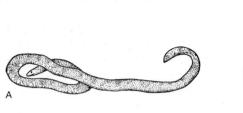

Fig. 24

A, the primitive snake *Cylindrophis* with tail in 'aggressive' posture;
after Mertens (1946). B, male rattlesnakes in ritual combat; per-
mission of San Diego Zoological Gardens.

secretions are concerned in courtship, but this has not been
certainly proved.

There are many observations in the literature which suggest
that accounts of snakes fascinating their prey may not always
be groundless. In certain tree snakes (e.g. *Thelotornis*) the
brightly coloured tongue apparently acts as a lure for lizards and
birds, the organ being waved about and its tips opened and closed.
It is probable that the coloured tail-tip of some pit-vipers may
act in the same way.

Enemies and exploitation by man

Although many lizards and snakes can defend themselves by
bluff or the more effective weapons of lashing tail, strong teeth or
venom, even the most powerful and dangerous species are beset
with enemies. Among these must be numbered others of their
own kind; monitor lizards, for example, eat many smaller
reptiles, and some snakes such as the king cobra and the non-
venomous king snakes (*Lampropeltis*) of America specialize in
eating other snakes, the king snakes sometimes attacking the
poisonous rattlesnakes. Many birds will kill small lizards and
snakes, and the African secretary bird, a kind of large cursorial
hawk, attacks large and dangerous snakes, beating them to death
with its powerful legs. Among mammals, pigs, hedgehogs and the
smaller Carnivora, especially the mongooses, often attack

snakes and lizards, but the main enemy of these creatures is of course man.

The skins of some species such as monitors and pythons make attractive leathers and the drain on them caused by the demands of the leather trade must be considerable. Iguanas, pythons and other forms are eaten in some parts of the world and there is a certain demand for the canned meat of rattlesnakes. Some lizards and snakes are kept as pets or used for scientific medical purposes, such as the study of venoms; snake venoms are occasionally used in the treatment of certain diseases, apart from their role in the preparation of antisera against snake bite (see Minton and Minton 1969).

The main human threat to these reptiles, as to many other animals, is from the destruction of their habitats by building and agricultural operations, especially in densely populated countries such as Britain. Here two of our native reptiles, the smooth snake (*Coronella austriaca*) and the beautiful sand lizard (*Lacerta agilis*) are seriously threatened and in urgent need of conservation. The effects of pollution and insecticides may also be important in some places, and road accidents are a special hazard to snakes in certain parts of America.

Snake-charming

Snakes, and to a lesser extent other kinds of reptiles, evoke in many people powerful emotions of fear mixed with fascination. These feelings, so well described by D. H. Lawrence in his famous poem in *Birds, beasts and flowers,* find expression in the part played by snakes in primitive religion, folklore and in the dream symbolism of the psychopathological literature. The general awe in which reptiles are held has, indeed, been capitalized by certain individuals in many communities. The schoolboy's pet grass snake may lend a certain kudos to its owner, and in countries such as India persons who are prepared to exhibit a public familiarity with venomous reptiles are assured of a living and even of a kind of professional status as snake-charmers.

At its best snake-charming is a risky and exacting art which involves the skilful taming of deadly snakes through continued and cautious handling. Too often, however, the performance is debased and only poisonous snakes bereft of their fangs, sometimes with seriously damaged jaws, are used. Snake-charmers usually carry a variety of snakes in their baskets and in addition to venomous species such as cobras, they often exhibit harmless types, especially those which are both spectacular and docile, such as the Indian python. The cobra is of course the *pièce de résistance* of the charmer's repertoire, since it obligingly rears up with erect hood and sways its head in an attempt to keep the charmer's moving hand within striking range. Although it is unwise to be dogmatic in view of recent work (see p. 207) it seems unlikely that the music of the snake-charmer's pipe has much effect on the snake's behaviour. Sometimes fights between a mongoose and a cobra are staged, but the thrifty charmer will often remove the mongoose and save his snake for another show before the combat reaches its conclusion.

In some parts of the world snakes feature in ritual dances practised by the natives. Among the best known of these are the summer snake dances of the Hopi Indians of northern Arizona who hold rattlesnakes in their hands and mouths during the performance and seldom if ever incur serious injury. The Indians claim that their snakes are not treated in any way, but evidence has accumulated that sometimes at least the fangs are removed or broken off; this was found to be the case by Bogert who succeeded in recovering one of the reptiles liberated by the snake-priests after the dance (Klauber, 1972). In their fascinating book *Men and Snakes* (1965), Ramona and Desmond Morris discuss the role of snakes in religious ceremony, and in various types of secular entertainment, from oriental snake-charming to occidental striptease. Their accounts of the snake-handling Christian sects of the twentieth century in rural parts of the USA are particularly interesting. During the 1940s (and perhaps more recently), members of 'The Dolley Pond Church of God with Signs Following', in Grasshopper Valley, Tennessee, bore witness to the Lord with copperheads and rattlesnakes held to their faces. The occurrence of accidents and the introduction of prohibitory legislation suggests that the venom apparatus of these reptiles had not been tampered with.

Bibliography

Subtitles of books are not given and the titles of some of the papers are abbreviated (as indicated by ...).

ATTRIDGE, J., and CHARIG, A. J. 1967. Crisis in evolution: the Stormberg series, *Sci. J.* **3**, 48–54.

AUFFENBERG, W. 1966. On the courtship of *Gopherus polyphemus*, *Herpetologica* **22**, 113–17.

AUFFENBERG, W. 1972. Komodo dragons. *Nat. Hist. N.Y.* **81**, 53–9.

AVERY, R. A. 1973. ...functional studies on the stomach of the lizard *Lacerta vivipara*, *J. Zool. Lond.* **169**, 157–67.

AXELROD, D. I., and BAILEY, H. P. 1968. Cretaceous dinosaur extinction, *Evolution* **22**, 595–611.

BAKKER, R. T. 1971. Ecology of the brontosaurs, *Nature, Lond.* **229**, 172–4.

BAKKER, R. T. 1972. ...endothermy in dinosaurs, *Nature, Lond.* **238**, 81–5.

BAKKER, R. T., and GALTON, P. M. 1974. Dinosaur monophyly and a new class of vertebrates, *Nature, London.* **248**, 168–72.

BALL, D., and BELLAIRS, A. D'A. 1972. Reptiles, in *UFAW* (Universities Federation for Animal Welfare) *Handbook on the care and management of laboratory animals*, Churchill, Livingstone, Edinburgh & London (4th ed.)

BELKIN, D. A. 1963. Anoxia: tolerance in reptiles, *Science, N.Y.* **139**, 492–3.

BELLAIRS, A. [D'A.] 1969. *The life of reptiles*, Weidenfeld & Nicolson, London, 2 vols.

BELLAIRS, A. [D'A.], and CARRINGTON, R. 1969. *The world of reptiles*, Chatto & Windus, London (2nd impr.).

BELLAIRS, R. 1971. *Developmental processes in higher vertebrates*, Logos Press, London.

BENEDICT, F. G. 1932. *The physiology of large reptiles*, Carnegie Institution, Washington.

BENTLEY, P. J. 1971. *Endocrines and osmoregulation*, Springer, Berlin, etc.

BERGMAN, R. A. M. 1962. Die Anatomie der Elapinae, *Z. wiss. Zool.* **167**, 291–337.

BOGERT, C. M. 1943. Dentitional phenomena in cobras..., *Bull. Am. Mus. nat. Hist.* **81**, 285–360.

BOGERT, C. M., and DEL CAMPO, R. M. 1956. The Gila monster and its allies..., *Bull. Am. Mus. nat. Hist.* **109**, 1–238.

BOGERT, C. M., and ROTH, V. D. 1966. Ritualistic combat of male gopher snakes, *Pituophis melanoleucus...*, *Am. Mus. Novit.* No. 2245, 1–27.

BOLTT, R. E., and EWER, R F. 1964. The functional anatomy of the head of the puff adder, *Bitis arietans*..., *J. Morph.* **114**, 83–106.

BOYCOTT, B. B., and GUILLERY, R. W. 1962. Olfactory and visual learning in the red-eared terrapin, *Pseudemys scripta*..., *J. exp. Biol.* **39**, 567–77.

BRADSHAW, S. D., and MAIN, A. R. 1968. Behavioural attitudes and regulation of temperature in *Amphibolurus* lizards, *J. Zool. Lond.* **154**, 193–221.

BRAGDON, D. E. 1953. ...surgical anatomy of the water snake, *Natrix sipedon*..., *Anat. Rec.* **117**, 145–61.

BRAMWELL, C. D. 1970, The first hot-blooded flappers, *Spectrum,* **69**, 12–14.

BRAMWELL, C. D., and FELLGETT, P. B. 1973. Thermal regulation in sail lizards, *Nature, Lond.* **242**, 203–5.

BRAMWELL, C. D. and WHITFIELD, G. R. 1974. Biomechanics of *Pteranodon, Phil. Trans. Roy. Soc. Lond. B.* **267**, 503–81.

BRYANT, S .V., and BELLAIRS, A. D'A. 1967. Tail regeneration in the lizards *Anguis fragilis* and *Lacerta dugesii, J. Linn. Soc. (Zool.),* **46**, 297–305.

BÜCHERL, W., BUCKLEY, E., and DEULOFEU, V. (Eds.). 1968–71. *Venomous animals and their venoms,* Academic Press, New York & London, 3 vols.

BUCKLEY, E. E., and PORGES, N. (Eds.). 1956. *Venoms,* Am. Ass. Adv. Sci., Washington.

BUSTARD, [H.] R. 1970. *Australian lizards,* Collins, London & Sydney.

BUSTARD, [H.] R. 1972. *Sea turtles,* Collins, London & Sydney.

BUSTARD, [H.] R. 1973. *Kay's turtles,* Collins, London & Sydney.

CARR, A. 1952. *Handbook of turtles,* Comstock, Ithaca; Constable, London.

CARR, A. 1964. *The reptiles,* Time-Life, (Nederland) N.V.

CARR, A. 1968. *The turtle,* Cassell, London.

CHARIG, A. J., ATTRIDGE, J., and CROMPTON, A. W. 1965. On the origin of the sauropods and the classification of the Saurischia, *Proc. Linn. Soc. Lond.* **176**, 197–221.

CLOUDSLEY-THOMPSON, J. L. 1971. *The temperature and water relations of reptiles,* Merrow, Watford.

CLOUDSLEY-THOMPSON, J. L. 1972. Temperature regulation in desert reptiles. *Symp. Zool. Soc. Lond.* No. 31, 39–59.

COLBERT, E. H. 1962. *Dinosaurs,* Hutchinson, London.

COLBERT, E. H. 1965. *The age of reptiles,* Weidenfeld & Nicolson, London.

COLBERT, E. H. 1968. *Men and dinosaurs,* Evans Bros., London.

COLBERT, E. H. 1970. The Triassic gliding reptile *Icarosarus, Bull. Am. Mus. nat. Hist.* **143**, 85–142.

COLBERT, E. H. 1973. *Wandering lands and animals,* Dutton, New York.

COLE, C. J. 1966. Femoral glands in lizards... *Herpetologica,* **22**, 199–206.

COOPER, J. S., and POOLE, D. F. G. 1973. The dentition...of the agamid lizard *Uromastyx, J. Zool. Lond.* **169**, 85–100.

COTT, H. B. 1961. ...the ecology...of the Nile crocodile..., *Trans. Zool. Soc. Lond.* **29**, 211–356.

COULSON, R. A., and HERNANDEZ, T. 1964. *Biochemistry of the alligator,* Louisiana State University Press, Baton Rouge.

COX, C. B. 1969. The problematic Permian reptile *Eunotosaurus, Bull. Brit. Mus. nat. Hist., Geol.* **18**, 167–96.

COX, [C.] B. 1969. *Prehistoric animals,* Hamlyn, London.

CROMPTON, A. W. 1963. The evolution of the mammalian jaw. *Evolution,* 17, 431–9.

CROMPTON, A. W. and CHARIG, A. J. 1962. A new ornithischian from the Upper Triassic of South Africa, *Nature, Lond.* 196, 1074–7.

CROMPTON, A. W., and JENKINS, F. A. 1968. Molar occlusion in late Triassic mammals, *Biol. Rev.* 43, 427–58.

CROMPTON, A. W., and JENKINS, F. A. 1973. Mammals from reptiles; a review of mammalian origins, *Annual Reviews of Earth and Planetary Sciences,* 131–55.

CUELLAR, O. 1966. Oviducal anatomy and sperm storage structures in lizards. *J. Morph.* 119, 7–20.

CUELLAR, O., and KLUGE, A. G. 1972. Natural parthenogenesis in the gekkonid lizard *Lepidodactylus lugubris, J. Genetics,* 61, 14–26.

DAREVSKI, I. S. 1966. Natural parthenogenesis in a polymorphic group of Caucasian rock lizards..., *J. Ohio herpet. Soc.* 5, 115–52.

DARLINGTON, P. J. 1948. The geographical distribution of cold-blooded vertebrates, *Quart. Rev. Biol.* 23, 1–26 & 105–23.

DAWBIN, W. H. 1962. The tuatara in its natural habitat, *Endeavour,* 21, 16–24.

DE BEER, G. [R.] 1954. *Archaeopteryx lithographica.* Brit. Mus. (Nat. Hist.), London.

DERANIYAGALA, P. E. P. 1939. *The tetrapod reptiles of Ceylon,* Dulau, London.

DOWLING, H. G., and SAVAGE, J. M. 1960. A guide to the snake hemipenis... *Zoologica, N.Y.* 45, 17–28.

EDINGER, L. 1908. *Vergleichende Anatomie des Gehirns,* Vogel, Leipzig.

ESTES, R., FRAZZETTA, T. H., and WILLIAMS, E. E. 1970. Studies on the fossil snake *Dinilysia...Bull. Mus. Comp. Zool. Harvard,* 140, 25–74.

ETHERIDGE, R. 1967. Lizard caudal vertebrae, *Copeia,* 699–721.

EWER, R. F. 1965. The anatomy of the thecodont reptile *Euparkeria...,* *Phil. Trans. Roy. Soc. Lond.* B. 248, 379–435.

FITCH, H. S. 1963. Natural history of the racer *Coluber constrictor, Univ. Kansas Publ. Mus. nat. Hist.* 15, 351–468.

FITCH, H. S. 1970. Reproductive cycles in lizards and snakes. *Univ. Kansas Publ. Mus. nat. Hist. Misc. Publ.* No. 52, 1–247.

FOXON, G. E. H., GRIFFITH, J. and PRICE, M. 1956. The mode of action of the heart of the green lizard, *Lacerta viridis. Proc. Zool. Soc. London.* 126, 145–57.

FRAIR, W., ACKMAN, R. G., and MROSOVSKY, N. 1972. Body temperature of *Dermochelys coriacea:* warm turtle from cold water, *Science, N.Y.* 177, 791–3.

FRAZZETTA, T. H. 1966. Studies on...the skull in the Boidae..., *J. Morph.* 118, 217–96.

FRAZZETTA, T. H. 1968. Adaptive problems...in the temporal fenestration of tetrapod skulls, *J. Morph.* 125, 145–58.

GABE, M., and SAINT GIRONS, H. 1964. *Histologie de* Sphenodon punctatus, Centre National de la Recherche Scientifique, Paris.

GALTON, P. M. 1970. Ornithischian dinosaurs and the origin of birds, *Evolution,* 24, 448–62.

GALTON, P. M. 1971. *Hypsilophodon,* the cursorial non-arboreal dinosaur, *Nature, Lond.* 231, 159–61.

GAMOW, R. I., and HARRIS, J. F. 1973. The infra-red receptors of snakes, *Sci. American,* **228,** 94–100.

GANS, C. 1952. The functional morphology of the egg-eating adaptations in the snake genus *Dasypeltis, Zoologica, N.Y.* **37,** 209–44.

GANS, C. 1960. Studies on amphisbaenids..., *Bull. Am. Mus. nat. Hist.* **119,** 129–204.

GANS, C. 1966. Locomotion without limbs, *Nat. Hist. N.Y.* **75,** 2, 10–17; No. 3, 36–41.

GANS, C. 1967. The chameleon, *Nat. Hist. N.Y.* **76,** 4, 52–9.

GANS, C. 1969. Amphisbaenians..., *Endeavour,* **28,** 146–51.

GANS, C. 1970. ...evolution of the external gas exchangers of ectothermal vertebrates, *Forma et Functio,* **3,** 61–104.

GANS, C. 1973. Uropeltid snakes—survivors in a changing world, *Endeavour* **32,** 60–5.

GANS, C., and ELLIOTT, W. B. 1968. Snake venoms: production, injection action, *Adv. oral. Biol.* **3,** 43–80.

GANS, C., and LATIFI, M. 1973. Another case of presumptive mimicry in snakes, *Copeia,* 801–2.

GANS, C., (BELLAIRS, A. D'A., v. **1** only), and PARSONS, T. S. (Eds.). v. **1** (1969); v. **2** & **3** (1970); v. **4** (1973). *Biology of the Reptilia,* Academic Press, London & New York. This important publication containing articles by various authors is referred to in the text as Gans *et al.* Further volumes are expected.

GASC, J. P. 1970. Reflexions sur le concept de 'régression' des organes, *Rev. des questions scientifiques,* **141,** 175–95.

GASC, J. P. 1974. L'interprétation fonctionelle de l'appareil musculo-squelettique de l'axe vertébral chez les serpents (Reptilia), *Mém. Mus. nat. d'Hist. naturelle, A,* **83,** 1–182.

GEORGE, J. C., and SHAH, R. V. 1965. Evolution of air sacs in Sauropsida, *J. Anim. Morph. Physiol.* **12,** 255–63.

GINGERICH, P. D. 1973. Skull of *Hesperornis* and early evolution of birds, *Nature, Lond.* **243,** 70–73.

GOIN, C. J., and GOIN, O. B. 1971. *Introduction to herpetology* (2nd Ed.), W. H. Freeman, San Francisco & London.

GOLDBY, F., and GAMBLE, H. J. 1957. The reptilian cerebral hemispheres, *Biol. Rev.* **32,** 383–420.

GRASSÉ, P. P. 1970. *Traité de Zoologie,* v. **14,** fasc. 2 & 3, Masson, Paris. Contains articles by various authors.

GRAY, J. 1968. *Animal locomotion,* Weidenfeld & Nicolson, London.

GREGORY, W. K. 1951. *Evolution emerging,* Macmillan, New York (2 vols.).

GRUBB, P. 1971. The growth, ecology and population structure of giant tortoises on Aldabra, *Phil. Trans. Roy. Soc. Lond. B.* **260,** 327–72.

GUGGISBERG, C. A. W. 1972. *Crocodiles,* David & Charles, Newton Abbot.

GUIBÉ, J. 1949. Revision du genre *Langaha..., Mem. Inst. Sci. Madagascar,* **3,** 147–55.

HAINES, R. W. 1952. The shoulder joint of lizards and the primitive reptilian shoulder mechanism, *J. Anat.* **86,** 412–22.

HARRIS, V. A. 1963 *The anatomy of the rainbow lizard* Agama agama (L.), Hutchinson, London.

HARRIS, V. A. 1964. *The life of the rainbow lizard,* Hutchinson, London.

HEILMANN, G. 1926. *The origin of birds,* Witherby, London.

HENDRICKSON, J. R. 1958. The green sea turtle *Chelonia mydas* (Linn.) in Malaya and Sarawak *Proc. Zool. Soc. Lond.* **130**, 455–535.

HOPSON, J. A. 1969. The origin and adaptive radiations of mammal-like reptiles and nontherian mammals *Ann. N.Y. Acad, Sci.* **167**, 199–216.

HOPSON, J. A. 1973. Endothermy, small size and the origin of mammalian reproduction, *Amer. Nat.* **107**, 446–52.

HUGHES, G. M. 1965. *Comparative physiology of vertebrate respiration,* Heinemann, London.

JOFFE, J. 1967. The 'dwarf' crocodiles of the Purbeck formation..., *Palaeontology,* **10**, 629–39.

JOYSEY, K. A., and KEMP, T. S. 1972. *Studies in vertebrate evolution,* Oliver & Boyd, Edinburgh.

KERMACK, D. M., and KERMACK, K. A. Eds. 1971. Early mammals, *Suppl. l, Zool. J. Linn. Soc.* **50**. [A symposium.]

KLAUBER, L. M. 1972. *Rattlesnakes,* University of California Press, Berkeley & Los Angeles. (2 vols.) (2nd ed.)

KLUGE, A. G. 1967. Higher taxonomic categories of gekkonid lizards..., *Bull. Am. Mus. nat. Hist.* **135**, 1–59.

KURTÉN, B. 1968. *The age of the dinosaurs,* Weidenfeld & Nicolson, London.

LICHT, P., HOYER, H. E., and VAN OORDT, P. G. W. J. 1969. Influence of photoperiod and temperature on testicular recrudescence and body growth in the lizards *Lacerta sicula* and *Lacerta muralis, J. Zool. Lond.* **157**, 469–501.

LOWE, P. R. 1928. ...observations bearing on the phylogeny of the ostrich, *Proc. zool. Soc. Lond.* 185–247.

LULL, R. S. 1947. *Organic evolution,* Macmillan, New York (rev. ed.)

MCDOWELL, S. B. 1972. The evolution of the tongue of snakes, in *Evolutionary Biology* (Eds. T. Dobzhansky *et al.*), Appleton-Century-Crofts, New York. vol. 6.

MCDOWELL, S. B., and BOGERT, C. M. 1954. The systematic position of *Lanthanotus...*, *Bull. Am. Mus. nat. Hist.* **105**, 1–142.

MCGOWAN, C. 1973. The cranial morphology of...ichthyosaurs..., *Bull. Br. Mus. nat. Hist. Geol.* **24**, 1–109.

MADERSON, P. F. A. 1966. ...observations on the foot-pads of the tokay (*Gekko gecko), Mem. Hong. Kong. nat. Hist. Soc.* No. 7, 6–10.

MADERSON, P. F .A. 1968. Observations on the epidermis of the tuatara, *J. Anat.* **103**, 311–20.

MADERSON, P. F. A., FLAXMAN, B. A., ROTH, S. I., and SZABO, G. 1972. Ultrastructural contributions to the identification of cell types in the lizard epidermal generation, *J. Morph.* **136**, 191–210.

MARSHALL, A. J. (Ed.) 1960. *Biology and comparative physiology of birds,* Academic Press, New York & London. vol. 1.

MERTENS, R. 1946. Die Warn- und Droh-Reaktionen der Reptilien, *Abh. Senckenb. naturf. Ges.,* No. 471, 1–88.

MERTENS, R. 1960. *The world of amphibians and reptiles,* Harrap, London.

MILSTEAD, W. W. (Ed.) 1967. *Lizard ecology. A symposium,* University of Missouri Press, Columbia.

MINER, R. W. 1925. The pectoral limb of *Eryops...*, *Bull. Am. Mus. nat. Hist.* **51**, 145–312.

MINTON, S. A. (Ed.) 1971. *Snake venoms and envenomation,* Marcel Dekker Inc., New York.

MINTON, S. A., and MINTON, M. R. 1969. *Venomous reptiles,* Scribners, New York.

MOLL, E. O., and LEGLER, J. M. 1971. The life history of a ... turtle *Pseudemys scripta...*, *Bull. Los Angeles Co. Mus. nat. Hist. Sci.* No. 11, 1–102.

MORRIS, R., and MORRIS, D. 1965. *Men and snakes,* Hutchinson, London.

MROSOVSKY, N. 1972. The water-finding ability of sea turtles, *Brain, Behaviour and Evolution,* **5,** 202–25.

NEILL, W. T. 1971. *The last of the ruling reptiles,* Columbia University Press.

NOBLE, G. K. 1937. The sense organs involved in the courtship of...snakes, *Bull. Am. Mus. nat. Hist.* **73,** 673–725.

OELRICH, T. M. 1956. The anatomy of the head of *Ctenosaura pectinata* (Iguanidae), *Misc. Publs. Mus. Zool. Univ. Michigan,* No. 94, 1–122.

OLIVER, J. A. 1955. *The natural history of North American amphibians and reptiles,* Van Nostrand, Princeton, etc.

OSBORN, J. W. 1973. The evolution of dentitions, *Am. Sci.* **61,** 548–59.

OSTROM, J. H. 1962. The cranial crests of hadrosaurian dinosaurs, *Postilla,* No. 62, 1–29.

OSTROM, J. H. 1964. A reconsideration of the paleoecology of hadrosaurian dinosaurs, *Am. J. Sci,* **262,** 975–97.

OSTROM, J. H. 1966. Functional morphology and evolution of the ceratopsian dinosaurs. *Evolution,* **20,** 290–308.

OSTROM, J. H. 1973. The ancestry of birds, *Nature, Lond.* 242, 136.

OSTROM, J. H. 1974. *Archaeopteryx* and the origin of flight, *Qu. Rev. Biol.* **49,** 27–47.

PARKER, H. W. 1965. *Snakes,* R. Hale, London.

PARKER, W. K. 1885. On the skull...in the Mammalia. *Phil. Trans. Roy. Soc. Lond.* **176,** 1–275.

PARRINGTON, F. R. 1958. The problem of the classification of reptiles, *J. Linn. Soc. (Zool.),* **44,** (*Bot.*), **56:** 99–115.

PARRINGTON, F. R. 1971. On the Upper Triassic mammals, *Phil. Trans. Roy. Soc. Lond. B.* **261,** 231–72.

PARRINGTON, F. R., and WESTOLL, T. S. 1940. The evolution of the mammalian palate, *Phil. Trans. Roy. Soc. Lond. B.* **230,** 305–55.

PHISALIX, M. 1922. *Animaux venimeux et venins,* Masson, Paris.

POPE, C. H. 1956. *The reptile world,* Routledge & Kegan Paul, London.

POPE, C. H. 1958. Fatal bite of...(*Dispholidus*), *Copeia,* 280–2.

POPE, C. H. 1962. *The giant snakes,* Routledge & Kegan Paul, London.

PORTER, K. R. 1972. *Herpetology,* Saunders, Philadelphia, London, etc.

PRESTT, I. 1971. An ecological study of the viper *Vipera berus* in southern Britain, *J. Zool. Lond.* **164,** 373–418.

PRITCHARD, P. C. H. 1967. *Living turtles of the world,* T.F.H. Publications, Jersey City, New Jersey.

RAO, M. K. M., and RAMASWAMI, K. S. 1952. The...chondrocranium of *Mabuya...*, *Acta Zool.* **33,** 209–75.

RAYNAUD, A. 1972. Morphogenèse des membres rudimentaires chez les reptiles..., *Bull. Soc. Zool. France,* **97,** 469–85.

REICHENBACH-KLINKE, H.-H., and ELKAN, E. 1965. *The principal diseases of lower vertebrates,* Academic Press, London & New York.

ROBINSON, P. L. 1973. A problematic reptile from the British Upper Trias, *J. Geol. Soc.* **129,** 457–79.

ROMER, A. S. 1946. The primitive reptile *Limnoscelis* re-studied, *Amer. J. Sci.* **244,** 149–88.

ROMER, A. S. 1956. *Osteology of the reptiles,* University of Chicago Press.

ROMER, A. S. 1966. *Vertebrate paleontology*, University of Chicago Press (3rd ed.). See also *Notes and comments on* Vertebrate Paleontology (1968), Chicago (a supplementary volume).

ROMER, A. S. 1968. An ichthyosaur skull from the Cretaceous of Wyoming, *Contr. Geol. Univ. Wyoming*, **7**, 27–41.

ROMER, A. S. 1970. *The vertebrate body*, Saunders, Philadelphia & London.

ROMER, A. S. 1973. The Chanares (Argentina) Triassic reptile fauna, XVIII, ...*Breviora*, No. 401, 1–4.

RUIBAL, R., and ERNST, V. 1965. The structure of the digital setae in lizards, *J. Morph.* **117**, 271–93.

RUSSELL, F. E., and SCHARFFENBERG, R. S. 1964. *Bibliography of snake venoms and venomous snakes*, Bibliographical Associates Inc., Covina, California.

SAINT GIRONS, H. 1971. ...rhythme circadien...chez les lépidosauriens ..., *Bull. Soc. Zool. France*, **96**, 317–30.

SAINT GIRONS, H., and PFEFFER, P. 1971. Le cycle sexuel des serpents du Cambodge, *Ann. Sci.. Nat.* **13**, 543–71.

SAUNDERS, J. T., and MANTON, S. M. 1972. *Practical vertebrate morphology*, Clarendon Press, Oxford (4th ed.).

SCHMIDT, K. P., and INGER, R. F. 1957. *Living reptiles of the world*, Hamish Hamilton, London.

SENN, D. G., and NORTHCUTT, R. G. 1973. The forebrain and midbrain of some squamates..., *J. Morph.* **140**, 135–52.

SHARELL, R. 1966. *The tuatara, lizards and frogs of New Zealand*, Collins, London.

SHEPPARD, L., and BELLAIRS, A. D'A. 1972. The mechanism of autotomy in *Lacerta, Br. J. Herpetology*, **4**, 276–86.

SMITH, H. M. 1946. *Handbook of lizards*. Comstock, Ithaca, New York.

SMITH, J. M. 1962. The importance of the nervous system in the evolution of animal flight, *Evolution*, **6**, 127–9.

SMITH, M. [A.] 1973. The British amphibians and reptiles, Collins, London (5th ed.).

SNYDER, R. C. 1949. Bipedal locomotion of...*Basiliscus, Copeia*, 129–37.

SNYDER, R. C. 1962. Adaptations for bipedal locomotion of lizards, *Am. Zool.* **2**, 191–203.

SPELLERBERG, I. F. 1972. Thermal ecology of allopatric lizards..., *Oecologia (Berlin)*, **11**, 1–16.

ŠPINAR, Z. V., and BURIAN, Z. 1972. *Life before man*, Thames & Hudson, London.

STEBBINS, R. C., and COHEN, N. W. 1973. The effect of parietalectomy on the thyroid and gonads in...lizards (*Sceloporus occidentalis*), *Copeia*. 662–68.

STEWARD, J. W. 1971. *The snakes of Europe*, David & Charles, Newton Abbot.

SWINTON, W. E. 1970. *The dinosaurs*. Allen & Unwin, London.

TEMPLETON, J. R. 1970. In *Comparative physiology of thermoregulation* (Ed. G. C. Whittow), v. **1**, Academic Press, New York & London.

TEMPLETON, J. R. 1972. Salt and water balance in desert lizards, *Symp. Zool. Soc. Lond.* No. 31, 61–77.

THOMPSON, D'A. W. 1968. *On growth and form*, Cambridge University Press, 2 vols (2nd ed.).

THORNTON, I. 1971. *Darwin's Islands. A natural history of the Galápagos*,

Publ. for the Am. Mus. nat. Hist., Natural History Press, Garden City, New York.

TINKLE, D. W. 1967. The life and demography of the side-blotched lizard, *Uta stansburiana*, *Misc. Publ. Mus. Zool. Univ. Michigan*, No. 132, 1–182.

UNDERWOOD, G. 1957. On lizards of the family Pygopodidae..., *J. Morph.* **100**, 207–68.

UNDERWOOD, G. 1967. *A contribution to the classification of snakes*, Brit. Mus. (Nat. Hist.), London.

UNITED STATES DEPARTMENT OF THE NAVY. 1968. *Poisonous snakes of the world*, Washington.

VOLSØE, H. 1944. ...male reproductive organs of *Vipera berus* (L.), *Spolia Zool. Mus. Hauniensis, Copenhagen*, V, 1–172.

WALKER, A. D. 1972. New light on the origin of birds and crocodiles, *Nature, Lond.* **237**, 267–63.

WALLS, G. L. 1942. *The vertebrate eye*..., Cranbrook Institute of Science, Michigan.

WIEDERSHEIM, R. 1909. *Vergleichende Anatomie der Wirbeltiere*, Fischer Jena.

WERMUTH, H., and MERTENS, R. 1961. *Schildkröten. Krokodile. Brückenechsen*, G. Fischer, Jena.

WETTSTEIN, O. VON, and LÜDICKE, M. 1931–64. In *Handbuch der Zoologie*, de Gruyter, Berlin, v. 7.

WEVER, E. G. 1971. Hearing in the Crocodilia, *Proc. nat. Acad. Sci.* **68**, 1498–1500.

WEVER, E. G., and GANS, C. 1973. The ear in Amphisbaenia..., *J. Zool. Lond.* **171**, 189–206.

WEVER, E. G., and VERNON, J. A. 1960. The problem of hearing in snakes, *J. Auditory Res.* **1**, 77–83.

WHITE, F. N. 1968. Functional anatomy of the heart in reptiles, *Am. Zool.* **8**, 211–19.

WILLIAMS, E. E. 1950. Variation and selection in the cervical central articulations of living turtles, *Bull. Am. Mus. nat. Hist.* **94**, 505–62.

YALDEN, D. W. 1971. The flying ability of *Archaeopteryx, Ibis* **113**, 349–56.

ZITTEL, K. A. VON. 1932. *Textbook of palaeontology*, v. 2 (2nd English ed.), Macmillan, London.

Specialized periodicals such as the *British Journal of Herpetology, Copeia* and *Herpetologica,* contain much material of interest while a bibliography of most of the literature published each year is given in the volumes of the *Zoological Record*. The *Dictionary of Herpetology* by J. A. Peters (1964; Hafner, N.Y.) contains useful definitions of many terms.

Addenda

FLORKIN, M., and SCHEER, B. T. (Eds.). 1974. *Chemical Zoology*. v. 9; Amphibia and Reptilia. Academic Press, New York & London. [Contains important articles on digestion, excretion, pituitary, venom, *etc.*]

GANS, C. 1974. *Biomechanics*. Lippincott, Philadelphia & Toronto. [Deals with functional anatomy of egg-eating snakes, limbless locomotion, amphisbaenian burrowing, *etc.*)

WELLNHOFER, P. 1974. The fifth . . . *Archaeopteryx, Palaeontographica,* Abt. A., *147*, 169–216.

Index

Main references to page numbers in bold print; f denotes figure.